Stalin

PROFILES IN POWER

General Editor: Keith Robbins

LLOYD GEORGE
Martin Pugh

HITLER
Ian Kershaw

RICHELIEU
R. J. Knecht

NAPOLEON III
James McMillan

OLIVER CROMWELL
Barry Coward

NASSER
Peter Woodward

GUSTAVUS ADOLPHUS
(2nd edn)
Michael Roberts

CHURCHILL
Keith Robbins

DE GAULLE
Andrew Shennan

FRANCO
Sheelagh Ellwood

JUÁREZ
Brian Hamnett

ALEXANDER I
Janet M. Hartley

MACMILLAN
John Turner

JOSEPH II
T. C. W. Blanning

ATATÜRK
A. L. Macfie

CAVOUR
Harry Hearder

DISRAELI
Ian Machin

CASTRO (2nd edn)
Sebastian Balfour

PETER THE GREAT
(2nd end)
M. S. Anderson

FRANCIS JOSEPH
Stephen Beller

NAPOLEON
Geoffrey Ellis

KENNEDY
Hugh Brogan

ATTLEE
Robert Pearce

PÉTAIN
Nicholas Atkin

THE ELDER PITT
Marie Peters

CATHERINE DE' MEDICI
R. J. Knecht

GORBACHEV
Martin McCauley

JAMES VI AND I
Roger Lockyer

ELIZABETH I (2nd edn)
Christopher Haigh

MAO
S. G. Breslin

BURGHLEY
Michael A. R. Graves

NEHRU
Judith M. Brown

ROBESPIERRE
John Hardman

LENIN
Beryl Williams

WILLIAM PENN
Mary Geiter

THE YOUNGER PITT
Michael Duffy

KAISER WILHELM II
Christopher Clark

TANAKA
David Babb

PORFIRIO DÍAZ
Paul Garner

CATHERINE THE GREAT
Simon Dixon

ADENAUER
Ronald Irving

GANDHI
David Arnold

JAMES II
W. A. Speck

LINCOLN
Richard J. Cawardine

WOODROW WILSON
John A. Thompson

THE GREAT ELECTOR
Derek Mckay

TALLEYRAND
Philip G. Dwyer

WILLIAM III
A. M. Claydon

IVAN THE TERRIBLE
Andrei Pavlor and
Maureen Perrie

HENRY VIII
Michael A. R. Graves

BISMARCK
Katharine Anne Lerman

MUSSOLINI
Martin Clark

EISENHOWER
Peter G. Boyle

MARTIN LUTHER KING
John Kirk

FERDINAND AND
ISABELLA
John Edwards

STALIN
Hiroaki Kuromiya

Stalin

Hiroaki Kuromiya

PEARSON

Longman

Harlow, England • London • New York • Boston • San Francisco • Toronto
Sydney • Tokyo • Singapore • Hong Kong • Seoul • Taipei • New Delhi
Cape Town • Madrid • Mexico City • Amsterdam • Munich • Paris • Milan

PEARSON EDUCATION LIMITED

Edinburgh Gate
Harlow CM20 2JE
United Kingdom
Tel: +44 (0)1279 623623
Fax: +44 (0)1279 431059
Website: www.pearsoned.co.uk

First edition published in Great Britain in 2005

© Pearson Education Limited 2005

The right of Hiroaki Kuromiya to be identified as author
of this work has been asserted by him in accordance
with the Copyright, Designs and Patents Act 1988.

ISBN-13: 978-0-582-78479-6
ISBN-10: 0-582-78479-4

British Library Cataloguing in Publication Data
A CIP catalogue record for this book can be obtained from the British Library

Library of Congress Cataloging in Publication Data
Kuromiya, Hiroaki.
    Stalin / Hiroaki Kuromiya.
    p. cm. – (Profiles in power)
    Includes bibliographical references and index.
    ISBN 0-582-78479-4
1. Stalin, Joseph, 1879–1953. 2. Heads of state—Soviet Union—Biography.
3. Soviet Union—History—1925-1953. I. Title. II. Series: Profiles in power
(London, England)
DK268.S8K868 2005
947.084'2'092–dc22
[B]   2005050972

10   9   8   7   6   5   4   3   2   1
09   08   07   06   05

Set by the author using TEX
Printed and bound in Malaysia (CLP)

The Publisher's policy is to use paper manufactured from sustainable forests.

Contents

Preface   vii
Chronology   xv

1 From Georgia to Russia   1
   Soso   1
   Koba   11
   Stalin   19

2 Revolution and Civil War   26
   From February to October   26
   Civil War   36

3 Struggle for Power   50
   The New Economic Policy   50
   Battle Royal   58

4 'Revolution from Above'   74
   The Crisis of the NEP   74
   Industrialisation and Collectivisation   85

5 Famine and Terror   101
   Famine   102
   Great Terror   113

6 War   133
   Struggle for Survival   133
   Uncertainty   143
   War   150

7 Twilight of the God   169
   Victory   169
   Cold War   180
   Death   191

   Conclusion   201

   Bibliography   212
   Index   217

Preface

Stalin, like all political leaders, was a complex figure. Although numerous biographies have been written, anyone who attempts to write Stalin's life finds him an enigma. One biographer, writing in 1967 on Stalin's early life, despaired: 'the more that has been written about Stalin's pre-revolutionary life, the less clarity has emerged; the more details that have been supplied, the deeper one must dig for facts'.[1] The Soviet dissident writer Andrei Siniavskii wrote in 1990: 'Ultimately, everything connected with Stalin is so involved and obscure that it's often impossible to know how to interpret the facts. . . . In short, the figure of Stalin, given the opacity of his machinations, becomes lost in the murk.'[2] Moreover, in the case of Stalin, unlike most other individuals, biographers generally dislike the subject instead of liking him. One such biographer loathed Stalin so much that he wondered why Stalin's colleagues failed to act when they 'must have known then that Stalin, like a mad dog, had to be destroyed'. 'Sometimes,' he wrote in 1983, 'in the quiet of my study I have found myself bursting out to their ghosts: "For God's sake, stab him [Stalin] with a knife, or pick up a heavy object and bash his brains out, the lives you save may include your own".'[3] Writing about Stalin is not as easy as writing about tyrants of the remote past, because his era is still a lived experience for many people. It is only half a century since Stalin died.

Fortunately, the 1991 collapse of the Soviet Union has led to the opening up of the formerly closed Soviet archives. Not all archives are open or accessible, and an unknown portion of Stalin's personal archives and a large part of his personal library are believed to have been destroyed or lost.[4] Still, a tremendous amount of new information has become available in recent years, and historians, both inside and outside the former Soviet Union, have taken advantage of the new opportunities and written a great deal on Stalin and his era. Recent major English-language biographical studies (including translations from other languages) include Dmitri Volkogonov, *Stalin: Triumph and Tragedy* (1991), Edvard Radzinsky, *Stalin* (1997), Erik van Ree, *The Political Thought of Joseph Stalin* (2002), Simon Sebag Montefiore, *Stalin: The Court of the Red Tsar* (2003), Miklós Kun, *Stalin: An*

Unknown Poet (2003), Donald Rayfield, *Stalin and His Hangmen* (2004) and Robert Service, *Stalin: A Biography* (2004). In addition, numerous memoirs by Stalin's entourage have recently been published. Some, such as Andrei Gromyko, *Memoirs* (1989) and *Molotov Remembers: Inside Kremlin Politics* (1993), are available in English translation. Although the subject himself has in no way become easy to grasp, new information and new research have made Stalin less enigmatic.

Of course, historical evidence always poses vexing questions as regards reliability and meaning. There is no foolproof way of resolving these questions. New archival documents do help, even though they do not provide fail-safe solutions.[5] Stalin's own writings, remarks, comments, speeches and conversations are the most important sources and are examined carefully in the present book. The testimonies of those, such as V.M. Molotov, L.M. Kaganovich, Georgii Dimitrov, Andrei Gromyko and Svetlana Allilueva, who lived or worked closely with him, are also very useful. From a perusal of them emerges a more or less coherent picture of Stalin. Much has necessarily to remain provisional. At the very least, however, I have endeavoured here to reflect the current state of knowledge as much as possible and incorporate my own research as well. Given the scope of the book, I have not been able to examine every aspect of Stalin's life in detail, so I have focused on Stalin the politician.

There is hardly any need to dwell on the importance of Iosif Stalin (1878–1953) in the modern history of the world. He was a contemporary of Adolf Hitler (1889–1945), Benito Mussolini (1883–1945), Franklin D. Roosevelt (1882–1945), Winston Churchill (1874–1965) and Mao Zedong (1893–1976). After the death of Vladimir Lenin (1870–1924), Stalin represented the first socialist country in history, which lasted not for sixty-odd days as the 1871 Paris Commune did but for 74 years. Stalin became the symbol of the country. The emergence of the Soviet Union, an explicitly anti-capitalist and atheist state, appears to have realised the worst nightmare of capitalists who had battled the spectre of communism for a century. Many capitalist countries tried to intervene to quash the Bolshevik revolution. They failed. The world order changed completely with the establishment of the Soviet Union. The spectre of Communism began to haunt the capitalist world with a vengeance after the Great Depression of 1929. In sharp contrast to the terrible economic crisis in the capitalist world, Stalin's violent 'revolution from above' appeared to transform human society in a new fashion.[6] Untold numbers of people in the capitalist world as well as in the less developed societies were smitten with Stalin's 'revolution'. Even though it was patently clear that the revolution took a terrible toll, the socialist alternative appeared to many people to be the future of human society. When liberal democracy did not appear to have the will to fight the rising tide of fascism and Nazism, the first socialist country appealed to many as a real, alternative defence. Western spies for the Soviet Union (including the infamous Cambridge spies) were true believers in the country Stalin had built and the future it promised.

By a curious turn of events, however, in 1939 the anti-Nazi bulwark suddenly became a sort of Nazi fortification, confusing the world. By another curious turn of events, the long-time enemies, Churchill and Stalin, became allies in 1941. On the day Hitler invaded the Soviet Union, Winston Churchill, who had once admired fascism, made a historic broadcast in which he acknowledged, 'No one has been a more consistent opponent of Communism than I have in the last twenty-five years. I will unsay no word that I have spoken about it.' Churchill declared, however, that 'the Russian danger' is 'our danger'. By yet another curious turn of events, after the victory the friends turned foes in the Cold War. Stalin's death in 1953 did not end the war, nor did the regime Stalin had created collapse immediately. For those who lived through the events of the Cold War, the 1989 fall of the Berlin Wall, the 1991 collapse of the Soviet Union and the end of the Cold War all seemed sudden and unexpected, yet it is evident that the 'short twentieth century' is symbolised by the birth and death of the Communist regime in the largest country in the world. Stalin represented the country in both a literal and figurative sense, and it would not be an exaggeration to state that without understanding Stalin one cannot understand the twentieth century.

Stalin's biographers have presented many interesting pictures of him, ranging from Stalin as a blind follower of Lenin to Stalin as a betrayer of the revolution, to Stalin the Russian nationalist and to Stalin a 'man of the borderlands'.[7] I shall not engage in polemics in the present book. Instead, I emphasise a different aspect of Stalin's life, one that overrode all other aspects but one that has been insufficiently articulated by his biographers. It is that Stalin lived by politics alone. This may appear obvious, but it is not: almost all politicians live by politics, but not by politics alone, while Stalin, devoid of any sentimentality, lived literally by politics alone. He lived for the purpose of shaping the body politic through the pursuit and exercise of power. Whatever private emotions (such as affection, hatred, lust and vindictiveness) he had, he subordinated them to political ends and to his quest for power. Stalin played politics masterfully, far more so than did any of his rivals in the party, who often fell victim to their intellectual pretensions or other human failings. This is how Stalin rose to power.

Some biographers argue that Stalin was a pathological figure: a neurotic, a megalomaniac, a paranoiac, a sadist, and so on.[8] This is a deceptively attractive proposition – deceptive because what appears utterly irrational and even pathological to outside observers often turns out to be thoroughly rational in the mind of the person in question. However pathological and irrational Stalin's mental universe may seem, the present book suggests that it had not so much a psychological as a political rationale, a rationale shared not only by Stalin's lieutenants but also by a significant segment of the Soviet population.

To one degree or another, all politicians are probably Machiavellian, following, wittingly or not, some of the political precepts of the sixteenth-century Florentine diplomat Niccolò Machiavelli, developed in, among other writings, *The Prince* (1513). Whatever his intentions in writing his precepts, in doing so Machiavelli described an almost universal state of affairs in politics. Even though he defended republicanism and criticised tyranny, his precepts have come to be associated with the amorality of politics and the use of violence. Stalin appears to have read Machiavelli and followed some of his precepts. He may even have been a 'natural Machiavellian'.[9] Stalin even imagined himself as a new prince or tsar. Yet Stalin was much more than a mere reprobate and violent Machiavellian. Stalin followed what he regarded as the objective laws of history as expressed in Marxism.

Once in power, Stalin maintained that he was the personification of the epic struggle for socialism. He even said that he, the person, was not Stalin. He judged everything (including human values and human lives) from a political point of view. His identification with the Soviet regime was such that he did not distinguish between the personal and the public. Therefore anyone against him, the embodiment of the inevitability of history, became *ipso facto* an enemy of the Soviet regime. His will for power, revenge and all other personal issues became matters of the Soviet state. He thus with impunity conflated his own needs with the needs of the state. Killing people close to him did not evoke any special emotion in Stalin, because he deemed it a necessity for the higher order, that is, politics. By comparison, even ruthless dictators like Mao Zedong and Vladimir Lenin appear somewhat more human than Stalin.[10] Stalin was even critical of the sixteenth-century Muscovite Tsar Ivan the Terrible for taking pity on his enemies. As dictators go, Stalin appears to be unique in that he lived by political considerations alone.

It is not that Stalin did not comprehend human relations. In fact he did, but he used his understanding for political purposes. As many foreigners who dealt with Stalin have testified, Stalin was capable of understanding human sentiment. Stalin's monstrosity lay as much in his subsumption of everything human under politics as in his ghastly terror.

In transliterating Russian and other Cyrillic names, I have used the most prevalent Library of Congress system for the sake of consistency. Some may appear odd: Beriia instead of Beria or Beriya, Trotskii instead of Trotsky, Zinov'ev instead of Zinoviev. I hope, however, that the reader will soon get used to them. The only exceptions are the familiar, Anglicised names of tsars (e.g. Alexander, Nicholas and Catherine). Non-Russian personal names present a complicated problem. More than a hundred languages were used in the Soviet Union. Stalin's real name in Georgian is Ioseb Jughashvili (in Latin transliteration), Feliks Dzerzhinskii, a Pole, is Feliks Dzierżyński in Polish, and the prevalent personal name Nikolai is Mykola in Ukrainian. I do not know how to deal with non-Russian (Uzbek, Azerbaijani, and many other) names in their original languages. To be fair (or to be equally unfair) to everyone, I have used the Russian names of Soviet people since Russian was the lingua franca of the country. For non-Russian place names, I have tried to respect current local usage with the exception of Moscow and Yalta. Hence Kyiv instead of Kiev, L'viv instead of L'vov or Lwów but Moscow instead of Moskva.

On 31 January 1918 the Soviet government switched from the Old Style (Julian) calendar to the New Style (Gregorian) calendar (thereby losing 13 days when 1 February 1918 O.S. became 14 February 1918 N.S.). In this book I have used the Russian calendar (i.e. the Julian calendar) until 1 February 1918 and the Gregorian calendar thereafter unless otherwise noted.

Whenever there is an English translation of foreign-language sources, I have tried to quote it instead of the original. I have occasionally changed the translation slightly to be accurate, however. All emphases in quotes are in the original unless otherwise noted.

This book was completed during a sabbatical leave from teaching in 2004–5, for which I am grateful to Indiana University. A 'Mellon grant-in-aid of research' from Indiana's Russian and East European Institute enabled me to travel to Tbilisi and Gori, Georgia, in the summer of 2004. For published sources, I have relied mainly on the Indiana University Library, Harvard University's libraries and the Wellesley College Library. I am grateful to these libraries as well as Harvard's Davis Center and Ukrainian Research Institute for various assistance. I should also like to thank the Russian State Archive of Socio-Political

History (RGASPI) in Moscow for granting me access to its archival documents.

'RGASPI', 'CC' for the Central Committee, 'SRs' for the Socialist Revolutionaries, 'NEP' for the New Economic Policy, 'OGPU' (later 'NKVD') for the Soviet secret police, and the 'USSR' for the Union of Soviet Socialist Republics (or the Soviet Union) are the only acronyms used repeatedly in the book.

Several people have read drafts and have given me detailed comments. I should like to express special thanks to two of my long-time friends, Dr Lars T. Lih of Montreal and Professor Norman M. Naimark of Stanford University, who as a Russian and East European specialist kindly scrutinised my manuscript. I should also like to thank James W. Morley, my father-in-law and an expert on Asia who took an interest in this book, and Carolyn Morley, my wife, who had to endure my constant rewriting. I am fortunate to have their companionship and am beholden to them for whatever strengths this biography may have. It goes without saying that I alone am responsible for the arguments and interpretations of the present book.

My editors at Pearson, Heather McCallum, Christina Wipf Perry, Hetty Reid and particularly Julie Knight and Ron Hawkins, have been very supportive.

Finally, I am very grateful to whoever recommended me to Professor Keith Robbins, General Editor of *Profiles in Power*, for the opportunity to write this political biography. It is almost 30 years since I began to read Stalin and to read about him – even so writing his biography has been daunting. Without this opportunity, I might not have undertaken it.

Notes

[1] Edward Ellis Smith, *The Young Stalin* (New York, 1967), 7.

[2] Andrei Sinyavsky, *Soviet Civilization: A Cultural History* (New York, 1990), 87.

[3] Robert C. Tucker, 'Memoir of a Stalin Biographer', *University* (Princeton, NJ), 88 (Winter 1983), 7.

[4] Roy Medvedev and Zhores Medvedev, *The Unknown Stalin: His Life, Death, and Legacy* (New York, 2004), ch. 3.

[5] For an instructive discussion of new archival documents on Stalin, see Norman M. Naimark, 'Cold War Studies and New Archival Materials on Stalin', *Russian Review*, 61:1 (January 2002).

[6] Stephen Kotkin, *Magnetic Mountain: Stalinism as a Civilization* (Berkeley, Calif., 1997).

[7] No comprehensive historiographical work of Stalin's biographies, particularly those of very recent years, seems to be available, but see Christoph Mick, 'Frühe Stalin-Biographien 1928–1932', *Jahrbücher für Geschichte Osteuropas*, 36:3

(1988), Ronald Grigor Suny, 'After the Fall: Stalin and His Biographers', *Radical History Review*, 54 (Fall 1992) and 'Beyond Psychohistory: The Young Stalin in Georgia', *Slavic Review*, 50:1 (Spring 1991), and Alfred J. Rieber, 'Stalin, Man of the Borderlands', *American Historical Review*, 106:5 (December 2001).

[8]See Tucker, 'Memoir of a Stalin Biographer', his *Stalin as Revolutionary, 1879–1929* (New York, 1973) and Daniel Rancour-Laferriere, *The Mind of Stalin: A Psychoanalytic Study* (Ann Arbor, Mich., 1988).

[9]E.A. Rees, *Political Thought from Machiavelli to Stalin* (Basingstoke, 2004), 239. Boris Souvarine, in his *Stalin* (New York, 1939), said that Stalin had 'obviously not read Machiavelli', but that 'on all points an intuitive Machiavellism guides him' (583, 585).

[10]For Mao, see Li Zhisui, *The Private Life of Chairman Mao: The Memoirs of Mao's Personal Physician* (New York, 1994), and, for Lenin, see Tamara Deutscher (ed.), *Not by Politics Alone: The Other Lenin* (London, 1973).

Chronology

1878	Born in Gori, Georgia, 6 December OS.
1894	Graduated from Gori church school and entered Tbilisi theological seminary.
1898	Joined the the Russian Social Democratic Workers' Party (RSDRP).
1899	Left the Tbilisi theological seminary and became a professional revolutionary.
1902	Arrested.
1903	Exiled to Siberia.
1904	Fled from exile.
1904–5	Russo-Japanese War.
1905	Participated in the 1905 Revolution in Transcaucasia.
1906	Married Ekaterina Svanidze.
1907	Son Iakov born. Ekaterina died.
1908–12	Repeatedly arrested, exiled and escaped.
1912	Co-opted to the RSDRP Central Committee. Helped to publish the party organ *Pravda*.
1912–13	Adopted the pseudonym 'Stalin'.
1914–18	First World War.
1917	In exile in Siberia when the February Revolution took place. Returned to Petrograd immediately. Participated in the October Revolution. Appointed People's Commissar of Nationalities in the Soviet government.
1918	Married Nadezhda Allilueva. Took the Menshevik leader Martov to court. Ruled Tsaritsyn as dictator.
1918–20	Participated in the Civil War as political commissar.
1921	New Economic Policy launched. Son Vasilii born. Heckled by workers in Tbilisi.
1922	Elected General Secretary of the party.
1923	Defeated Trotskii in a power struggle.
1925	Defeated the Leningrad Opposition (Zinov'ev and Kamenev).
1926	Daughter Svetlana born.

1927   Defeated the United Opposition (led by Trotskii, Zinov'ev and Kamenev).

1928   First Five-Year Plan launched retroactively.

1928–9   Defeated the 'rightists' (led by Bukharin and Rykov).

1929   The Great Depression assaulted the capitalist world.

1929–30   Wholesale collectivisation and dekulakisation.

1930   Temporarily retreated from wholesale collectivisation ('Dizzy from Success'), March.   Collectivisation resumed in the autumn.

1932   Manchukuo founded as a Japanese puppet government. Nadezhda committed suicide.

1932–3   The Great Famine.

1933   Hitler's rise to power in Germany.

1934   'Congress of Victors'. Joined the League of Nations. Kirov murdered, December.

1935   Adopted the 'People's Front' against Nazism and fascism.

1936–8   Staged three Moscow show trials and the Great Terror.

1938   The Lake Khasan battle with Japan-Manchukuo, July-August. The Munich Accord, September.

1939   The Khalkin Gol (Nomonhan) battle with Japan-Manchukuo, May–August. The Molotov–Ribbentrop pact signed, August.   Second World War began, September.   Incorporated western Ukraine and western Belarus into the Soviet Union.

1939–40   The Soviet–Finnish War ('Winter War').

1940   Incorporated the Baltic states into the Soviet Union. Annexed Bessarabia and the northern Bukovyna.

1941   Signed a non-aggression treaty with Japan. Became Chairman of the Sovnarkom (cabinet). Germany invaded the Soviet Union, June. Son Iakov taken prisoner. Survived the Battle of Moscow.

1942–3   Won the Battle of Stalingrad.

1943   Participated in the Tehran Conference.   Son Iakov killed in captivity.

1944   The Second Front opened. Failed to help the Warsaw Uprising.

1945   Participated in the Yalta Conference, February, and the Potsdam Conference, July. Germany surrendered, May. Occupied much of East–Central Europe. Entered the war against Japan, August. Japan surrendered, and Second World War ended, August.

1946   Launched 'Zhdanovshchina'.
1947   Rejected the Marshall Plan and formed the Com-
        inform. The Cold War began.
1948   Broke with Tito, the communist leader of Yugoslavia.
        Blockaded Berlin.
1949   Met with Mao of China.
1950   Sanctioned Kim to stage war in Korea.
1953   Died, 5 March.

Chapter 1

From Georgia to Russia

Soso

Iosif Vissarionovich Dzhugashvili, later to be Stalin, was born in Gori, Georgia, an old-established Christian area in the Transcaucasian region of the old Russian Empire, on 6 December 1878 and was christened eleven days later.[1] This simple fact was not widely known until quite recently. According to Soviet official biographies, his birth date was 9 (21 according to the New Calendar adopted after the Russian Revolution of 1917) December 1879. So the Soviet dictator was actually a year older than people had thought. What was the purpose of this misinformation? Stalin is known to have offered different birth dates on different occasions. Perhaps he wanted to present himself as younger than he was: 1879 would have made him nine years younger than Vladimir Ul'ianov (Lenin) and a year younger than his arch-rival Lev Bronshtein (Trotskii). Whatever the reason, this type of minor deception was characteristic of a politician who, as a dictator, would rule the largest country in the world for three decades.

Unlike Lenin, whose father was an intellectually gifted nobleman, Stalin was born into a peasant 'estate'. His father Vissarion and his mother Ekaterina (Keke) were born serfs. Even after the emancipation of serfs, however, the legal system of estates continued to exist until 1917, hence the Dzhugashvilis belonged legally to the peasant estate. The peasant Vissarion became a cobbler. He prospered for a while, even owning his own workshop and hiring workers, thus qualifying as an 'exploiter', as Stalin said later.[2] By the time Stalin was 10 years old, however, his father had failed in his trade and become an employee in a shoe factory in Tiflis, or Tbilisi, the capital of Georgia. Very little is known about Vissarion, but it is widely believed that he became a drunkard, beat his only child, and at some point forced Stalin, if only briefly, to leave school to train as a cobbler, like himself. Vissarion left (or was forced to leave) his household while Stalin was still a child, and little is known of him after this. Stalin seems to have had very little to do with him, and rarely spoke of him. Vissarion died a lonely man, probably a vagabond, in Tbilisi in 1909.

His mother, by contrast, is the only person (apart from his two future wives) for whom Stalin is said to have ever felt love. Keke had given birth to two (or three) boys before Stalin, but all of them died in infancy. Stalin himself was weak as an infant and Keke looked after her only child carefully. Many observers have noted her devotion to Stalin. After Vissarion left, Keke, unlike her neighbours, was forced to seek menial jobs such as house cleaning and sewing to support her family. By all accounts, the family was poor. Keke had 'a strict, decisive character', and became even more so after Vissarion's departure.[3]

Apparently, Keke was not averse to beating her son. In 1935, two years before she died, in what was to be their last meeting, Stalin asked her 'Why did you beat me so hard?' She responded, 'That's why you turned out so well.' It is said that she was devout and had dreamed of her son becoming a priest.[4] In the 1935 meeting, she asked, 'Joseph [i.e. Iosif] – who exactly are you now?' She did not understand what her son had become. Stalin answered, 'Remember the tsar? Well, I'm like a tsar.' Keke responded, 'You'd have done better to have become a priest.'[5] Her reaction amused Stalin. His daughter Svetlana noted that Stalin 'used to recount this with relish'.

Inevitably, some elements of Stalin's later personality were already evident in childhood. One of his childhood friends, I. Iremaschwili (who later turned against him politically), recounted how patient and hard-working Soso was (Soso, a diminutive of Iosif, was Stalin's childhood name). Iremaschwili recalled that, although Soso liked nature, he was incapable of compassion for animals and humans, and attributed this trait to Soso's having been beaten by his father. Stalin came to entertain a defiant attitude towards his superiors. According to Iremaschwili, from childhood on, Soso was driven by a desire for revenge: 'To be victorious and be feared was to triumph for him.'[6] Yet another childhood friend, Joseph Davrichewy, in a more positive anecdote, recounted how Soso was once praised anonymously by a priest in a sermon for being a good Samaritan by helping a woman in the street to carry her heavy packages. Davrichewy soon found out that the Samaritan was Soso, and he and another friend tried to emulate him by helping an old peasant woman carry her bag. Unfortunately, she mistook them for robbers, and Davrichewy was slapped by his father for this 'chivalry' inspired by Soso. However, Davrichewy also related, like Iremaschwili, that Soso could not easily accept authority, and he would, for example, disobey and undermine the leader of the gang of children to which he belonged.[7]

In retelling Stalin's life, many observers have made much of Stalin's physical characteristics, for example, his height and its impact on his character. In fact he grew to be 170 centimetres (164 centimetres according to some data),[8] probably taller than Lenin. He also suffered from a variety of minor physical deformities: in childhood he suffered from smallpox, which left his face pockmarked; the second and third toes of his left foot were congenitally joined; his left arm was deformed, probably as a result of being run over by a phaeton in childhood; and his legs were injured permanently by another phaeton accident. Moreover, like many of his contemporaries, he suffered from tuberculosis. Yet he was a relatively strong child, a fierce fighter, according to his childhood friends.[9] In adulthood, Stalin suffered constant muscular pain and frequent bouts of diarrhoea. He also suffered from neurasthenia (some around him, including doctors, suspected 'paranoia').

Although Stalin did not enjoy the reputation of being an intellectual or a theorist in his adult political life (there were indeed more brilliant intellectuals, including Lenin and Trotskii), he was nevertheless bright. His mother was keen on his education. With the support of her employers and patrons (one of whom some people suspect may have been Stalin's real father, the father of his friend Iosif Davrichewy), Keke had him taught the Russian language (at which he did very well after initial difficulties) and he entered the Gori church school to prepare to become a priest. According to one childhood friend, Soso was devout and his ideal was to become a monk.[10] Interestingly, when he heard the story of Jesus's crucifixion, Soso demanded to know why Jesus did not take up his sword and why his comrades had not defended him.[11] Another incident may have influenced Soso's psyche in some way. In February 1892, when he was 13 years old, he and his friends witnessed the public executions in Gori of two Ossetian peasants accused of robbery (curiously, the future writer Maksim Gor'kii also happened to be there to witness the executions). One of them had to be hanged twice because the first time the rope snapped. Soso and his friends found it hard to reconcile the executions with the teachings of the church.[12]

Soso proved to be the best student in the class at the Gori school, although Iremaschwili noted that Soso was defiant. In school the use of Russian was compulsory, and pupils were beaten and fined routinely for speaking Georgian. One day the despised school inspector became the object of ridicule by the pupils: he was greeted with whistles and boos. The students were punished for their behaviour, including their ringleader Soso.[13]

In 1894 Soso graduated with distinction from the Gori school. His mother turned down the opportunity for him to study at the Tbilisi normal school at the expense of the state. She wanted him to train as a priest. With the aid of a scholarship and Keke's patrons, Soso matriculated to the Tbilisi theological seminary, the most prestigious institution in Georgia at that time. Even though it is said that in his Gori years Soso had ceased to believe in God after reading Charles Darwin, in his first year in the Tbilisi seminary Soso appeared to be a good candidate for the priesthood. His penchant for mischief gave way to studiousness; he performed all his duties, including religious services and rites, sang in the church choir, and academically did well (if not brilliantly), eighth out of the 29 students in his class. The seminary students' lives were regimented according to strict and harsh rules. In particular, their contact with the outside world, including their reading, was severely restricted. According to Stalin's own account in 1931, it was a 'humiliating regime' based on 'Jesuitical methods' with surveillance and spying. The 'humiliating regime' in the seminary fostered discontent and rebellion. As in Gori, the use of the Russian language was enforced rigorously at the seminary. Many of the teachers were politically conservative or even reactionary Russian Orthodox priests. The year before Stalin began his study, the school was forced to shut down for almost nine months owing to student unrest and rebellion. Nevertheless, Soso behaved well, gaining the highest score, a five, in 'conduct'.

Yet Soso was keenly interested in other subjects. More than likely he had already been exposed in Gori to some literature on the Georgian national revival. He began to read Georgian literature and history intently. In 1895, without the knowledge or permission of the seminary, Soso published patriotic poems under a pseudonym in the Georgian daily *Iveriia*.[14] One poem ended with

> Be full of blossom, O lovely land,
> Rejoice, Iberians' country,[15]
> And you, O Georgian, by studying
> Bring joy to your motherland.

Another proclaimed the victory of the oppressed:

> The Lord's Providence is great . . .
> Know for certain that once
> Struck down to the ground, an oppressed man

> Strives again to reach the pure mountain,
> When exalted by hope.

Yet another echoes this theme:

> When the man driven out by his enemy
> Again becomes worthy of his oppressed country
> And when the sick man, deprived of light,
> Again begins to see sun and moon;
> Then I, too, oppressed, find the mist of sadness;
> Breaks and lifts and instantly recedes
> And hopes of the good life
> Unfold in my unhappy heart!

These poems suggest that the beginnings of Soso's political life are to be found in Georgian cultural nationalism.[16] Donald Rayfield, who has analysed the poems, notes that if any of his poems 'contained an *avis au lecteur*', the following one on the 'opposition of poet–wanderer and the mob' does. It ends with:

> Wherever the harp was plucked,
> The mob set before the outcast
> A vessel filled with poison . . .
> And they said to him: 'Drink this, o accursed,
> This is your appointed lot!
> We do not want your truth
> Nor these heavenly tunes of yours!'

Rayfield sees in this poem 'a paranoiac conviction that great prophets could only expect conspiracy and murder: a conviction that is only too obvious in the last twenty years of Stalin's rule, marked by recurrent poisonings, real and imaginary'. All the same, Soso's poetic talent was such that Rayfield speculates that had Stalin become a poet, the history of the Soviet Union would have been very different, just as, had Hitler become a painter, the history of twentieth-century Europe would have been very different.[17]

Soso's political life soon evolved from a romantic, literary nationalism into socialism. It is in these years, 1895–6, that social democratic (Marxist) circles began to form in Tbilisi. The Tbilisi seminary was a hotbed of revolutionaries. Soso, with others, organised an underground socialist circle in the seminary around this time. After publishing another poem in 1896, Soso stopped writing poems to engage in politics. In 1898, when the Russian Social Democratic Workers' Party (RSDRP) was formed, Soso joined. He was 18 in 1896 and 20 in 1898, contradicting his later account that he began his revolutionary career at the age of 15. By the end of his third year at the seminary (1897)

Soso's academic performance had begun to fail, falling to sixteenth place (with the grade of 3.5 for 'conduct') and, by the end of his fourth year (1898), to twentieth place (with the grade of 3 for 'conduct').

Unfortunately, little is known about what attracted Soso to social democracy. Nationalism could have provided a solution to the problems he saw in Georgia: salvation through a particular group called a 'nation'. Indeed, Soso so admired the hero and avenger, Koba, of the Georgian nationalist writer A. Kazbegi's *The Patricide* that he later took his name. Marxism offered a different solution, however: the universal salvation of human society through a particular group called a 'class'. Many in Georgia as elsewhere attempted to reconcile these two major ideologies that had emerged in reaction to the Enlightenment, so the two schools of thought may have appeared to Soso and his Georgian contemporaries as to some extent compatible. Clearly, Soso, of humble origin, was keenly aware of social injustice, not just national injustice: at the seminary he had been caught with works by the French writer and republican Victor Hugo and was punished accordingly. Moreover, the complex national life of the capital of Georgia at that time – in which only about a quarter of its population were Georgians, with Armenians and Russians accounting for about one-third each – may have contributed to Soso's thinking. In his native town of Gori, too, Georgians were a minority with Armenians as a dominant group. Did Soso and others envisage a nationally reordered Transcaucasia? Was it feasible? Most likely, Marxism, with its universal salvation for all mankind, proved more attractive than nationalism, cutting across national lines and presenting a radical, international solution: a new rule by the oppressed and exploited class of workers. 'Universal' may not have meant literally universal or even European in practical terms, however. The term referred at least to the Russian Empire, not just Georgia or Transcaucasia. Unlike some other Georgian social democrats, according to an account by a childhood friend, Soso transcended the narrow political and ideological confines of Georgia thanks to his association with more cosmopolitan Marxists (such as Lev Kamenev who was to become a prominent Bolshevik, only to be executed by Stalin in 1936).[18] According to his daughter, Soso would become 'completely Russian' to the extent that his son Vasilii once said to her, 'You know, Papa used to be a Georgian once.'[19]

Soso did not appear to have discarded his commitment to national issues, however. According to a Bolshevik contemporary, he was interested in organising a territorially demarcated Marxist party. Only in 1904, after he fled his first exile in Siberia, did Soso renounce his earlier position openly in a document called 'Credo'. This document has never been found. According to Robert Service, Soso 'retained a strong feeling that the national sensitivities of the Georgians and other peoples should be respected'.[20] Later he wrote a major treatise on the nationality questions in the Russian Empire, and became a specialist on the nationality question in the All-Russian Communist Party.

It is often said that Soso's Marxist learning was shallow, or at least was deeply affected by the simplistic catechism of his ecclesiastical education. This is not entirely fair. As will be seen, he was not a blind follower of Lenin or anyone else: he had his own views, beliefs and convictions. His intellectual ambitions led him at one point to consider the idea of entering a university and becoming a professor. The 1902 massacre in Batumi, to be discussed later, would mark a major change in his life.[21] Soso was an avid reader but, as Iremaschwili noted, Soso's socialism derived not from reflective understanding but from a fanatic hatred for authority and the propertied classes. Soso was already a 'little dictator' who refused to be subordinate to anyone. *His* socialism deviated from the ideals of socialism (people's power); *his* power was what mattered. The proletariat, which Iremaschwili admitted Soso knew well in Tbilisi, was merely a tool to serve his will. His atheism was born of his love for violence. His understanding of socialism was such that even before the 1903 split of the RSDRP into Bolsheviks and Mensheviks, he had already managed to split the Tbilisi Marxists into factions.[22] Soso did, however, learn something valuable at the seminary, as he later noted: 'One thing priests teach you is to understand what people think.'[23]

From the very beginning of his revolutionary career, it is often said that Soso did not tolerate those who disagreed with him, often reacting with fists even to innocent remarks. Yet he was also known to be an extraordinarily patient listener, an 'ideal listener'. 'Patience is a rare trait in men of action,' as one observer noted. 'That rare combination is the principal key to his character.'[24] Gregorii Uratadze, who spent some time in prison with him in 1903, noted that he was unsociable and that nothing 'human' seemed to interest him. Yet Uratadze also recalled that he was 'completely imperturbable' and that not once did he see him become angry, lose his temper, or swear: he was always completely composed. He never laughed, only smiled. His voice, too, corresponded exactly with his 'icy character', as those who knew him closely said of him.[25]

Some people detect a deeper (or at least an ironic) meaning in Soso's idolisation of Koba, Kazbegi's hero modelled on the Persian king Kabadh, who, having conquered Georgia in the late fifth century, moved its capital to Tbilisi. Kabadh initially supported the proto-communistic sect of Mazdakites in demanding that the rich should share their wealth with the poor, in the hope of breaking the power of the magnates. The magnates, in turn, conspired to oust Kabadh. Yet he escaped, returned to the throne, and dealt with the magnates. In the end, Kabadh also eliminated his erstwhile allies, the Mazdakites. Soso went by the name Koba for a few years from 1903 (and some continued to call Stalin Koba even in the 1930s), but, of course, one does not know whether he consciously emulated the Persian king. What is clear is that he was well versed in Georgian literature, including its most famous twelfth-century epic poem, Shota Rustaveli's *The Knight in the Panther's Skin*. Soso–Koba–Stalin's favourite aphorisms included the following from Rustaveli: 'My life is pitiless, like the beast' and 'A close [friend] turned out to be an enemy more dangerous than a foe.'[26]

In addition to literature, he was keenly interested in history. A Russian history textbook that has been preserved in his personal library reveals that he marked with a pencil the following statement made by Genghis Khan: 'The deaths of the conquered are necessary for the conquerors' peace of mind.'[27] Although it would be patently simplistic to explain Stalin's rule as Caucasian or non-European and futile to argue whether European history is more, or less, bloody than non-European history, Stalin was nevertheless a product of Georgia, a Christian land at the crossroads of the Russian, Persian and Ottoman powers. He himself believed that he was not a 'European' (whatever he might have meant by that). At the height of the terror in 1937, he declared: 'I'm not a European, but a Russified Georgian-Asiatic.'[28]

Stalin may have had romantic views of the life of a revolutionary, but the pattern of his early life was often prosaic and mundane. He later recounted that he was expelled from the seminary in 1899 for his Marxist propaganda, an atheist ideology, but, in fact, he was expelled in the spring of 1899 for not taking the required examination to advance to the sixth (and final) year. Why did he fail to take that examination? It appears that he was no longer interested in continuing his religious education. Moreover, '[c]aptivated by illegal literature, he began to read all night by candlelight. From this curious habit he developed a sickly pallor and a bad cough'. When interviewed by an American journalist in 1930, his mother noted: 'I brought him home on account of his health. When he entered the seminary he was strong as a boy could be. But overwork up to the age of nineteen pulled him down, and the doctors told me that he might develop tuberculosis. So I took him home away from school. He did not want to leave. But I took him away. He was my only son'.[29] His departure may also have been related to the birth of his suspected illegitimate child at that time.[30] Whatever the case, both his formal education and Keke's dream of her only son becoming a priest ended in 1899.

After recuperation, Soso plunged into the revolutionary movement from the autumn of 1899 onwards. In late 1899 he acquired a part-time clerical position in the Tbilisi observatory. Within the Russian Social Democratic Workers' Party he had so recently joined a struggle had been brewing over the importance of the general political education of workers versus their agitation for direct political action. Soso supported the latter, criticising the leaders for favouring education and threatening, if necessary, to take the matter to the workers themselves. Thus, by 1900, leaflets calling for direct political action began to appear in Tbilisi, and workers began to strike here and there. It was then, in early 1900, that Soso was arrested for the first time. Whether or not it was related to his political activity is not known, but he was soon released and returned to work. When workers at several Tbilisi factories struck from the summer of 1900 to the spring of 1901, the police began to take note of Soso's activity in the clandestine political party. He escaped a raid in March 1901 in which many party members were arrested, and went underground at the cost of his observatory job. Thereafter, Soso never held a steady job, living the life of a professional revolutionary mainly at the expense of his supporters and the party. He later acknowledged that being able to become a professional revolutionary and not having to worry about making a living was his great fortune. Otherwise, he would have 'inevitably succumbed to petit-bourgeois influence, lost his sharpness and depleted his revolutionary energy'.[31]

In 1901 the May Day demonstration in Tbilisi was massive (with the participation of, perhaps, 2,000–3,000 workers). The RSDRP sought to politicise it, calling for 'Down with Tyranny! Long Live Freedom!' Soso again escaped the police raid that followed the demonstration. The arrest of many party leaders elevated Soso from the rank and file to a leadership position in Tbilisi, though his tenure was short-lived. It was not that he lacked leadership – on the contrary, he possessed important leadership skills. As both his friends and his foes noted, Soso had a remarkable talent for identifying, promoting and using people who supported him.[32] His daughter Svetlana recalled: 'All his life he was very good at finding people and promoting them, and this is why so many remained devoted to him, often young people whom he would pull out and promote over the heads of the old guard. . . . That was quite a part of him, his sociability and being with people.'[33] Trotskii's famous characterisation of Stalin as 'outstanding mediocrity' was certainly mistaken at least in this regard. Yet Soso also gained a reputation as a terrible troublemaker owing to his rudeness and ruthlessness. (He tended to polarise people into his friends and foes, a phenomenon that would characterise his political career.) It was probably for this reason that he was forced to leave Tbilisi and move to Batumi, Georgia, in the autumn of 1901.

Batumi on the Black Sea coast was becoming an important port city that exported oil transported through a pipeline from the oil city of Baku on the Caspian Sea in the east. A number of big factories supported the export industry in the city. Soso managed to set up a social democratic organisation with the help of local activists, and proved himself a militant organiser in Batumi. In January 1902, for instance, he staged a strike by workers against what he regarded as an injustice: the workers had been mainly responsible for extinguishing a fire that took place at their factory a few days earlier, but the factory administration rewarded only their supervisors. The strike was a success and the workers received two roubles each. This incident was soon followed by conflicts over lay-offs. Strikes led to the arrests of workers, and in March demands for the release of arrested comrades ended with the deaths of 13 people by mobilised soldiers. Soso's role in these incidents was central: it was he who set up the printing shop that produced the leaflets. The tone of his agitation was intense: 'Others live off our labour; they drink our blood; our oppressors quench their thirst with the tears of our wives, children and relatives.' Yet Soso's behaviour antagonised people: 'the despotism of Dzhugashvili' split the party in Batumi.[34]

Soon, in April 1902, Soso was arrested. Accused of sedition, he was sentenced to three years in eastern Siberia. According to Davrichewy, while he was awaiting deportation in 1903, he was conscripted but was saved from military service by Davrichewy's father (who some suspected was Stalin's real father).[35] Subsequently Stalin, like other revolutionaries, would boast of his fight against autocracy, a life filled with arrests, exiles, and escapes. Yet, unknown to the party, Soso twice tendered obsequious petitions for release to the governor of the Caucasus, Prince G.S. Golitsyn, an act tantamount to treason in the eyes of revolutionaries: 'A humble petition. / My choking cough is worsening. My old mother, abandoned by her husband twelve years ago and in a hopeless situation, sees me as the sole support of her life. . . . I beg the chancellery of the chief authorities not to ignore me and answer my petition.'[36] In the end, however, Tsar Nicholas approved the sentence. While awaiting transport, Soso, known now as Koba, organised a prison uprising. He was exiled to Novaia Uda, in the north of the Irkutsk region, in November 1903.

Koba

In early January 1904 Koba fled Novaia Uda and returned straight to Tbilisi and then to Batumi. That he fled so quickly and with such apparent ease made him politically suspect. His colleagues wondered how he secured the funding for it, and how he made it through police checks along the way. Some suspected that Koba might be one of the numerous police agents planted in revolutionary circles. Indeed, much is still unknown about his flight. Koba also appeared to have extraordinary luck in escaping the police on many subsequent occasions. He explained that his flight was made possible by forging the identification card of a police agent. Rumours and theories persist even today about Stalin's possible role as a police provocateur, resulting in a voluminous literature.[37] Yet no hard evidence has emerged to support a dual life. It is true that wherever Koba went, all kinds of rumours and innuendos followed him, because, as his contemporaries noted, he believed that in the name of revolution the ends justified the means and he had little or no sense of shame or morality when it came to politics.[38] Although, as was often alleged, Koba may have betrayed his former comrades by denouncing them to the police, he was almost certainly not a paid police informer. His luck in avoiding apprehension or in securing light punishment was more likely because of the fact that many wealthy and powerful people in Transcaucasia, dissatisfied with the Russian autocracy, surreptitiously funded the revolutionary movements and assisted their activists. The family of a Baku oil baron, Abraham Nussimbaum, apparently helped Koba. (The Nussimbaums, however, fled to Germany after the 1917 Revolution. The son, Lev Nussimbaum, wrote a biography of Stalin in 1931 under the pen-name of Essad-Bey.)[39] Friendships and connections also helped (for example, Koba's old friend David Matchavariani, who worked as an administrator in Gori, helped to supply him with forged documents, as did the father of his friend Davrichewy.)[40] Extortion of the wealthy by revolutionaries may have taken place, too. It should also be noted that just as the police penetrated subversive circles, so the revolutionaries infiltrated the police.

In any event, Koba left Batumi but returned later to take part in the 1904 May Day. Critical of the Batumi party committee's insufficiently militant position, Koba sought to mobilise the workers he had known before. He did not, however, find much sympathy among them and, after a fight, he left Batumi again.

He became widely known as a cunning schemer, everywhere getting into fights with those who disagreed with him. Uratadze noted that there was no party organisation in which Koba's presence did not result in a party trial.[41] Koba had become an ardent supporter of Lenin, whose work he had been reading since the late 1890s. When the RS-DRP split into two factions (Bolsheviks and Mensheviks) in 1903, Koba attached himself to the Bolsheviks, led by Lenin. The party split had occurred owing to, among other reasons, differing views of the party. The Bolsheviks wanted to create a centralised, disciplined party of dedicated revolutionaries, whereas the Mensheviks preferred a more open party of people with differing levels of commitment. Koba's views were indeed supremely Bolshevik: 'Only when we join one of the party organisations and thus *merge our personal interests with the interests of the party* can we become party members and, consequently, real leaders of the proletarian army.'[42]

Koba proved more ruthless than Lenin. He spoke rudely and crudely, a habit he retained until his death and justified as the speech of workers who spoke the truth straightforwardly and bluntly and were unfamiliar with the delicacy of manners. Koba's characterisation of the Mensheviks astonished his party colleagues: 'Lenin is outraged that God sent him such comrades as the Mensheviks. What kind of people are they, really? Martov, Dan, Axelrod – circumcised Jews. And the old woman V. Zasulich. Cowards and peddlers'; 'Do Georgian workers really not know that the Jewish people are cowardly and no good for fighting?'[43] It is not that Koba was inherently anti-Semitic. He knew well that there were many Jews among the Bolsheviks and he did not discriminate against the Jews (until late in his life). Some of his closest associates were Jews. Jewishness was of no concern to him personally, but he was not unwilling to use any popular prejudice for political purposes. A party colleague who met him in Batumi in 1904 detected something unusually cruel about him. Seeing no sincerity in Koba, he wondered whether he was a dedicated revolutionary or a heartless machine in the form of a human being, bent on destroying everything and building something else in its place.[44]

Another party activist, whose 1904 private correspondence was intercepted by the police, left an extremely unflattering description of Koba. Branding him a 'Don Quixote' and a liar, he expressed his surprise to a colleague at Koba's impudence:

> I know in general the worth of people like this gentleman, but I have to confess I do not expect such 'courage' from them. It turns out that they are capable of anything. . . . God did not endow these people with the talent needed for honest work, so they have to resort to intrigue, lies and other such pleasantries in order to realise their ambitions. . . . I think that we

should rebuff such 'filthy' characters when they try to smear our great and sacred cause with dirt and filth.[45]

After Batumi, Koba roamed around the Transcaucasus – Gori, Chiatura, Kutaisi, Imereti, Tbilisi, Baku. In the course of 1904–5, in spite of the trouble he had created, vacancies due to the arrests of Marxist leaders in Transcaucasia helped to elevate him to leadership positions. He sought out Lenin abroad through correspondence, and Lenin in turn took note of this fiery revolutionary from Georgia.

An important year for Koba, as it was for many Russian revolutionaries, was 1905. War broke out with Japan in the Far East in 1904, in the wake of a decade of rapid industrial development that ripped apart the traditional fabric of a mainly rural Russian Empire. Opposition to an autocracy that allowed no organised political expression of the people had been mounting. The loss of a war against a tiny Asian country had a devastating political impact on Russia. Lenin had formulated his strategy of 'revolutionary defeatism': the defeat of Russia in the war was beneficial to the cause of revolution. It was a doctrine that would cause a decisive break within the socialist movement in 1914. Indeed Lenin welcomed Russia's surrender at Port Arthur in January 1905. What political stance Koba took during the war is not clear, although 40 years later he would declare that the Soviet victory over Japan in August 1945 cleared a dark stain from the country marked by the 1905 defeat.

Soon after the fall of Port Arthur, on Sunday, 9 January 1905, a peaceful procession of St Petersburgers to the Winter Palace to petition for economic concessions and political representation ended in bloodshed: the guard troops fired on the marchers, scores of whom died. Ironically, the forces that had organised the march were controlled by the police. This scheme of 'police socialism', which had been intended to divert the mounting political discontent in a direction safe to the autocracy, led to a loss of control by the police. Thus with Bloody Sunday began the 1905 revolution. It was a rare instance in which almost all opposition forces in the country, from moderate liberals to radical Marxists, were united in their demands for concessions from the Tsar. Overwhelmed by the opposition to the autocracy, Tsar Nicholas II was forced to promise a quasi-constitutional democracy based on a parliament. This concession broke the unity of the opposition.

Koba was in his element in 1905. He moved about Transcaucasia, one day in Tbilisi, another in Batumi or Baku or Kutaisi, giving speeches to workers' meetings and organising their strikes, demonstrations and street actions. His January 1905 appeal was 'Workers of the

Caucasus! It is time to take revenge'.[46] How successful he was in these activities is not known. It appears that, as would be the case in 1917, he was not among the most visible of the social democratic leaders. He does seem, however, to have worked very hard and energetically. He was a skilful organiser, often acting behind the scenes. Koba's agitation was bellicose, even bloody: 'When the enemy sheds tears, is killed, moans and writhes with pain, then we must beat the drums and be happy.' He may have been involved in organising the 29 August action in Tbilisi in which some hundred workers were murdered by the police and Cossacks. Koba proclaimed, 'Blood for blood and death for death – that is how we will answer! To arms, on to revenge, long live the insurrection!'[47] In Baku, he witnessed the mutual pogroms of Armenians and 'Tatars' (Muslim Azeris) and was said to have organised military detachments to prevent further pogroms in Baku. (No doubt the detachments were also used for 'expropriations', robberies of banks and other sources of funds.)

The year 1905 was important for Koba in another respect. He was elected a delegate from Transcaucasia to a party conference held in Tampere (Tammerfors) in Finland in December 1905. There Koba met Lenin for the first time. It is said that Koba was deeply disappointed to find that Lenin, whom he had admired as the 'mountain eagle of our party', was, unlike himself, 'of privileged birth'. Koba entertained a class prejudice towards the privileged and intellectuals, whose very social position, in his view, determined their political wavering. By contrast, he equated the proletariat with firmness. Moreover, on several issues of critical importance, Koba clashed with Lenin. The first concerned the State Duma, a parliament set up by the decree of the Tsar in October 1905. It was to be a parliament based on indirect, unequal and incomplete male suffrage, a curia or council system discriminating heavily in favour of the propertied classes (one gentry vote equalled 15 peasant votes and 45 worker votes). Nevertheless, it had progressive elements as well, such as the creation of the worker council, an acknowledgement by the autocracy that the old estate system, which did not include a category of people as 'workers', was anachronistic. In addition to the new parliament the 1905 Revolution gave the nation a degree of freedom of the press and of association. All this afforded the revolutionaries an opportunity to bring their underground work into the light and engage in open politics. While attacking parliamentary politics, Lenin was also tempted to use the Duma elections for the party cause. Koba took the opposite position, supporting the boycott of the Duma. Before the party conference, Koba attacked the Duma as 'a negation of the people's revolution'. After the conference, he called the Duma a 'parliament of enemies of the people', contrasting it with the 'street' and the 'dictatorship of the street', which the autocracy could not disband.

Lenin hesitated and then reversed his position, ultimately supporting the boycott of the Duma. The party congress approved of the boycott. Koba appears to have seen Lenin's apparent lack of resolve as typical of 'intellectual vacillation'. Many years later, in 1920, Stalin took advantage of the occasion of Lenin's fiftieth birthday to recall the incident. Lenin, 'that giant', is great, Stalin noted, because he is modest and ready to acknowledge his mistakes. When Lenin shifted his position in 1905 regarding the boycott of the Duma, 'We were astonished. It had the effect of an electric shock. We cheered him to the echo.'[48] It was a golden opportunity for Stalin to promote himself at the cost of the living 'giant'.

A few months after the boycott resolution, at the fourth congress of the party held in Stockholm in April 1906, Koba again clashed with Lenin, this time on the issue of land reform. This was a particularly thorny issue for the Bolsheviks, who tended to regard the peasants as a petite bourgeoisie, a large segment of which would turn conservative, once their dreams of acquiring land came true. Given that, in general, European peasants had become politically conservative once they had acquired land after their emancipation, this was not an entirely unreasonable assumption. Yet Russia was still an overwhelmingly agrarian country with more than 85 per cent of the population residing in the countryside. Land reform was not an issue to be taken lightly. Many workers belonged in legal terms to the peasant estate and retained stakes in land reform in the countryside. Moreover, the Bolsheviks had to compete with the Socialist-Revolutionary (SR) Party, a party of agrarian socialists that was by far the most popular political force in the countryside. The SR party, a loosely knit party of diverse orientations, was known as a fighting party with a proven record of political terrorism. If proletarian revolution was to succeed in Russia, a country with a very small working class, the peasantry would play a key role. The peasant question thus posed a formidable challenge for the Bolsheviks. By 1906, even after the revolution in the cities had subsided, the countryside was still in turmoil: the peasants, demanding land, rebelled and seized landed estates and property. At the congress, Koba supported the confiscation of land and its redistribution among the peasants, an affirmation of peasant revolution. It appears that Lenin did not approve of Stalin's position as it sanctioned the demands of small proprietors, a bulwark of conservatism. Moreover, at the 1906 congress, the party (including Lenin) reversed its previous position and resolved to participate in the Duma elections in order to take advantage of legal opportunities. According to one account, Koba's disenchantment with Lenin was such that he soon stopped referring to Lenin's work in his writings: there are only two citations of Lenin in Stalin's writings from the Fourth Congress [1906] through to 1913.[49]

Back in the Transcaucasus, taking advantage of the limited freedom gained in the wake of the 1905 revolution, Koba actively worked in publishing party newspapers and literature. When newspapers were banned or print shops closed by the government, he opened new ones. Meanwhile, in the summer of 1906, Koba married Ekaterina (Kato) Svanidze in Tbilisi. Little is known about her except that the Svanidzes were a Georgian Bolshevik family. Her brother, Aleksandr, became an important Soviet official, only to be executed by Stalin in 1941. The atheist Koba had a religious marriage. Although he was a fugitive, living without a proper passport, a former classmate of Koba's at the seminary married them. Soon after the marriage, Koba left for work in Baku. In the meantime, the pregnant Kato, who had kept her maiden name for safety, was arrested by the police and detained for a month and a half. In March 1907 a son, Iakov, was born to the couple. Koba soon departed for Copenhagen, and from there to London, to attend the fifth party congress, probably visiting Berlin and Paris as well.

The 1907 congress resolved to disband armed detachments and proscribe 'expropriations' in view of the new political situation at the time. However, everyone suspected that Lenin had not abandoned expropriations to support the party and that he relied on Koba to carry them out. According to Davrichewy, who himself had participated in expropriations, Koba had long been involved in numerous expropriations.[50] Certainly, the party was in dire need of money. The first two Dumas had proved too radical for the autocracy to accept, with the result that on 3 June 1907 Prime Minister Petr Stolypin staged a 'coup'. A new electoral law, supplanting the constitution, ensured that a conservative majority be elected to the Duma. Now 1 gentry vote equalled 260 peasant votes and 543 worker votes (instead of 15 and 45 respectively).

Soon after the 1907 congress Koba returned to Tbilisi from Europe. His return coincided with a raid in broad daylight on 12 June 1907 by a group of Bolshevik terrorists on mail coaches delivering a large sum of banknotes and coins to the Imperial Bank of Tbilisi in the city centre. Using bombs, which killed several bystanders and wounded scores of them, the group managed to escape with some 250,000 roubles. The raid, led by the famous 'Kamo' (Semen Ter-Petrosian) and engineered by Leonid Krasin (who later became a prominent Soviet diplomat), became famous as the Erevan Square robbery. Historians concur that, even though he did not participate directly in it, Koba controlled the 'expropriation' from behind the scenes.[51]

The incident, a blatant violation of party discipline, became a scandal inside and outside the party. True, it is only one of numerous terrorist acts at the time. Russia had a long tradition of political terrorism. Lenin's elder brother had been implicated in an 1887 assassination attempt on Tsar Alexander III and was hanged.[52] Almost all revolutionary parties, including the Mensheviks and the Bolsheviks but particularly the SRs and anarchists, practised political terror. Between 1905 and 1907 as many as 4,500 state officials were killed or injured by terrorists, with an additional 2,180 private citizens slain in terrorist attacks. In the following two and a half years, 732 government officials and 3,051 private citizens were likewise killed. The government responded in kind: from 1905 to 1909 it executed nearly 3,000 civilians for political crimes.[53] Terror was not limited to the revolutionaries, however. Revolutionary upheaval had also led to large-scale anti-Jewish pogroms with the loss of more than 3,000 lives, mainly within the Pale of Settlement, the western region of the Russian Empire where Jews were legally allowed to reside.[54] In 1911 the then Prime Minister, Stolypin, was himself assassinated by a terrorist. Yet the Erevan Square robbery, coming so soon after the decision of the party congress against expropriation, became a serious problem for the entire party.

Koba was held responsible for the robbery and was expelled from the party by its Tbilisi organisation (he was also suspected of being involved in a number of other political killings), but it is not clear whether the decision to expel him was sanctioned by the party centre. In any case, Koba found it difficult to stay in Tbilisi and in July 1907 moved to Baku with his wife and son. Koba later noted that his three years of experience with the Baku oil workers made him 'a practical fighter': he became 'a journeyman for the revolution' in Baku.[55]

Baku, the centre of Azerbaijan, was an oil town. Like the coal and steel centre of the Donbas, Baku was a thriving industrial dynamo. It was also ethnically complex, with Armenians, Russians and Muslim Azeris working side by side. Baku's foreign capital which ran much of its oil industry was 'enlightened', as the Baku industrialists, eager to ensure a steady flow of oil, were willing to make certain concessions to labour. They sought to maintain institutional formalities for negotiation with labour (such as collective agreements), and the wages of Baku workers were high by national standards. As a result, Baku offered much more room for open, legal work than elsewhere. It was in Baku that Koba became associated with some of his future supporters, including the Red Army leader K.E. Voroshilov, the industrial leader G. (Sergo) K. Ordzhonikidze and the prosecutor of the Moscow trials A.Ia. Vyshinskii.

In the autumn of 1907, not long after Koba took his family to Baku, his wife became gravely ill. She was taken back to Tbilisi, but died there of typhoid at the age of 22. She had a Christian funeral. Devastated by her death, Koba said to his former classmate Iremaschwili, 'This creature has softened my heart of stone. She died and with her died my last warm feelings for people'. Then putting his right hand on his chest, he said, 'It is all so hollow here inside, so indescribably empty.'[56] According to another account, Koba said, 'My personal life is damned. I have nothing more that ties me to life, save socialism. From now on I'm going to dedicate all my life to it.'[57] His remarks would prove prophetic. After Kato's death Koba continued to work underground. He displayed no special interest in his son Iakov, who was raised by the Svanidzes. Fourteen years later, when Iakov moved to Moscow, Stalin treated him with apparent displeasure. Stalin did not want to be reminded of his tragic marriage.

In Baku, Koba's view of revolutionary activity changed in the direction of open politics, at least to some extent. Although he did not disband the fighting detachments of Baku Bolsheviks (against the party resolution), he dropped his opposition to the Duma and accepted parliamentary work as a legal theatre of agitation. On other issues, too, Koba came to adopt a more realistic stance. In the philosophical debate between the 'proletarian purist' A.A. Bogdanov and Lenin the intellectual pragmatist, for example, Koba had initially sympathised with Bogdanov, yet by 1908–9 Koba came to criticise both sides, famously characterising it as 'a tempest in a teapot': 'if our party is not a sect – and it is definitely no sect – it should not divide itself into groups according to philosophical (gnoseological) tendencies'. Koba's realism was fostered during his work in Baku, but it was also consistent with his view that the unity of the party (at least that of the Bolshevik faction) was of critical importance.[58]

Koba's growing prominence in the party attracted the attention of the police; in March 1908 he was arrested in Baku, and in early 1909 he was exiled to Sol'vychegodsk, Vologda, for two years. This was a relatively mild sentence: Vologda, in northern European Russian, was far closer to St Petersburg or Moscow than Siberia was. Koba prepared to flee again and succeeded in June 1909. He hid in St Petersburg for a while and then returned to Baku. Everywhere Koba went, personal conflict followed him. In Baku, Koba and his colleagues clashed, accusing each other of being police provocateurs. The professional revolutionary Koba often violated the basic rules of conspiracy, jeopardising the safety of other party members. Then in March 1910 he was arrested in Baku again. Koba tried to evade another exile by seeking marriage to a woman named S.L. Petrovskaia. He also petitioned the authorities for clemency on the grounds of his tuberculosis, but was nevertheless returned to Sol'vychegodsk in the autumn of 1910.

In early 1911 Koba attempted another flight, but apparently he failed and is said to have voluntarily returned to Sol'vychegodsk. Many revolutionaries considered such voluntary submission to authority beneath their dignity. At any rate, during his stay there, Koba is said to have fathered a child by a local widow, Mariia O. Kuzakova.[59] In June 1911 Koba's term of exile expired and he was allowed to move to Vologda, a provincial capital. Barred from living in the Transcaucasus or any of the major cities, he stayed in Vologda for a time. His stay in Vologda was probably also because of his relationship with a young woman, Pelageia G. Onufrieva, the fiancée of a fellow comrade in exile.

Koba fled to St Petersburg in September 1911 but was caught there almost immediately and returned to Vologda in December 1911. In Vologda he met and became close to a fellow exile, his future right-hand man, Viacheslav M. Skriabin (Molotov). While in Vologda, Koba was co-opted in absentia on to the party Central Committee (CC) and its Russian Bureau at the January 1912 party conference in Prague. In February 1912 he fled from Vologda to St Petersburg, where he helped to publish the party's newspaper, *Pravda*. The day it began publication, 22 April 1912, Koba was arrested again; by the summer he was banished to Narym, western Siberia, for three years, whereupon he fled again. In the autumn of that year, he campaigned for the Fourth Duma elections in St Petersburg and Moscow. The campaign helped Roman Malinovskii to be elected as a Bolshevik delegate; subsequently, however, Malinovskii was revealed to be a police agent, although no one had known about it at the time of the campaign.

Stalin

From the autumn of 1912 to February 1913 Koba lived in Europe (probably with a brief return to the capital in between), in Cracow (Kraków) in Habsburg Poland, and Vienna. He was 34 years old. It was then that Koba began to use the pen name Stalin by which he would be known for the rest of his life. Numerous commentators have made much of this name, which means 'steel' or 'man of steel' in Russian, because it turned out to symbolise his iron rule. Stalin later commented that the name was given to him by his comrades because they thought it suited him and thus it stuck.[60] Yet it is also possible that Koba had been seeking an appropriate name that would suit him not as a Transcaucasian but as a Russian revolutionary at a time when Russia, not Transcaucasia, had become the main theatre of his activity. It is possible that Stalin took the name from E.S. Stalinskii, the Polish-born translator of the 1888 multilingual edition of Rustaveli's epic poem.[61]

It was in Vienna that Stalin completed his first major theoretical work, 'Marxism and the National Question'.[62] Published under his new pen name in a Bolshevik monthly in March–May 1913, this treatise elevated Stalin to a leading position in the party on the national question. His detractors insist that it was written by ghost writers (possibly Lenin or Nikolai I. Bukharin). To be sure, Stalin's knowledge of foreign languages was good but not brilliant. Even though he spoke Armenian and Azeri (in addition to Georgian and Russian), his knowledge of German (and French) was limited at most to reading. (He also read Greek and studied English and Esperanto with very limited results.) It is possible that he received some help from others in reading German literature on the subject, but the treatise itself is almost certainly his own. Hailing from the small and conquered nation of Georgia, he became a believer in a centralised multinational state such as Germany and Russia, which he contended were 'unifiers of nationalities'. Like Lenin, Stalin acknowledged the right of nations to self-determination (including secession), but, also like Lenin, he believed that nations were obsolete, ultimately to be absorbed into 'a larger universality'. Stalin also implicitly acknowledged, to the great chagrin of Lenin, that the Austrian Marxists, Lenin's opponents, were right in insisting that nations possess 'cultural identities' and constitute 'communities of culture'.[63] Both ideas were to be reflected in Soviet nationality policy.

Before his treatise was published, Stalin returned to Russia. Perhaps he could have stayed in Europe – many of the Bolshevik leaders apparently preferred emigration to exile – but Stalin was temperamentally against the émigré intellectuals with their pronounced tendency to squabble. Whatever theoretical ambitions he may have had, Stalin always prided himself on being a *praktik*, a man of action. Clearly, for all its hardships and dangers, Stalin preferred underground work in Russia. Upon returning to Russia in February 1913, he was arrested. This time, the punishment was harsh: four years in Turukhansk on the Yenisei River, Siberia, near the Arctic Circle. In fact, Stalin had to live in Kureika, north of the Arctic Circle, which had only eight (or ten, according to some accounts) houses. It was well nigh impossible to escape from this forlorn place (although it may be that in the summer of 1916 he attempted to flee, but was detained and returned there).

Stalin was a difficult man even for fellow exiles. For a while he shared living quarters in exile with Ia.M. Sverdlov, the future nominal head of the Soviet government. According to Sverdlov, Stalin turned out 'too much of an individualist' in everyday life (which meant that Stalin did no cleaning, cooking or other necessary duties). Their ways parted and they saw each other very rarely in this backwater (their break-up may have had something to do with Stalin's relationship with an underage girl, with whom he is said to have fathered a son). Completely isolated, Stalin grew despondent. However, he also seems to have been resigned to his exile. His daughter Svetlana noted that Stalin 'always looked back on his years of exile as if they were nothing but hunting, fishing and walks through the taiga'.[64] Unlike other 'politicals', Stalin is known to have associated with common criminals while in exile. 'There were some nice fellows among the criminal convicts,' Stalin once remarked, they 'were nice, salt-of-the-earth fellows. But there were lots of rats among the political convicts. They once organised a comrades' court and put me on trial for drinking with the criminal convicts, which they charged was an offence.'[65] (Given the isolation of Kureika, this incident probably took place during an earlier exile.) To be sure, compared with the penal regime under Stalin's rule, exile under Nicholas was almost heaven. Stalin was able to hunt, fish, drink and even correspond with his comrades abroad. In correspondence Stalin whined constantly, complaining about his difficult life and bad health and asking for money and books. In one of his letters to Malinovskii, Stalin wrote: 'I don't have rich relatives or acquaintances, I have absolutely no one to whom to turn [for help].'[66]

Because Stalin did not abide by the most basic rules of conspiracy, he did not always get the sympathy of his comrades when he was arrested. When he was first sent to Turukhansk, Lenin and other leaders sought to organise his escape, but they did not succeed. Lenin considered Stalin important to the Central Committee as a non-Russian expert on the national question. With much disdain, Trotskii later stated:

These four years of exile should have been the years of intense intellectual activity. The exiles, under such conditions, keep diaries, write treatises, elaborate theses, platforms, exchange polemical letters, etc. It is hardly conceivable that Stalin did not write anything during four years of exile on the basic problems of war, the International and the revolution. Yet one would seek in vain for any traces of Stalin's intellectual labors during those four amazing years.[67]

Stalin may have tried to work but his isolation probably prevented him from doing much reading or writing.

When war began in 1914 in the Balkans, it quickly spread over Europe and beyond, becoming an event of world-historical significance known as the Great War, or the First World War. At the beginning, four empires controlled much of central and eastern Europe: the German, the Austro-Hungarian, the Russian and the Ottoman. When the war ended, none existed. Instead, an explicitly anti-capitalist and atheist government had emerged in Russia, the largest country in the world. On the other hand, the war split the international socialist movement. Whereas most of the European socialists supported the war in a patriotic outburst, tiny groups of internationalist socialists agitated against the war. Other equally small groups denounced the war as imperialist and advocated defeatism. Lenin and his small group of Russian Marxists openly contended that the defeat of tsarist Russia would be beneficial to the cause of revolution.

Stalin, however, was in exile and missed most of the turbulence. It is not clear what stand he took on the war, the most pressing issue of the day. He may have learnt something valuable in exile, however: politics as an art. According to one account, 'he spent many hours during his final Siberian exile poring over a copy of that classic manual of advice for the power-seeker, Machiavelli's *The Prince*'.[68] The book is said to have been given to him by his old friend from Tbilisi and fellow exile, Lev Kamenev.

In late 1916 Stalin was called up by the army and taken to Krasnoiarsk, a provincial capital. In February 1917, however, he was declared unfit for military service owing to his deformed arm. It was in Achinsk, near Krasnoiarsk, that the news of a revolution in the capital reached Stalin.

Stalin was 38 years old then. Did he know that he would become the ruler of the first socialist country in history? Did he have the ambition? It is not easy to know because Stalin left no autobiography or diaries. Clearly, however, he had proved himself cunning, ruthless and vindictive. He recognised no morality in politics and had a 'heart of stone'. Stalin also had nerves of steel. When he was in gaol in Baku, nocturnal executions, and particularly the screams and moans of the condemned, strained the nerves of the other prisoners to the extreme. Stalin, however, 'slept peacefully or quietly studied Esperanto'.[69] Wherever he went, he caused trouble. Yet he was good at finding people, and his political allies were devoted to him. Stalin had made it to the Central Committee of the Bolshevik party, but few would have believed then that one day he would become *the* undisputed Leader.

Notes

[1] *Izvestiia TsK KPSS*, 1990, 11, 132–4.

[2] *Istochnik*, 2001, no. 1, 55.

[3] Svetlana Alliluyeva, *Twenty Letters to a Friend* (New York, 1968), 164.

[4] There is a different account, however: 'Stalin did not love his mother . . . the old lady . . . was not devout. On the contrary, she had views that were progressive for that period. . . . One day, when she [Sergo Beriia's grandmother] exhorted her friend [Keke] to pray to God, pleading for mercy for the sins of their respective sons, Ekaterina laughed in her face.' Sergo Beria, *Beria, My Father* (London, 2001), 20.

[5] Edvard Radzinsky, *Stalin* (New York, 1997), 24. In 1930, however, she said to an American interviewer, 'Soso was always a good boy. I never had to punish him.' 'Stalin's Mother: "Soso was Always a Good Boy"' *Literary Digest*, 20 December 1930, 26.

[6] J. Iremaschwili, *Stalin und die Tragödie Georgiens* (Berlin, 1931), 6, 12, 40.

[7] Joseph Davrichewy, *Ah! Ce qu'on rigolait bien avec mon copain Staline* (Paris, 1979), 40–1, 46, 76.

[8] B.S. Ilizarov, *Tainaia zhizn' Stalina* (Moscow, 2002), 102, 366 and Aleksandr Ostrovskii, *Kto stoial za spinoi Stalina* (Moscow, 2002), 194.

[9] Iremaschwili, 5, and Davrichewy, 76, 82.

[10] Davrichewy, 47, 60.

[11] Ibid., 39.

[12] *Antireligioznik*, 1939, no. 12, 17, and *Molodaia gvardiia*, 1939, no. 12, 48–9.

[13] Iremaschwili, 8.

[14] The poems cited here are discussed in Donald Rayfield, 'Stalin the Poet', *PN Review*, 11:3 (1984).

[15] Iberia refers to Georgia, not Spain.

[16] Erik van Ree, *The Political Thought of Joseph Stalin* (London, 2002), 60.

[17] Rayfield, 46. The first poem was included in various editions of the Georgian primer *Mother Language* 'from which almost every Georgian child has learnt to read and write'.

[18] Davrichewy, 123.

[19] Alliluyeva, 43.

[20] Robert Service, *Stalin: A Biography* (London, 2004), 51, 54–5.

[21] *Slovo tovarishchu Stalinu* (Moscow, 2002), 462.

[22] Iremaschwili, 19–22, 25, 38.

[23] Donald Rayfield, *Stalin and His Hangmen* (London, 2004), 12.

[24] Alexander Barmine, *One Who Survived* (New York, 1945), 257.

[25] Grigorii Uratadze, *Vospominaniia gruzinskogo sotsial-demokrata* (Stanford, Calif., 1968), 66, 68, 69.

[26] V.V. Pokhlebkin, *Velikii psevdonim* (Moscow, 1996), 47–8, 76.

[27] RGASPI, f. 588, op. 3, d. 11, l. 33.

[28]V.A. Nevezhin, *Zastol'nye rechi Stalina* (Moscow, 2003), 158.

[29]'Stalin's Mother', 26 and Edward Ellis Smith, *The Young Stalin* (New York, 1967), 54.

[30]Ilizarov, 284–8. This child has yet to be confirmed, however.

[31]Ernest Ozolin'sh, 'Kakim ia pomniu Stalina', *Daugava*, 2002, no. 4, 130–1.

[32]P. Arsenidze, 'Iz vospominanii o Staline', *Novyi zhurnal*, 72 (1963), 235.

[33]Quoted in Rosamond Richardson, *The Long Shadow* (London, 1994), 211.

[34]Ostrovskii, 197, Arsenidze, 227 and Erik van Ree, 'Stalin's Bolshevism: The First Decade', *International Review of Social History*, 39:2 (August 1994), 368.

[35]Davrichewy, 31.

[36]Ostrovskii, 197.

[37]The most recent English book on this subject is Roman Brackman, *The Secret File of Joseph Stalin: A Hidden Life* (London, 2001).

[38]Arsenidze, 223–4.

[39]See Tom Reiss, *The Orientalist* (New York, 2005) and Essad-Bey, *Stalin* (Berlin, 1931) or the English edition: *Stalin: The Career of a Fanatic* (London, 1932).

[40]Davrichewy, 31, 35.

[41]Uratadze, 210.

[42]Stalin, *Works*, 1:67 (emphasis added).

[43]Arsenidze, 220–1.

[44]Ibid.

[45]*Otechetsvennye arkhivy*, 1995, no. 4, 79.

[46]Stalin, *Works*, 1:75.

[47]Van Ree, 'Stalin's Bolshevism', 369.

[48]Stalin, *Works*, 4:329. For the 1905 encounter, see Robert Himmer, 'First Impressions Matter: Stalin's Initial Encounter with Lenin, Tammerfors 1905', *Revolutionary Russia*, 14:2 (December 2001).

[49]Robert Himmer, 'On the Origin and Significance of the Name "Stalin"', *The Russian Review*, 45:3 (July 1986), 273.

[50]Davrichewy, 174–5, 177, 181, 213, 237–8.

[51]For the most recent work, see Miklós Kun, *Stalin: An Unknown Poet* (Budapest, 2003), 59–94.

[52]Norman M. Naimark, *Terrorists and Social Democrats: The Russian Revolutionary Movement under Alexander III* (Cambridge, Mass., 1983), 150.

[53]Anna Geifman, *Thou Shalt Kill: Revolutionary Terrorism in Russia, 1894–1917* (Princeton, NJ, 1993), 21, 228.

[54]John D. Klier and Shlomo Lambroza (eds), *Pogroms: Anti-Jewish Violence in Modern Russian History* (Cambridge, 1992), 228.

[55]Stalin, *Works*, 8:183, and Ronald Grigor Suny, 'A Journeyman for the Revolution: Stalin and the Labour Movement in Baku, June 1907–May 1908', *Soviet Studies*, 23:3 (January 1972).

[56]Iremaschwili, 40.

[57]Davrichewy, 35.

[58]Van Ree, 'Stalin's Bolshevism', 375–9.

[59]For this child, Konstantin S. Kuzakov, see 'K. Kuzakov – syn I.V. Stalina', *Argumenty i fakty*, 1995, no. 39, 12.

[60]*Istochnik*, 1999, no. 5, 79.

[61] Pokhlebkin, 81–89. Under Stalin's rule, this particular version of the epic poem was completely withdrawn from the Soviet public.

[62] Stalin, *Works*, 2:300–81.

[63] See Erik van Ree, 'Stalin and the National Question', *Revolutionary Russia*, 7:2 (December 1994).

[64] Alliluyeva, 131.

[65] *Khrushchev Remembers* (Boston, Mass., 1970), 301.

[66] Ostrovskii, 397.

[67] Leon Trotsky, *The Stalin School of Falsification*, tr. by John G. Wright (New York, 1962), 184.

[68] Robert C. Tucker, *Stalin as Revolutionary, 1879–1929* (New York, 1973), 212. The Russian politician N.I. Ryzhkov claims that he had read the 1869 Russian edition of *The Prince* containing Stalin's marginalia. Nikolai Ryzhkov, *Perestroika: istoriia predatel'stv* (Moscow, 1992), 354–6.

[69] *Dni* (Paris), 24 January 1928, 2 (Semen Vereshchak).

Chapter 2

Revolution and Civil War

At the beginning of 1917, Stalin was suffering in exile. He was not to
be the chief architect of the October 1917 Revolution, thus 'missing'
the critical event, as his critics have observed, yet by the summer of
1917 he would become one of the most important figures in the party.
The October Revolution, like other pivotal events in any nation, was
the defining moment for the Bolsheviks. It proved painful for Stalin
that he, a drab orator, did not stand out as prominently as Lenin and
Trotskii. (According to Molotov, 'in his youth, Stalin had once made an
effort to improve his abilities in this regard'. Andrei Gromyko, to whom
Molotov recounted this story after Stalin's death, noted that his efforts
were 'evidently without success. He couldn't conquer his nature.')[1]
Nor did Stalin possess the intellectual or literary flair of Trotskii. Yet
he continued to rise, becoming the People's Commissar (Minister) of
Nationality Affairs in the revolutionary government and a member of
the all-powerful Politburo (Political Bureau) of the party in 1919 when
it was set up. His dictatorship in Tsaritsyn in 1918 introduced all the
characteristics of his later rule in the 1930s. One of these was the 'ability to "exert pressure" ' which 'Lenin prized so highly in Stalin', according to Trotskii.[2] 'Exerting pressure' is surely too mild an expression for
Stalin's political style. In any case, whatever disagreements and conflicts Stalin may have had with Lenin, he climbed the ladder of power
with Lenin's support. It was during these critical years of revolution
and civil war that Stalin also experienced acute conflicts with Trotskii.

From February to October

Much historical literature maintains that the February Revolution
which led to the collapse of the centuries-old autocracy caught the revolutionaries by surprise. In January 1917, just a few weeks before the
revolution, Lenin famously noted that 'We, the old people, won't survive to see the decisive battles of the forthcoming revolution'. When

the news of revolution in Petrograd (with which Russia replaced the German-sounding name of St Petersburg/Petersburgh in 1914) reached him in Zurich, Switzerland, he uttered: 'It's staggering! It's so incredibly unexpected!'[3] How Stalin reacted to the news is not known, but the revolution may well have been a pleasant surprise to a revolutionary cut off from the capital and suffering in exile.

Revolution should not have been altogether unexpected, however, considering that, like the Russo-Japanese War, the war against Germany and Austria had become a losing battle for Russia. Whatever enthusiasm might have existed in the population at the beginning, Russia's military might proved less than adequate. By 1917 the front line had been pushed far inside the pre-war borders in the west. On 16 February 1916 a German general noted in his diary, 'It would seem that she [Russia] cannot hold out longer than the autumn.' The British military attaché with the Russian Army, Colonel Knox, described Russia's military losses: 'More than a million men had been killed. A further two million were either missing (that is to say, dead) or prisoners-of-war. More than half a million were in hospital. Nearly a million and half were on extended leave or had been excused all further service. A further million men had deserted.'[4] Consequently, Tsar Nicholas II found it difficult to deal with the Duma, instead relying on his close entourage (which by then included the Siberian charlatan Rasputin) in affairs of the state. As in the previous war, Russia appeared to every observer to be headed in the wrong direction. The Right deemed it urgent to save Russia from the crisis, murdering Rasputin in December 1916. Others, including concerned business leaders, were hatching plans for a 'palace coup', and numerous Leftist groups were organising the masses of discontented people.

There are many indications that Lenin had eagerly anticipated revolution in Russia, 'having bet his entire political reputation on the outbreak of revolution and on turning the imperialist war into a civil war'.[5] In the January 1917 speech quoted earlier, Lenin said, 'Europe is pregnant with revolution.'[6] Nadezhda Krupskaia, Lenin's wife, wrote of him on the eve of the February Revolution: 'Never before had Vladimir Ilyich [Lenin] been in such an uncompromising mood as he was during the last months of 1916 and the early months of 1917. He was positively certain that the revolution was impending.'[7]

War-weariness had permeated Russian society. Procurement of grain was becoming increasingly difficult: the peasants proved loath to part with their produce because the government had nothing to give them in return. This was a relatively new problem. For centuries the government simply squeezed the peasants in order to run the country (including financing wars). It used the collective responsibility of the peasant communes for tax payments and other duties. After the 1905 Revolution the tsarist government under Stolypin realised that Russia, like West European countries, needed independent, well-off peasants to create a stable political base in the country and began to dismantle the communes, which would loosen the tight reins on the peasants. Once loosened, however, the reins appeared to be lost forever: the Government found it difficult if not impossible to exploit the peasants as it had done for centuries. The 'peasant question' thus crippled the tsarist government as it would, later, the 1917 Provisional Governments and the Soviet Government under Lenin and Stalin.[8] People, especially the urban population, were hungry. Industrial actions, both spontaneous and organised, were rising. The country was becoming unruly. When the women of Petrograd demonstrated on 23 February, International Women's Day, demanding bread, followed by the hungry and striking men, disturbances turned quickly into revolution. Anger filled the streets. Over the following days, although dozens of demonstrators were shot dead, in general the capital's military guards proved unwilling to follow the orders of their superiors. The authority of Nicholas, then far away from the capital, at the Army HQ in Mahiliou (Mogilev), in present-day Belarus, evaporated almost overnight. On 2 March, on the advice of his military commanders Nicholas abdicated in favour of his brother, the Grand Duke Mikhail. Mikhail, worried about his own safety, declined the throne.

Thereupon a Provisional Government formed, mainly from Duma deputies of diverse political persuasion ranging from conservatives to liberals to one socialist. Within weeks Russia, however chaotic, had become the 'freest country in the world', as Lenin exclaimed. Censorship disappeared altogether. Basic civil rights and universal suffrage were granted, as was a generous amnesty.

Stalin, in common with all other revolutionaries, welcomed the revolution and took advantage of the new freedom. On 8 March, along with his fellow exiles Kamenev and M.N. Muranov, he left Achinsk for the capital by the Trans-Siberian railway. They arrived in Petrograd four days later. Stalin immediately sought out the family of an old acquaintance from Tbilisi, the Alliluevs. (In 1918 he was to marry one of them, Nadezhda Allilueva.) The Bolsheviks in the capital were divided in their assessment of the political situation. The party newspaper *Pravda*, now legal and under Molotov's editorship, regarded the Provisional Government as bourgeois and advocated no support for it, while the Petersburg (the Bolsheviks did not follow the official name change and continued to use the old name on the grounds that

the change was chauvinistic) party committee took the more conciliatory position of supporting the Provisional Government 'in so far as
its actions correspond to the interests of the proletariat and the broad
democratic masses of the people'.[9] Stalin sought a position in the Russian Bureau of the Central Committee, which published *Pravda*, but
failed initially to gain full membership 'in view of certain personal
characteristics'. What the bureau meant by these characteristics is not
known, but the following day, 13 March, the bureau 'reversed itself
and accepted him as a full member, at the same time naming him a
member of the editorial board of *Pravda*'. Stalin, along with Kamenev
and Muranov, were also designated as Bolshevik representatives to the
Executive Committee of the Petrograd Soviet.[10]

The Soviet (the word 'soviet' means 'council' in Russian) was *the* organ of the Petrograd people. Soviets were elected by the people themselves (workers, soldiers, peasants) as an alternative power to official
authority. They had first emerged in 1905 under the leadership of the
Mensheviks. In 1917, even before the Provisional Government formed,
the Petrograd Soviet was organised. As the old power structure van-
ished, Soviets quickly appeared at various levels (region, city, factory
and so on) all over the country. Unlike the Provisional Government,
which had virtually no means of enforcement (the old police organisation had fallen part), the Soviets became an organ of popular power
nearly everywhere. In this way, the Provisional Government became
dependent on the Soviets for its legitimacy. The Soviets were the locus
of actual power, but the Soviet leaders, dominated by the Mensheviks
and the SRs, were willing to work with the Provisional Government 'in
so far as' it conformed to the wishes of the Soviets. This configuration
of power, especially in the capital, was referred to as 'dual power'.

Once on the *Pravda* editorial board, Stalin pushed aside Molotov
and others (at least, Molotov felt it to be that way), and began to control the newspaper. Stalin, along with Kamenev, took critical steps immediately. Kamenev published essays that supported the Provisional
Government and defended the position of 'revolutionary defencism'
with regard to the war. Similarly, Stalin followed with an article that
proclaimed that the slogan 'Down with war' was 'absolutely unsuitable
as a practical means' and agitated instead 'to bring pressure on the Provisional Government to declare its consent to start peace negotiations
immediately'.[11] More than half a century later, still irked by the move
by Stalin and Kamenev, Molotov criticised them: 'As long as I was on
the [editorial] board, such things [publishing defencist and pacifist es-
says] did not happen.' Molotov, surprised that Stalin's 1917 pacifist essay had made its way into his *Works* in 1953, maintained that the essay

was a mistake.[12] Whether Stalin was aware that his conditional support of the Provisional Government and pacifist position were closer to the Mensheviks than to Lenin who urged 'turning the imperialist war into a civil war' is not known. Within a few days, however, Stalin was reminded that Lenin's position was much more radical and uncompromising. 'Letters from Afar' by Lenin, who was still in Zurich, were brought over to the *Pravda* editors. They did not publish his first letter *in toto*, but in edited form to suit their positions, and completely ignored his second letter.

Meanwhile, Lenin worked hard to return to Russia from Switzerland. It was not possible for him and his companions to cross the war zone from the west to Russia. Pavel Miliukov, a noted historian and the liberal Minister of Foreign Affairs in the Provisional Government, was opposed to having the well-known defeatist back in Russia. By contrast, Germany, like Japan during the Russo-Japanese War, found it politically expedient to assist revolutionaries opposed to their own government. Thus, on 27 March, with the approval and assistance of Germany, Lenin, his close associate Grigorii Zinov'ev and other Russian revolutionaries left Switzerland in what is known as a 'sealed' train (in fact it was not sealed). By way of Germany, Sweden and the Grand Duchy of Finland, they arrived in Petrograd a week later.

In anticipation of Lenin's return, Stalin became somewhat more cautious. In his report to the All-Russian Conference of Bolsheviks on 29 March, Stalin finally proposed not to support the Government, Lenin's stance. The conference, nonetheless, resolved to support the Government. As to the question of seeking the unification of the Bolsheviks with the left-wing Mensheviks (those who did not take the defencist position), however, Stalin, like the majority of the Bolsheviks present, was in favour of exploring the possibility, a position that Stalin had taken since 1912 or so and which Molotov had denounced.

When Lenin, Zinov'ev and others arrived in Petrograd on the evening of 3 April, the Bolsheviks (and others) present at the Finland Station were astonished by Lenin's militancy. (Stalin, attending a meeting to explore the merger of the Bolsheviks and the left-wing Mensheviks, was not among those who welcomed Lenin.) Lenin's programme for action, known as the 'April Theses', the gist of which had already been expressed in his 'Letters from Afar', were indeed radical. Russia was passing from the first, 'bourgeois' stage of revolution to its second stage, 'which must place power in the hands of the proletariat and the poorest sections of the peasantry'. Therefore no support should be given to the Provisional Government. The Soviets were the only possible form of revolutionary government (a parliamentary republic would be 'a retrograde step'), so 'All Power to the Soviets'. The Soviets had to be won over to the Bolshevik side. Only by overthrowing capital would it be possible to end the imperialist war. All landed estates were to be confiscated.

Lenin's agenda for the revolution passing to the second stage was very similar to Trotskii's theory of 'permanent revolution'. In the wake of the 1905 revolution Trotskii, a left-wing independent Menshevik, had published a theoretical treatise 'Results and Prospects' in which he explained why in Russia, with its relatively weak bourgeoisie, a bourgeois-democratic revolution had to be carried out by the proletariat (and the peasants) to the end; this process would inevitably evolve into a socialist revolution, yet the survival of socialism would be possible only when socialist revolution took place in Europe. Trotskii's ideas may not have been totally original, but it was he who first formulated the theory clearly and systematically.[13] This was not standard Marxist theory, which supposed two distinct stages of revolution, bourgeois and socialist. Lenin's position on this is not entirely clear: if anything, he tended to be dismissive of Trotskii's theory. Yet it was clear to everyone in April 1917 that Lenin's position had come very close to Trotskii's. This rapprochement made it possible for Trotskii to join the Bolshevik party in July 1917. In April Trotskii hurriedly left New York for Russia but was promptly detained in Canada by the British authorities in Halifax. He returned to Petrograd only in May.

It is possible that Stalin's weak theoretical background distinguished him from Lenin and Trotskii. Yet there were many prominent theorists among the Mensheviks as well (including the father of Russian Marxism, Georgii Plekhanov), and Stalin's position towards the revolutionary process in Russia was an 'orthodox' Marxist one. After all, who could believe that Russia, barely out of feudalism, was ready for a proletarian revolution against Marx's prediction? Stalin did not accept Lenin's theses immediately. *Pravda* did not publish them promptly, and when it did on 7 April, it attached an editorial note, indicating that they represented Lenin's personal opinion, not the party's.[14]

There were increasing signs that Lenin and Trotskii might well be right in anticipating that the revolution would pass quickly to the second, proletarian stage. The Provisional Government proved weak. It was bent on carrying out Russia's war obligation to the Entente against the pacifist mood of the soldiers. (It is widely speculated that many cabinet members, including Miliukov, pledged Russia's continued contribution to the war until victory as members of international Freemasons.) The first Provisional Government fell quickly, and in May a new, coalition government formed in which both Mensheviks and SRs participated. Popular suspicion that the new Provisional Government was still 'bourgeois' died hard, however; as the countryside fell into chaos with peasants confiscating lands without anyone's sanction, the Government could only postpone the solution of the land question, to be decided at a future constituent assembly. Chaos in the countryside did nothing to assuage the food shortages in the towns, which remained hungry and unruly. Numerous former policemen were lynched by angry crowds, and so were untold numbers of criminals. A.H. Birse, Churchill's Russian interpreter and a native of Petrograd, wrote about his experience of 1917: 'The intensely hated police were hounded out of their stations and shot on the spot. Those who took refuge on the roofs of houses became engaged in a shooting match with soldiers, workers and students; they were hunted down and mercilessly slaughtered. Police stations were set on fire.'[15] Isaiah Berlin, a Petrograd resident in 1917, recalled events in the capital many years later:

> The only people who remained loyal to the Tsarist government, I recollect, were the police. I do not think that there is much about this in the literature. The police in the streets were called Pharaohs – oppressors of the people. Some of them sniped at the revolutionaries from rooftops and attics. I remember seeing a policeman being dragged off, pale and struggling, by a mob, obviously to his death – that was a terrible sight that I have never forgotten; it gave me a lifelong horror of physical violence.[16]

Soldiers and sailors refused to obey their superior officers. They were democratising the supremely hierarchical military by electing their own officers. Discipline broke down everywhere – at the front, on the shop floor, in the street and in the countryside. The 'bourgeois' Government had to rely on socialist parties simply to survive. A perspicacious observer would have wondered whether (and how) this 'bourgeois' revolution could be settled at all.

What Stalin thought of all this is not known. By late April, he had come to accept Lenin's views. One historian has observed that 'Working side by side with Lenin in the *Pravda* office, Stalin readily absorbed the older man's point of view.' At the seventh party congress in late April, Stalin, to the surprise of many present, came out in support of Lenin against Kamenev. Stalin acted at the congress as if he were Lenin's spokesman. On the question of nationality, with the exception of Stalin, 'not a single representative of the national minorities supported Lenin': the proposition of Lenin and Stalin on the right of nations to self-determination met with stiff resistance from non-Russian Bolsheviks (such as the Pole F.E. Dzerzhinskii) on the grounds that it was against proletarian internationalism. In any case, Stalin emerged as one of the top leaders at the congress, the third most popular in the election to the party Central Committee.[17]

The summer of 1917 radicalised the political process. In June, Aleksandr F. Kerenskii, the socialist Minister of War who admired Napoleon, resumed a military offensive. It ended in a fiasco with hundreds of thousands of casualties. The mood of soldiers and sailors turned even more militantly against the Provisional Government, which provided no tangible solution to either the question of peace or to the questions of food and land. Neither the Bolsheviks nor the Soviets could contain the popular anger. Lenin was cautious about spontaneous mass street actions (which the party could not readily control), whereas Stalin was more supportive (as he was in 1905). Popular anger exploded in early July in the form of a mass, armed uprising in the capital. The crisis prompted the Government to declare the July Incident a Bolshevik conspiracy, though Lenin did not in fact support it. The frustration of the people was such that when the head of the SRs, a leader of the Soviets and the Minister of Agriculture Viktor Chernov, came out to calm things down, he was detained by the crowd. One angry worker shouted at him in a now famous line: 'Take power, son of a bitch, when it's handed to you.'[18] The Government attacked the Bolsheviks, portraying Lenin as a German spy. Lenin and Zinov'ev were forced underground, and Trotskii and Kamenev were arrested. *Pravda* was banned (though it soon began publication again under a different title). Stalin, who had maintained working relations with the Soviet leaders, was not arrested. Instead, along with the Alliluevs, he aided Lenin's escape and negotiated the disarming of soldiers and sailors.

The July Incident signified the failure of the Government. The Prime Minister Prince Georgii L'vov resigned, noting that 'The only way to save the country now is to close down the Soviet and shoot at the people. I cannot do that. But Kerenskii can.'[19] Kerenskii took over as Prime Minister and formed a second coalition government. Yet his new government could not save the situation. Lenin now abandoned the slogan 'All Power to the Soviets' (the Mensheviks and SRs, which dominated the Soviets, had 'betrayed' the revolution, Lenin claimed). He saw only two ways out of Russia's predicament: Bolshevik seizure of power by an armed uprising or a military dictatorship.

Stalin was cautious regarding Lenin's call for an armed uprising. Stalin was, after all, a Bolshevik representative to the Soviets, whereas Lenin had little to do with them and could not control them. Stalin must have found it tactless, to say the least, to rescind the wildly popular slogan 'All Power to the Soviets'. Meanwhile, from his hideout Lenin pressed the party hard for a change of course. When the sixth party congress met in late July, with other leaders hiding or in gaol, Stalin took charge and gave the Central Committee (CC) report to the congress. He did not discuss Lenin's new call. It was symbolic of his rise to power that Stalin had become the main speaker at the congress, but his rise was balanced by the acceptance into the party of Trotskii and his followers; Trotskii proved more popular than Stalin in the election to the CC.[20]

The other possibility Lenin foresaw, that of military dictatorship, failed, to the decisive advantage of the Bolsheviks. After the July Incident, Kerenskii replaced the Commander-in-Chief General Aleksei Brusilov with General Lavr Kornilov. Kerenskii and others believed that Kornilov was the man who could restore discipline and order to the military. Some hoped that Kornilov would overthrow the Provisional Government and establish a dictatorship, but Kerenskii hoped that Kornilov's authority would strengthen his own power and, if necessary, help to establish and support his position. Concerned about Kornilov's power, however, Kerenskii soon dismissed him, prompting Kornilov to rebel against the government. Few, even soldiers, were willing to join him. The Kornilov rebellion failed miserably, and ended up with the people in the capital being armed in its defence. Kerenskii lost his political credibility: the conservatives considered him a traitor, while the Left suspected that Kerenskii was a party to the Kornilov affair, a cunning scheme to enable him to become a dictator. In the summer, particularly after the Kornilov affair, it was the Bolsheviks that came to dominate many Soviets, including those in major cities such as Moscow and Petrograd. On 25 September, Trotskii became the chairman of the Petrograd Soviet.[21]

In the events leading up to the Bolshevik seizure of power on 25 October, Stalin's role was not as visible as that of Trotskii (who organised the uprising) or as decisive as that of Lenin (who directed the entire affair). On the one hand, Lenin sought to allay the fear of the Bolsheviks that their seizure of power, even if successful, would collapse into civil war. Lenin declared in September that if 130,000 landowners had governed the country by perpetrating 'endless violence against 150,000,000 people' in Russia, a party with 240,000 members surely would be able to govern the country. (From February to September, the membership of the Bolshevik party had increased sixfold from 40,000 to 240,000). On the other hand, Lenin comforted himself that were the revolutionary regime to survive longer than had the Paris Commune (just over two months), history would justify the Bolsheviks. On the eve of the uprising, Lenin urged the Bolshevik leaders to proceed without hesitation: 'History will not forgive revolutionaries for procrastinating when they could be victorious today (and they certainly will be victorious today), while they risk losing much tomorrow, in fact, they risk losing everything.'[22] In these critical weeks of the autumn of 1917 Stalin acted in favour of Lenin's plan (even if he disagreed on certain issues).[23] Yet when two prominent leaders, Zinov'ev and Kamenev, publicly opposed Lenin's plan, threatening to split the party, Stalin implicitly defended the two 'strikebreakers', most likely in order to preserve party unity.

In the end, the party did not split and the uprising succeeded. Lenin's plan was fraught with problems, however. The most serious concerned the legitimacy of the new revolutionary government in the event that his plan succeeded. Lenin did not trust the Soviets. Even though the Bolsheviks had grown much stronger, they still could not control the Soviets: at the first congress in June, the Bolsheviks accounted for only about 100 delegates out of over 600; at the second congress 300 out of the roughly 670 delegates were Bolsheviks. Lenin wanted to take power *before* the second All-Russian Congress of Soviets convened on 25 October, and to present a fait accommpli to the Congress. Other leaders feared that it would be tantamount to a coup d'état. Unlike the scenes depicted in the celebrated film *October* by Sergei Eizenshtein (Eisenstein), the armed uprising of 25 October proved largely peaceful and bloodless: it met little resistance. (Isaiah Berlin recalled that 'We – my family and its friends – hardly knew that it had happened').[24] The uprising began before the congress met and ended successfully while it was still in session.

Lenin and Trotskii were the leaders popularly associated with the Revolution, and their visibility eclipsed Stalin almost completely. It would be wrong to state, however, that Stalin missed it – by 1917 Stalin had become one of the central figures in the party but, like every other Bolshevik, he simply was not as visible as Lenin or Trotskii.

Whatever the misgivings of many Bolsheviks leaders, Lenin's gamble worked. When the Bolshevik uprising against the Government became known to the delegates of the Soviet Congress, most of the Mensheviks and SRs walked out in protest. Their desertion largely freed Lenin's hand. He did not have to form a government against or apart from the Soviets but to build one on them. After a number of twists and turns, a Soviet government was formed that was dominated by the Bolsheviks but which included members of the Left SR Party (a left-wing splinter from the SRs) willing to collaborate with them. Lenin became the chairman of the Council of People's Commissars (as the new Soviet cabinet was called), Trotskii the People's Commissar of Foreign Affairs and Stalin the People's Commissar of Nationalities.

Civil War

Stalin's post was not as powerful or prestigious as Lenin's or Trotskii's, but all the same it was a portfolio of no small import. As nearly everyone (including Lenin) feared, the Bolshevik seizure of power inevitably led to armed conflict with counter-revolutionary forces, ranging from monarchists to liberals, to socialists and to nationalists. Censorship was revived immediately after the Bolshevik Revolution. Berlin described the demise of a 'Liberal newspaper called *Day* – it reappeared as *Evening*, then as *Night*, then as *Midnight*, then as *Darkest Night*, and then, after four or five days or so it was finally suppressed'.[25] Petrograd was conquered relatively easily, but the provinces had yet to be won. (Even in Petrograd, however, people like Berlin, whose parents were 'bourgeois liberals', thought that 'the putsch might last at most for two or three weeks'.)[26] As in 1991 when the Soviet Union collapsed, in 1917 non-Russian areas of the Russian Empire began to break away from Russia. National sentiments ran high here and there. In December 1917, for example, Finland declared independence, which the Soviet government recognised based on the principle of self-determination. Yet when it came to Ukraine (which Russians referred to as 'Little Russia', part of Russia), the Soviet government proved much less generous, denouncing Ukraine's socialist Rada ('rada' is a Ukrainian word for 'soviet'). Even before the Rada declared independence in January 1918, war had broken out there between Bolsheviks and anti-Bolshevik forces. Similar situations obtained elsewhere.

The issue of war confounded the already complex political situation in the country. Immediately upon his seizure of power, Lenin issued the famous 'Decree on Peace'. It satisfied the popular yearning for peace and therefore proved hugely popular, but it caused serious international problems by calling for a 'just and democratic' peace without annexations and indemnities. Trotskii followed by publishing the tsarist secret treaties with the Allied Powers. When neither Britain nor France proved willing to participate in peace negotiations, the Soviet Government proposed a separate peace with the Central Powers (Germany and Austria–Hungary). The Ukrainian Central Rada, however, refused to be represented by the Bolsheviks at the Brest-Litovsk peace negotiations, and sent its own delegation. So did Finland, Poland and the Baltic states. A German proposal to dismember the old Russian Empire, which meant Russia losing Ukraine, Poland, Georgia, the Baltic states and other 'Russian' territory, was not acceptable to the Soviet Government. In the meantime, on 9 February 1918, the Rada signed a treaty with the Central Powers that resulted in the virtual military occupation of Ukraine by German forces. Trotskii's delay tactics ('Neither peace nor war'), which Stalin initially supported, led to the invasion of Soviet Russian territory by the German forces. After bitter debate, Lenin's Government had to accept humiliating terms and signed the Treaty of Brest-Litovsk with Germany on 3 March 1918.

Treaties did not settle the matter. Many Bolsheviks inside and outside the territorially diminished 'Russia' would not accept the humiliation, some resorting to guerrilla warfare against national governments. The Bolshevik partner, the Left SRs, regarded the Brest-Litovsk settlement as a treasonous abandonment of revolutionary war. In Ukraine, in April 1918 the Germans replaced the Rada with a dictatorship by a puppet government (of Hetman Pavlo Skoropadskii). This led to full-scale civil war among the Germans, the Bolsheviks, the various nationalists, the Russian counter-revolutionary forces bent on recovering Ukraine and numerous independent peasant armies. In July 1918, the Left SRs assassinated the German ambassador Count Mirbach in a failed attempt to provoke Germany to attack Russia and to incite popular revolt against the Bolsheviks. This incident ended with the collapse of the Bolshevik–Left SR coalition and the establishment of Bolshevik one-party dictatorship. Under these conditions, Stalin declared that the principle of self-determination had turned into a 'fiction' and had 'lost its revolutionary meaning' (even though he did not abandon it altogether).[27]

It was in the tense atmosphere of 1918, shortly before Lenin moved the capital from Petrograd to Moscow in March 1918, that Stalin married Nadezhda Allilueva, aged sixteen, the daughter of his long-time acquaintance.

It was also then, in the spring of 1918, that Stalin took the trouble to drag the Menshevik leader Iulii Martov to the revolutionary tribunal for slander. In March 1918 Martov noted in a Menshevik publication that Stalin had once been expelled from the party for his involvement in 'expropriation'. Stalin contended that he had never been tried by the party nor expelled from it. The revolutionary tribunal, modelled on the Jacobin institution, dealt with crimes against the state. Slandering the People's Commissar of Nationalities was considered a political crime. Martov protested that the matter should be dealt with by a 'people's court', not the revolutionary tribunal, which was a 'political court'. Stalin responded that it was a 'purely political case', instigated by the desperate leader of a bankrupt political group. Martov retorted by asking whether he could bring to the tribunal those who slandered him every day in the official Soviet press. After Martov's defence, Stalin contended that there was not a shade of truth in Martov's story and challenged him to produce documentary evidence. Martov asked that witnesses be called to testify to Stalin's involvement in the 1908 robbery of the steamship *Nicholas I*. His request was not granted because, given the situation, it would have been impossible to find and bring witnesses from the Caucasus. The tribunal was postponed for a week, however, to summon witnesses from Moscow and Petrograd. No witnesses appear to have testified. (One witness could not report from Petrograd owing to the lack of money.) On 18 April 1918, the tribunal found Martov guilty and censured him: all newspapers in Moscow were ordered to publish this censure.[28]

The court neither proved nor disproved Stalin's actual involvement in this particular example of expropriation. More importantly, this case is indicative of the way in which Stalin was to politicise everything (although it has to be admitted that Martov, too, used the case for political purposes). Martov got off lightly, but numerous Soviet citizens would pay with their lives for much more innocent 'slander' in the 1930s. Martov died in Germany in 1920 without witnessing the bloody Stalin era. It is said that when Lenin proposed monetary assistance to Martov upon learning of his illness in Germany, Stalin refused to comply on the grounds that he did not want to 'waste money on the enemy'.[29]

Like other Bolshevik leaders, Stalin became preoccupied with the fight for survival, more absent than present in his own commissariat. Peace was fragile at best. Workers remained militant, often against the new Government which, like the previous governments, could not feed the hungry urban population. Just before her marriage to Stalin, Nadezhda Allilueva wrote to Alisa Radchenko, the wife of an Old Bolshevik and a friend of her parents: 'There's real hunger in Petrograd. They hand out only an eighth of a pound of bread every day, and one day they gave us none at all. I've even cursed the Bolsheviks. But they promise to increase the ration on February 18. We'll see if they do or not.'[30] The promise was often not kept, because the Government could not procure enough grain to feed the city. After the October seizure of power, the Bolsheviks had handed over the landed estates to the peasants. Once they acquired land, a dream come true, the peasants, as the Bolsheviks had feared all along, appeared to turn conservative: they were loath to part with their produce at a time when industry was in shambles and they could buy precious little in return. The Government introduced what was called the 'food-supply dictatorship' in May 1918.[31] In the summer, Lenin declared war on the 'kulaks' (literally meaning 'fists' but referring to rich peasants) who were 'bloodsuckers'. Armed detachments of workers were dispatched to the countryside to requisition grain, and the peasants responded in kind.

Other measures taken by the Bolsheviks also antagonised large segments of the population. The constituent assembly, for example, which the Bolsheviks had supported before the October coup, actually met in January 1918 but was dissolved by the Bolsheviks. The election to the assembly, which took place in November 1917, was the only free and universal election in the entire history of Russia before 1989. The election results were not favourable towards the Bolsheviks. The party gained only about 23 per cent of the votes, and the SRs about 37 per cent (although the votes for the SRs did not distinguish between the SRs and the Left SRs). The Bolsheviks drew their support mainly from urban workers and soldiers and the SRs from the peasants. Given the overwhelmingly rural population of Russia, the Bolshevik performance was respectable, but they lost the election. So when the assembly finally met in January, the Bolsheviks dissolved it on the grounds that the assembly, falling into the hands of 'counter-revolutionaries', did not represent the actual political configuration of the country. The Bolsheviks stood accused of hypocrisy and treason.

The Bolshevik murder of Nicholas II and the Romanov family in July 1918 also marked a significant turning point. Armed conflict with anti-Bolshevik forces led the Bolsheviks to think that the former Tsar and his family could become a rallying point for counter-revolution. With the approval of Lenin, they were murdered in captivity in Ekaterinburg (later Sverdlovsk) in the Urals. Terror incited more terror. In August Lenin, in turn, was shot by Fanny Kaplan, an SR recruit. Lenin survived the attempt on his life, but Kaplan was executed. Thus by the summer of 1918 terror was in full swing on all fronts.

The terror regime Stalin set up in Tsaritsyn in the summer of 1918 presaged his bloody rule to come. Tsaritsyn, to be renamed Stalingrad in 1925, was an important trading centre on the river Volga, a gateway to the south. In early June 1918 Stalin, the government's special plenipotentiary, was sent to Tsaritsyn with Lenin's mandate to obtain food in the south. Some 450 armed men accompanied him.[32] Tsaritsyn was surrounded by anti-Bolshevik Cossack forces and Stalin soon found himself deeply involved in military affairs. He was opposed to the practice of Trotskii, now the head of the Red Army, of employing tens of thousands of old military officers for the civil war owing to the lack of Red commanders. Stalin reorganised the military front and conducted 'a ruthless purge of the rear, administered by an iron hand'.[33] Stalin wrote to Lenin on 7 July from Tsaritsyn: 'You may rest assured that we shall spare nobody, neither ourselves nor others, and shall deliver the grain by all means. If our military "specialists" (bunglers!) had not been asleep or loafing about, the [railway] line would not have been cut, and if the line is restored, it will not be thanks to, but in spite of them. . . . Be assured that our hand will not tremble.'[34] Stalin also made it clear that he would not subject himself to any authority. Writing to Lenin three days later, he said,

> For the good of the cause, I need military powers. I have already written about this, but have received no reply. Very well. In that case, I shall myself, without any formalities, dismiss army commanders and commissars who are ruining the cause. The interests of the work dictate this, and, of course, the absence of a paper from Trotskii won't deter me.[35]

Stalin, K.E. Voroshilov and other military operatives in Tsaritsyn, mostly from the lower social classes with a strong prejudice against the privileged, distrusted the loyalty of the former tsarist officers, many of whom had noble backgrounds. The Tsaritsyn Cheka (secret police) also maintained that 'All specialists are bourgeois and most are counter-revolutionaries.'[36] Numerous officers were thus arrested and executed. In many cases, there was little evidence of treason. Even the case of General Nosovich, whose 'treason' Stalin and Voroshilov used to justify their terror against the other officers, was not a clear-cut case. It is not clear whether Nosovich betrayed the Red Army out of conviction or was compelled to defect to the Whites (the counter-revolutionaries) by Stalin's terror against officers in general.[37] When Trotskii, alarmed by the situation in Tsaritsyn, sent a telegram of protest regarding the military staff, Stalin ordered: 'Disregard'. Executions went on. When reminded that disregarding an order from Moscow might cause problems, Stalin is said to have answered: 'Death solves all problems. No man, no problem.'[38] This remark may well be apocryphal, but it does reflect Stalin's conduct in Tsaritsyn.

Stalin ruled Tsaritsyn as a dictator, and Tsaritsyn became a black hole. Everything disappeared there: money, people and equipment designated for other purposes were expropriated by Stalin's orders. Mandatory daily reports did not go from Tsaritsyn to Moscow. 'Anti-Soviet conspiracies' instead arose everywhere in Tsaritsyn, which turned into a 'murderous bedlam'.[39] The military situation deteriorated, despite Stalin's assurances that everything was in order. Finally, on 27 September, he sent an alarming note to Lenin about the difficulties in Tsaritsyn owing to 'downright treachery'. On 3 October 1918, Trotskii sent an order to Stalin and Voroshilov not to let political commissars interfere with operational matters, and the same day Stalin sent back an angry telegram accusing Trotskii of disrupting the military front, declaring that the 'so-called military specialists from the bourgeoisie' (or 'military specialists from the camp of "non-party" counter-revolutionaries') deserved 'utter distrust': to trust the traitors would destroy the entire front. So Stalin asked Lenin to remove Trotskii. Trotskii, who had joined the party 'only yesterday', was trying to teach him, Stalin, party discipline: Trotskii's 'left' and 'red' discipline was making the most disciplined comrades nauseous.[40] Writing to Lenin on 4 October 1918, Trotskii finally demanded: 'I insist categorically on Stalin's recall. . . . Tsaritsyn must either submit or take the consequences. We have a colossal superiority of forces, but there is utter anarchy at the top. I can put a stop to it in twenty-four hours, provided I have your firm and clear-cut support. At all events, this is the only course I can see'.[41] Lenin had no choice but to recall Stalin.

Lenin avoided confronting the issue of Stalin's contumacy and his terror in Tsaritsyn, however. Even though he was critical of the Tsaritsyn affair, he gave Stalin the benefit of the doubt – after all, Lenin was not averse to terror in general. According to Trotskii, Lenin used to say about their enemies:

[T]hey run the risk of losing everything. And yet they have hundreds of thousands of men who went through the experience of war, who are well fed, courageous; they have officers, junkers, the sons of landlords and industrialists, sons of policemen and rich peasants who are ready for anything. And here are those, excuse the word, 'revolutionaries' who imagine that we shall achieve our revolution in a nice way, with kindness? What have they learned? What do they understand by 'dictatorship'? And what sort of a dictatorship will that be if they themselves are ninnies?[42]

In February 1918, when Lenin ordered that 'all profiteers, hooligans and counterrevolutionaries' should be summarily shot, the Left SR Commissar for Justice I.N. Steinberg 'immediately went to Lenin and protested'

'Then why do we bother with a Commissariat of Justice at all? Let's call it frankly the "Commissariat for Social Extermination" and be done with it!' Lenin's face lit up and he replied: 'Well put, that's exactly what it should be; but we can't say that.'[43]

Lenin, according to Trotskii, said, 'The Russian is tenderhearted and incapable of adopting resolute measures of revolutionary terror.'[44] Stalin appeared to Lenin to be resolute.

Lenin wanted to believe that Stalin's problem with Trotskii was a personal one, and continued to support both as indispensable leaders. Certainly, personal rivalry and antagonism was a factor, but the Tsaritsyn incident was much more than personal. As Robert Argenbright has noted, Stalin used terror as a 'natural and effective means of government' in Tsaritsyn. 'He was an inspired plotter':

> People who disagreed with Stalin were shot and then slandered afterwards.
> But other victims who were strangers to Stalin were treated the same way.
> They served as the necessary raw material for the formation of a regime
> of terror. Arrests were conducted in a virtually random manner, while
> charges were applied on the basis of completely distinct political or ideo-
> logical grounds. Prisoners were tortured or falsely promised clemency if
> they would name others. And the whole wretched mess was portrayed as
> a great victory.[45]

Trotskii considered 'Stalin's patronage of the Tsaritsyn policy a most
dangerous ulcer, worse than any treason or betrayal by military specialists'. Privately, Lenin understood that Stalin was a troublemaker
and his Tsaritsyn regime disputable, although it is not clear whether
he thought that the Tsaritsyn affair was merely a 'wretched mess'. According to Trotskii, Lenin noted in 1922, echoing Trotskii's sentiment
of the civil war period: 'Stalin will make a rotten compromise and then
he will deceive us.'[46]

Yet Lenin did not lose his faith in Stalin as a capable and authori-
tative leader.[47] Even though Stalin's contumacy [disobedience] was a problem, Lenin
valued his leadership and resoluteness. (In the eyes of Trotskii and others, however, Lenin was continually 'deceived' by Stalin.) In Lenin's
eyes, Stalin was as much a troubleshooter as a troublemaker. After
Tsaritsyn, Stalin was dispatched to many fronts of critical importance:
the Urals, Petrograd, the south, Smolensk, Minsk. Wherever he went,
he discovered conspiracies and proved willing to criticise Moscow's
policy (particularly with regard to military officers) and disobey orders.
Behind the scenes, he continued to inspire and support his Tsaritsyn
group (particularly Voroshilov) which sought to implement elsewhere
the Tsaritsyn experience as the proper 'proletarian' policy, thus out-
raging Trotskii. Lenin tended to accept Stalin's offence as political
'mischief'.[48] In 1919, at the eighth party congress where Lenin criticised Stalin's Tsaritsyn policy, Stalin was elected nonetheless to the
Politburo, a five-member CC subcommittee, which de facto became the
highest decision-making organ in the country. Stalin also became a
member of the Orgburo, another CC subcommittee, charged with the
appointment of party officials. When the Politburo decided to award
the Order of the Red Banner to Trotskii for his successful defence of
Petrograd against General Iudenich's offensive in the autumn of 1919,
Stalin's old pal Kamenev (who happened to be married to a sister of
Trotskii's), proposed that Stalin, too, be awarded. According to Trotskii, Mikhail Kalinin, a candidate member of the Politburo, asked 'For
what?' 'I can't understand why it should be awarded to Stalin.' The

awkward situation was saved with a jest, and Kamenev's proposal was adopted. After the meeting, according to Trotskii, 'Bukharin [another candidate member] pounced on Kalinin. "Can't you understand? This is Lenin's idea. Stalin can't live unless he has what someone else has. He will never forgive it".'[49]

Meanwhile, the Civil War expanded with the end of the First World War. Germany's defeat in the autumn of 1918 freed the Allied forces. Annoyed with the emergence of an 'extremist' regime in Russia, they intervened in the war against the Reds, prolonging the conflict and causing much damage to the country. Yet their intervention was generally half-hearted: they were weary of another war, a civil war in a distant Russia whose nature they did not understand very well. With the Treaty of Brest-Litovsk made defunct by the defeat of Germany, the Bolsheviks sought to reconquer some of the lost territory of the Russian Empire. Ukraine, for example, became a major theatre of war in which numerous Jewish pogroms were committed by all the parties concerned (including Red Army soldiers). Its capital Kyiv (Kiev), as Mikhail Bulgakov wrote in his famous *The White Guard*, changed hands numerous times. Stalin also caused problems in Ukraine by refusing Moscow's orders. In February 1920, when Stalin was asked by Lenin to transfer two divisions to the Caucasian front, Stalin responded: 'I am not quite clear as to why the chief concern about the Caucasian Front falls primarily upon me. The strengthening of the Caucasian Front properly and entirely falls upon the Military Council of the Republic, the members of which, according to my information, are in good health; it is their concern and not that of Stalin who is overburdened with work as it is.' Lenin had to reprimand Stalin: 'It is generally obligatory to give all possible assistance and not to bicker about departmental jurisdiction.'[50]

Stalin played some part in the Soviet defeat in the Polish campaign in 1920. In May 1920 the newly independent Poland, assisted by the Ukrainian nationalist forces ousted by the Bolsheviks, occupied the capital, Kyiv. The Bolsheviks staged a counter-attack, however, and marched all the way to the outskirts of Warsaw. (The writer Isaak Babel', originally from Odesa, wrote the famous *Red Cavalry* based on his experience of this Polish campaign.) The Polish campaign nevertheless ended in a debacle for the Bolsheviks. Against the advice of Trotskii and Stalin, Lenin ordered the march on Warsaw, in the hope that the Polish workers would rise up in support of the Red Army, the army of the workers' revolution, and that Polish revolution would lead to revolution in Europe. Contrary to Lenin's hopes, the Polish workers rallied to their national leader Józef Piłsudski. The march not only failed to rouse the Polish workers, it was a military failure as well. Stalin, then a political commissar on the south-western front, was fighting to take L'viv (L'vov, Lwów, Lemberg) in Galicia. On 11 August Stalin and his commander, A.I. Egorov, however, were ordered by the Red Army's Commander-in-Chief to redirect and attach a considerable part of their unit to the western front marching on Warsaw. The Warsaw campaign was commanded by the former tsarist army officer Mikhail Tukhachevskii. From a noble family, he was still only 27 years old. He had been captured by the Germans during the First World War, learnt French in captivity from the French POW Colonel Charles de Gaulle, then fled to revolutionary Russia to become a Bolshevik. Ironically, de Gaulle was assisting the Polish army in this war. Stalin did not move his unit as ordered. He took two days to respond to the order. On 13 August 1920, Stalin disingenuously stated that the order should have been given three days earlier or later, after the capture of L'viv.[51] Perhaps he did not trust or even wish to assist the noble officer Tukhachevskii. Perhaps he wanted to capture L'viv to gain credit. It is also possible that Moscow was sending conflicting signals, allowing Stalin to ignore the Commander-in-Chief.[52] In any case, four days later Stalin was recalled to Moscow. The delay in the transfer of the units exposed the flank of the Tukhachevskii front to the Poles. It was too late. The Red Army captured neither L'viv nor Warsaw, and was beaten out of Poland.

Available documents show that in the fighting against Poland, many Bolsheviks, even Stalin (who was initially sceptical about the march on Warsaw), came to be convinced that Poland was about to fall, whereas the military commanders were more cautious.[53] Criticised by Lenin and Trotskii, Stalin defended himself by criticising the commanders of the western front.[54] Subsequently, according to Trotskii, Stalin blamed in vain Ivan Smilga, the political commissar on the western front.[55] Clearly Stalin alone was not to blame for the debacle of the Polish campaign, but his conduct certainly did not gain the respect of the military commanders.

Stalin's reputation suffered in Transcaucasia as well. Like Ukraine, Transcaucasia underwent a complex process of war involving foreign powers (Turkey, Germany and Britain in particular), the nationalists, the Whites, the Bolsheviks and the Mensheviks. Once the Russian White forces were beaten in the northern Caucasus, Transcaucasia was open to the Bolshevik advance. A coup established a Soviet government in Azerbaijan in April 1920 and in Armenia in November 1920. On 6 November 1920, addressing the Baku Soviet, Stalin declared:

Undoubtedly, our path is not the easiest, but, just as undoubtedly, we are not to be frightened by difficulties. Paraphrasing the well-known words of [Martin] Luther, Russia might say: 'Here I stand on the border between the old, capitalist world and the new, socialist world. Here, on this border, I unite the efforts of the proletarians of the West and of the peasants of the East in order to shatter the old world. May the god of history help me.'[56]

Yet the god of history did not help him in Georgia, his homeland. It was in Georgia that Stalin was subjected to a humiliating welcome.

In Georgia, the Mensheviks had built a popular government. It was recognised by major Western powers (so Stalin called Georgia the 'kept woman of the Entente'),[57] and in May 1920 Russia even signed a treaty with it, thus *de jure* recognising it. However, in February 1921, violating the treaty, the Russian Red Army advanced into Georgia and crushed the resistance of the Georgians. The coup, directed by Stalin in Moscow and G.K. Ordzhonikidze on the spot, dismantled the Menshevik regime and set up a Georgian Soviet Republic. After the coup, Stalin's childhood friend Iremaschwili accosted Stalin's mother among those who gathered at a mass grave in Tbilisi to mourn the Georgian war dead. He said to her, 'Keke, this is your son's fault. Write to him in Moscow: he is no longer my friend. He is the enemy and murderer of the Georgian people.'[58] Whether she wrote to Stalin is not known.

The Menshevik Iremaschwili was arrested in May 1921. In July 1921 Stalin came to Tbilisi as a conqueror. Iremaschwili's sister, Aneta, went to Stalin to seek the release of her brother. Stalin replied, 'Too bad about Soso [Iosif (Soso) Iremaschwili, not Stalin]! His case pains me to the heart. We have similar ideas, but he stands on the other side of the barricade. He'd better fight on our side. I'll consider this matter. I hope he'll find his way back to me!' The following day, Iremaschwili and two others were freed by Stalin's order. Then, through a childhood common friend, Iremaschwili received an invitation from Stalin to meet, but declined the invitation, stating that he would not shake hands with a traitor.[59]

Meanwhile, a mass meeting was organised to honour Stalin in the working-class quarter of Tbilisi. Stalin appeared surrounded by Chekists (secret police guards), but he was greeted with cries of 'Traitor' and 'Murderer'. Then, the old, respected Georgian Marxist Isidor Ramishvili was welcomed with an ovation. Stalin was angry and astounded. So were his Chekists. According to Iremaschwili, Stalin stood still, accused by Ramishvili of treason. Then the leader of the Tbilisi workers, Dgebuadze, spoke, likewise attacked him. Stalin had to endure the condemnation silently for hours. The crowd did not let Stalin speak.

The meeting broke up with workers laughing and singing the 'International' and Georgian freedom songs.[60]

That night more than one hundred social democrats (Mensheviks) were arrested in Tbilisi. Amongst them were Ramishvili and Dgebuadze. Stalin then convened another mass meeting, only to face the same condemnation as before. After two days in Tbilisi, according to Iremaschwili, Stalin took to his heels to Moscow.[61] Before he left Tbilisi, he 'stormed into Tbilisi party headquarters and made a furious attack on Philip Makharadze, whom he professed to hold personally responsible for his humiliation'.[62] Stalin told the Georgian Communists that he was 'astounded by the absence of the former solidarity between the workers of the nationalities of Transcaucasia'. Blaming the Mensheviks and the nationalists, he told them to 'crush the hydra of nationalism and create a healthy atmosphere of internationalism'.[63] It was probably on this visit to Tbilisi that Stalin faced his mother's question: 'Son, the Tsar's blood is not on your hands?' Stalin said, 'I swear it is not!' and crossed himself in the presence of others.[64]

The 'relics' of nationalism died hard and continued to plague the Soviet government. Stalin's high-handed treatment of his homeland was symptomatic of the ways in which Stalin would deal with those suspected of nationalist heresy. Yet when the Civil War ended in 1921, the Soviet Government had not only won it but recovered much of the territory of the former Russian Empire save Poland, Finland and the Baltic States. This was no mean achievement. For all the problems Stalin brought about, Lenin valued him as a resolute leader. As such, Stalin commanded the respect of his followers.

The Civil War was a baptism by fire for the Bolsheviks, a 'great heroic period' against the class enemies, and Lenin and Trotskii played critically important roles in it. Not without reason were they the best-known leaders in the revolutionary government. Thus they 'were never referred to apart – "Lenin and Trotsky" were spoken of in one breath like the name of a firm'.[65] Stalin had become one of the top leaders but remained much less visible than his two 'elders'. His terror regime in Tsaritsyn, his deep mistrust of the tsarist army officers, his repeated insubordination – all this distinguished him – and his cunning, brutality and savagery presaged his terror of the 1930s. He had tasted personal dictatorship in Tsaritsyn. However, he was perhaps not very different from others in Lenin's entourage, or at least Lenin appeared to think so. The party as a whole accepted political terror as a necessary part of the revolutionary struggle against class enemies; the anti-officer sentiment was widespread; almost every leader dissented from Lenin on important issues and often fought against him. Stalin excelled in cultivating his followers (such as Voroshilov), and, most importantly, Lenin valued Stalin as an able leader as much as he did Trotskii. Even Trotskii understood that 'Lenin was "advancing" Stalin, valuing in him his firmness, grit, stubbornness, and to a certain extent his slyness, as attributes necessary in the struggle'.[66] Stalin could 'exert pressure' in a way no one else could.

Notes

[1] Andrei Gromyko, *Memoirs* (New York, 1989), 361.

[2] Leon Trotsky, *Stalin* (New York, 1967), 270.

[3] Orlando Figes, *A People's Tragedy: A History of the Russian Revolution* (New York, 1997), 385. For the events of 1917 I draw heavily on this book. For the February Revolution, see Tsuyoshi Hasegawa, *The February Revolution: Petrograd, 1917* (Seattle, Wash., 1981).

[4] Martin Gilbert, *The First World War: A Complete History* (New York, 1994), 309.

[5] Here I am quoting Lars Lih who has enlightened me on this point and directed me to the relevant literature on the subject.

[6] Robert C. Tucker (ed), *The Lenin Anthology* (New York, 1975), 292.

[7] N.K. Krupskaia, *Reminiscences of Lenin* (New York, 1970), 334–5. For the February Revolution, see also Michael Melancon, *Rethinking Russia's February Revolution: Anonymous Spontaneity or Socialist Agency?* (Pittsburgh, Pa.: Carl Beck Papers, no. 1408, 2000).

[8] Lars T. Lih, *Bread and Authority in Russia, 1914–1921* (Berkeley, Calif., 1990).

[9] Robert M. Slusser, *Stalin in October: The Man Who Missed the Revolution* (Baltimore and London, 1987), 8.

[10] Ibid., 11–12, 15–16.

[11] Stalin, *Works*, 3:7–8.

[12] *Molotov Remembers: Inside Kremlin Politics* (Chicago, Ill., 1993), 91–2.

[13] Leon Trotsky, *The Permanent Revolution and the Results and Prospects* (New York, 1969).

[14] Slusser, 60.

[15] A.H. Birse, *Memoirs of an Interpreter* (New York, 1967), 31.

[16] Isaiah Berlin and Ramin Jahanbegloo, *Conversations with Isaiah Berlin* (New York, 1991), 4.

[17] Slusser, 65, 76, 82, 94–5.

[18] Figes, 430.

[19] Ibid., 437. However, L'vov was proved wrong: Kerenskii was unable to shoot at the people.

[20] Slusser, 202.

[21] Figes, 436–59.

[22] V.I. Lenin, *Collected Works*, 26:235.

[23] For their disagreement in 1917, see Stalin, *Works*, 4:329.

[24] Berlin and Jahanbegloo, 4.

25 Ibid., 4.

26 Loc. cit.

27 Stalin, *Works*, 4:158.

28 RGASPI, f. 558, op. 2, d. 3, ll. 1–63.

29 An account by a sister of Lenin's in *Izvestiia TsK KPSS*, 1989, no. 12, 197.

30 Alliluyeva, *Twenty Letters*, 104.

31 Lih, 126.

32 Robert Argenbright, 'Red Tsaritsyn: Precursor of Stalinist Terror', *Revolutionary Russia*, 4:2 (December 1991), 158.

33 Tucker, 191.

34 Stalin, *Works*, 4:120.

35 Ibid., 4:123.

36 Argenbright, 165.

37 For Nosovich's alleged treason, see ibid., 174–5.

38 Quoted in Anatoli Rybakov, *Children of Arbat* (Boston and Toronto, 1988), 559. See also Robert Conquest, *Stalin: Breaker of Nation* (New York, 1991), 79 (no source is cited).

39 Argenbright, 175

40 *Sovetskoe rukovodstvo. Perepiska. 1912–1927* (Moscow, 1996), 52–3.

41 Ibid., 54 and Trotsky, *Stalin*, 288–9.

42 Leon Trotsky, *Lenin: Notes for a Biographer* (New York, 1971), 123.

43 Figes, 536.

44 Trotskii, *Lenin*, 139.

45 Argenbright, 178–80.

46 Leon Trotsky, *My Life* (Harmondsworth, 1975), 462.

47 Tucker, 208.

48 Dmitri Volkogonov, *Stalin: Triumph and Tragedy* (London, 1991), 44.

49 Trotsky, *My Life*, 450–1.

50 *Direktivy komandovaniia frontov Krasnoi armii, 1917–1922 gg.*, v. 2 (Moscow, 1972), 410, 790.

51 *Sovetskoe rukovodstvo*, 155.

52 Stephen Brown, 'Lenin, Stalin and the Failure of the Red Army in the Soviet–Polish War of 1920', *War & Society*, 14:2 (October, 1996).

53 *Sovetskoe rukovodstvo*, 147–54.

54 Ibid., 160–1.

55 Trotsky, *Stalin*, 329.

56 Stalin, *Works*, 4:406.

57 Ibid., 4: 393.

58 Iremaschwili, 57.

59 Ibid., 60.

60 Ibid., 60–2. Among those who shouted at Stalin were old women 'who had fed and sheltered Stalin when he was hiding from the tsarist secret police'. See David Marshall Lang, *A Modern History of Georgia* (New York, 1962), 239. (Unfortunately, however, Lang gives no source for this meeting.) According to another account, Stalin was lifted out of the meeting by the workers. Irina Chervakova, 'Pesochnye chasy', *Druzhba narodov*, 1997, no. 4, 92.

61 Iremaschwili, 60–2.

62 Lang, 239.

[63]Stalin, *Works*, 5:97, 101.
[64]Stanislav Gribanov, *Stalin v zhizni* (Moscow, 2001), 70.
[65]Berlin and Jahanbegloo, 4.
[66]Trotsky, *Stalin*, 243.

Chapter 3

Struggle for Power

The years between the end of the Civil War and the beginning of Stalin's 'revolution from above' at the close of the 1920s marked a period of intense struggle for power among the Bolshevik party leaders, particularly Stalin, Trotskii, Zinov'ev, Kamenev and Bukharin. The paralysis in 1922–3 and then the death of Lenin in 1924 made the fight for succession inevitable. The bitter struggles revealed much about the political personalities of the contenders as well as the political nature of the party. Perhaps to the surprise of those who questioned his intelligence, Stalin emerged victorious in the end. There are indications, however, that Lenin supported Stalin as his successor. In 1922, with Lenin's backing, Stalin was appointed General Secretary of the party, thus taking the first critical step towards a dictatorship. Whatever Stalin's intellectual acumen, he proved to be an extraordinarily skilful politician. Those who fought against him almost certainly underestimated Stalin's intellect as well. The struggle for power involved intellectual and theoretical debates on the future of the Revolution. In this regard, too, Stalin managed to convince the party that he was right: socialism could be established in Russia.

The New Economic Policy

Victory often divides the victors. Once it became apparent that the Civil War was coming to an end, the question of how to rebuild a society torn apart by war, revolution and civil war became a bone of contention within the victorious party. Gross industrial production had dropped by nearly 70 per cent between 1913 and 1921, and agricultural production by 40 per cent. Pig-iron production plummeted by 99.5 per cent between 1913 and 1920, because none of the 65 blast furnaces that had operated at full capacity in 1913 were working in 1920.

More seriously, the entire country appeared to be on the brink of rebellion against the Bolshevik government. Strikes took place everywhere, protesting against, among other things, the lack of food and jobs. There was a massive exodus of hungry workers back to the countryside, undermining the political base of the Bolshevik party. (The population of Petrograd declined by more than 60 per cent between 1910 and 1920.) The peasants were fighting against the forceful seizure of grain. Here and there their stand assumed the form of genuine war (the most famous being the Antonov rebellion in Tambov).[1] The last straw was the Kronstadt rebellion in February–March 1921. The sailors of the Kronstadt naval base, just across the Gulf of Finland from the city of Petrograd, had been among the staunchest supporters of the revolution (although many of them were anarchists), but now they were demanding political freedom from the dictatorship of the Bolsheviks. The rebellions were in every case mercilessly crushed after much bloodshed. Yet it also became evident to the Bolsheviks that something had to change if they were to survive. It was a crisis as serious as the German invasion that had led to the Brest-Litovsk peace treaty.

As he had earlier, Lenin once again forced a painful change on an unwilling party. This change, mainly in the economic sphere, came to be known as the 'New Economic Policy' (NEP), the crux of which was the reintroduction of market forces. It appeared to many party members as a 'retreat' from what was retrospectively called the 'war communism' of the Civil War period, which levelled the life of almost everyone, albeit to the level of dire poverty. The collapse of the economy had led to runaway inflation, which completely devalued the currency; this, in turn, had created a moneyless natural (barter) economy. It was a far cry from the supposed paradise of communism, but it appeared to have done away with money and market, the symbols of capitalism. The NEP was probably not as radical a break (or 'retreat') as has been portrayed in textbooks and scholarly literature. The Bolshevik leaders, even Bukharin, who became its most ardent supporter, seem to have meant to use the NEP in order to overcome eventually the necessity of the market.[2]

Lenin met resistance from within the party, however, just as he had at the time of the Brest-Litovsk treaty, and several factions actively fought against him. The NEP appeared to them to magnify the already serious problems extant in the country, especially the plight of workers, and, furthermore, to favour the peasants over the workers. By reintroducing trading relations between industry and agriculture, the NEP would allow the peasants to dispose of their produce in markets after payment of taxes. Although the 'commanding heights' of the national economy (heavy industry, rail transport, banking and financial institutions, and foreign trade) remained in the hands of the state, the NEP would allow small-scale producers and traders to operate for profit. Many 'negative' features associated with capitalism re-emerged, ranging from economic exploitation and economic stratification to prostitution and cabarets. Unemployment, the scourge of markets, remained a serious problem throughout the 1920s, but foreign trade with capitalist countries began to open up.

Despite all the changes designed to improve the economy, a severe setback took place when, in 1921–2, a dreadful famine struck the country, mainly the grain-producing Volga region and Ukraine, killing up to five million people. Half a century later, in the 1970s, the NEP was touted by those seeking alternatives to Soviet-type socialism as a promising market socialism. In fact, the reality of the NEP was complex and painful. The party as a whole accepted it as a political expediency but remained opposed to it emotionally. Many communists and Komsomol (Young Communist League) members were disoriented and disillusioned with the drab life of the NEP. In industry, the supposed bastion of Bolshevik power, it appeared to many to restore the old regime. The 'bourgeoisie' (factory owners), like the landed nobles, had largely gone (emigrated abroad), but the old industrial experts (engineers and technicians), like the old military officials during the Civil War, had to be employed to run the factories. The specialists, regarded by workers as representatives of the bourgeoisie, proved widely unpopular on the shop floor, leading to the ubiquitous phenomenon of 'specialist-baiting' (harassment and persecution of specialists by workers and communists). In the recollections of Soviet citizens who grew up in the 1920s, the NEP era is associated more with hunger, pain and bitterness than with pleasure.[3]

Stalin, like the other leaders, accepted the NEP as a necessary 're-treat', though there are indications that he only grudgingly accepted it and had many reservations about it. He (and other Bolsheviks) entertained a nostalgic view of the Civil War era as a 'great heroic period' and occasionally expressed their deep-seated anger at the prosaic life under the NEP. The resumption of foreign trade led Stalin to declare in December 1921 that 'it must not be forgotten that trade and all other sorts of missions and associations that are now pouring into Russia, trading with her and aiding her, are at the same time the most efficient spy agencies of the world bourgeoisie'. In the spring of 1923 Stalin attacked the 'corrupting influence of NEP elements', contending that the NEP and the private capital associated with it fostered all kinds of nationalisms (Great Russian chauvinism, Georgian and other national chauvinisms).[4]

The general sentiment in the party that the NEP was a 'retreat' assumed that at some point in the future the 'retreat' had to stop and an offensive to resume. Even those 'rightists' such as Bukharin (a former left Communist opposed to the Brest-Litovsk treaty) who came to embrace the NEP agreed on this issue. The question was, when and how?

The question stemmed from the contradiction inherent in the October Revolution itself. The contradiction was best described by the Italian Marxist Antonio Gramsci who famously welcomed the revolution as a 'revolution against *Das Kapital*'. If the first proletarian revolution took place in a relatively backward, predominantly agricultural country with a small working class and a less than fully developed capitalist infrastructure on which to build a superior system called socialism, then Russia's task was to overcome this contradiction. One answer was Trotskii's 'permanent revolution'. Trotskii was not an opponent of the NEP – he even boasted, incorrectly, that it was he who had already actually proposed the NEP in 1920. During the 1920s Trotskii and his supporters worked out sophisticated strategies for modernising and industrialising the country, which Richard Day has called 'integrationism'. Trotskii emphasised, according to Day's account, that 'socialism could only triumph if "we measure up not only to our own discoveries and inventions, but also to the progress of world technology"'. Economic 'disengagement from Europe' could only harm the country. An 'optimal planning strategy' could be gained through 'extensive trade links with the West and maximum foreign investments'.[5]

Yet Trotskii also implied that, unless proletarian revolution took place in Europe and came to assist the country of 'revolution against *Das Kapital*', the revolution would inevitably degenerate. The threat came both from the large peasant population and from an emerging Soviet bureaucracy. Without international revolution, the future of the country was doomed and, as in the French revolution, a Thermidorian reaction would be inevitable.

Against this internationalist and integrationist prognosis, Lenin and Stalin appeared to develop an alternative perspective on the future: an 'isolationist' position that would culminate in Stalin's 'socialism in one country'. It was this shared view that drew them together rather than forced them apart. Lenin suffered from minor heart seizures and strokes, drastically losing his capacity to work from the summer of 1921 to the spring of 1923, when he was totally incapacitated. In January 1924 he died. It has widely been accepted by historians that during the last few months of his working life, namely late

STALIN

1922 and early 1923, Lenin struggled against Stalin ('Lenin's last struggle'), but it now appears that they worked together. Certainly they
disagreed on several issues, such as the question of a foreign trade
monopoly and the formation of the Soviet Union from several constituent Soviet republics (including the Russian Federal Republic) in
1922. Yet neither took their disagreements on these issues too seriously, and they remained amicable.[6] Indeed, it was Stalin, of all the
Bolshevik dignitaries, who was received by Lenin most frequently in
1921–2,[7] and it was Stalin whom Lenin asked in the summer of 1922
to administer poison to him in case he could not recover physically.[8]
(Lenin meant to die like Marx's son-in-law Paul Lafargue. Lenin's sister Mariia noted that Lenin asked Stalin because he was 'firm, steel-
like [stal'noi] and free of any sentimentality'.)[9] Unquestionably, there
are many reports that Lenin disparaged and despised Stalin: his sister Mariia, for example, noted that Lenin said that Stalin was 'not
at all clever'.[10] According to Trotskii, Krupskaia told him that Lenin
thought that Stalin was 'devoid of the most elementary honesty, the
most simple human honesty'.[11] Yet these reports, like others, must
be taken with a pinch of salt. Both Lenin and Trotskii had sharp and
sometimes almost wicked tongues.

It was Lenin who in 1922 manoeuvred to have Stalin accepted by
the party as its General Secretary, because he trusted Stalin as a capable
man. Stalin was the only person to hold a position on all the three
CC subcommittees: the Politburo, the Orgburo and the Secretariat.
Whether or not Lenin believed that Stalin was a 'good man' is of little significance. Lenin might have thought that a good politician, especially the party General Secretary who had to deal with all kinds of
tough problems (including dissent within the party), should be a man
who was 'firm, steel-like and free of any sentimentality'. 'High-minded
and gentle men could not do the job that was required.'[12] Lenin nevertheless seems to have had some misgivings. He once confided to
Ia. Shatunovskii, an old Bolshevik who knew Trotskii, Stalin and Lenin
well, that 'As a politician I have a very big shortcoming. I have a poor
understanding of people, I don't understand people. But I know this
problem of mine and try to seek the advice of old comrades [such as
his wife and sister].' (Lenin was shaken when it was proved after the
Revolution that one of his trusted colleagues, Malinovskii, was a tsarist
police agent. Malinovskii was executed in 1918.) Then Lenin said,
'Stalin has the same shortcoming. It's only that he doesn't see it and
doesn't consult anyone.' Shatunovskii's wife, however, disagreed with
Lenin: 'Stalin knew very well how to pick people who were right for

him and necessary to him. It's only that his criteria of selection were completely different from Lenin's.'[13]

In any case, Lenin and Stalin thought similarly on the future of the Revolution: even without revolution in Europe, their Revolution would survive. Already in 1917, Stalin argued against the internationalist Preobrazhenskii:

> The possibility is not excluded that Russia will be the country that will lay the road to socialism. No country hitherto has enjoyed such freedom in time of war as Russia does, or has attempted to introduce workers' control of production. Moreover, the base of our revolution is broader than in Western Europe, where the proletariat stands utterly alone face to face with the bourgeoisie. In our country the workers are supported by the poorest strata of the peasantry. . . . We must discard the antiquated idea that only Europe can show us the way. There is dogmatic Marxism and creative Marxism. I stand by the latter.[14]

In October 1920 Stalin declared that there were some conditions that would guarantee the 'existence and progress of Soviet Russia'. First, 'Russia is a vast and boundless land, within which it is possible to hold on for a long time by retreating, in the event of reverses, into the heart of the country in order to gather strength for a new offensive.' If Russia were a small country like Hungary (where a 1919 socialist revolution led by Béla Kun was quickly crushed), 'it could hardly have held on for so long as a socialist land'. Second,

> Russia is one of the few countries in the world which abound in every kind of fuel, raw material and food – that is to say, a country which is independent of foreign lands for fuel, food, etc., a country that can do in this respect without the outside world. It is beyond doubt that if Russia had depended for its existence on foreign grain and fuel, as Italy, for instance, does, it would have found itself in a critical situation on the very morrow of the revolution.[15]

In Stalin's mind the vast land of Russia represented a world in itself.

Lenin had similar views. He no longer spoke of revolution in Europe as a prerequisite for the success of socialism in Russia. By 1922 he came to assert that 'economic power in the hands of the proletarian state of Russia is quite adequate to ensure the transition to communism'. The NEP was so successful and the 'position of the peasantry is now such that we have no reason to fear any movement against us from that quarter'.[16] In one of his last notes written in January 1923, Lenin criticised the Mensheviks and other dogmatic Marxists who claimed that 'we are not yet ripe for socialism' and that 'the objective economic premise of socialism does not exist in our country'.

Lenin insisted that it was possible to build socialism in Russia: 'You [Mensheviks] say that civilisation is necessary for the building of socialism. Very good. But why could we not first create such prerequisites of civilisation in our country as the expulsion of the landowners and the Russian capitalists, and then start moving towards socialism?' Then Lenin added:

> Napoleon, I think, wrote: 'On s'engage et puis . . . on voit.' Rendered freely this means: 'First engage in a serious battle and then see what happens.' Well, we did first engage in a serious battle in October 1917, and then saw such details of development (from the standpoint of world history they were certainly details) as the Brest Peace, the New Economic Policy, and so forth. And now there can be no doubt that in the main we have been victorious.[17]

The fate of the country would depend on 'whether the peasant masses will stand by the working class'. The danger of their turning against the Soviet government existed, but Lenin assured the party that it need not fear the peasants who were by and large satisfied with the outcome of the Revolution. The most important task, Lenin wrote in January 1923, was to organise the peasants into cooperatives. 'We went too far when we introduced the NEP, but not because we attached too much importance to the principle of free enterprise and trade – we went too far because we lost sight of the cooperatives'. The cooperatives were the key to socialism:

> we have now found that degree of combination of private interest, private commercial interest, with state supervision and control of this interest, that degree of its subordination to the common interests which was formerly the stumbling block for very many socialists.

Lenin noted, however, that to achieve socialism in the Soviet Union it would take 'a whole historical epoch', at best 'one or two decades'.[18] What if the capitalist countries decided to crush the Soviet Union before then? Lenin had no answer.

Thus, while hoping for world revolution, both Lenin and Stalin had come to see the outcome of revolution generally within the context of one country, the Soviet Union. The nationality policy devised after the Civil War under the direction of Stalin was also to some degree predicated on this premise. It was precisely in non-Russian territory on the periphery of the former Russian Empire that the revolutionary government met the stiffest resistance. Stalin feared that the NEP was fostering an array of nationalisms. To counter them and ensure civil peace (in place of civil war) in the areas where Soviet power was weak, a new policy called *korenizatsiia* (indigenisation or nativisation) was implemented. This entailed a degree of national-territorial autonomy in the sphere of language, education and administration. Terry Martin has compared the Soviet policy to the policy of affirmative action enacted in the USA from the 1960s onwards, calling the Soviet Union an 'affirmative action empire'.[19] Both external and internal peace was imperative for the construction of socialism in the Soviet Union.

By the mid-1920s the international situation had improved dramatically. The Soviet Union was recognised by major Western powers (save the USA). The Treaty of Versailles in 1919 did not include Soviet Russia which, however, concluded a treaty in 1922 (the Treaty of Rappalo) with Weimar Germany and restored diplomatic relations. In fact, the two countries also concluded a secret agreement on military cooperation. *Realpolitik* had set in. The failure of the 1923 revolution in Germany extinguished any flicker of hope for revolution in Europe. As it turned out, the Soviet Union, through the Comintern (Communist International), had encouraged German workers to insurrection and possibly helped them militarily as well, while maintaining cooperation with the Reichswehr! Stalin initially took a condescending attitude towards the Germans, but later had hopes of moving the 'centre of world revolution from Moscow to Berlin'. When the revolution failed, Stalin blamed, among others, Karl Radek (a Trotskii supporter sent illegally to Germany by the Comintern) and the German Social Democrats, whom he called the 'pillar' of fascism.[20]

The external detente did not lead to an internal detente. The NEP was no 'liberal' regime, and there was no let-up in political repression. The 1921 tenth party congress banned factions within the party, and open resistance was brutally crushed. Many intellectuals and politicians whom the government deemed harmful were deported abroad en masse. In 1922 Stalin's childhood friend Iremaschwili was expelled to Germany in the wake of large-scale prison riots against the government.[21] Taking advantage of the 1921–2 famine, Lenin ordered 'the confiscation of church valuables in the most decisive and rapid manner'. He believed that the clergy would not be able to resist the move at a time when millions of people were starving. Lenin thus sought to crush the resistance of the clergy to the atheist government 'with such brutality that it will not forget it for decades to come'.[22] Numerous political show trials, including a 1922 trial of the SRs, were staged, foreshadowing the Stalinist court spectacle of the 1930s.

As discussed earlier, the terror regime Stalin set up in Tsaritsyn 1918 presaged his bloody rule to come, though despite his warnings of spies and enemies, the Stalin of the early 1920s was not yet the Stalin of the 1930s. In February 1922, for instance, when the Cheka (secret police) informed Stalin of terrorist acts allegedly being planned against prominent Soviet leaders, he merely jotted down, 'Rubbish (*Pustiaki*)'.[23] Similarly, when he was notified of the alleged pan-Turkic 'counter-revolutionary' conspiracy of the Tatar national communist Mirsaid Sultan-Galiev, Stalin merely warned him and did not propose his arrest. Stalin's decision notwithstanding, however, Sultan-Galiev was arrested in May 1923.[24]

Battle Royal

Stalin's appointment in 1922 as the party's General Secretary was not considered by his rivals to be significant. Indeed, why the position was created is not clear, but the idea probably originated with Lenin. In spite of the ban on factionalism Lenin had imposed on the party, he himself engaged in factional activity to the exclusion of the politically suspect. Lenin proposed the position of General Secretary to Stalin in a factional meeting (which excluded Trotskii and others) at the 1922 eleventh party congress. Even Stalin had criticised Lenin for factionalism, but in turn Lenin retorted that Stalin was no stranger to factional politics.[25] In any case, neither Zinov'ev nor Kamenev aspired to what appeared to them to be mainly an administrative position. According to Boris Bazhanov, a former secretary of Stalin's, they initially regarded Stalin as politically insignificant and saw in him a convenient assistant and not a rival.[26] The purpose of the position was not explained to the congress, and more than half of the delegates abstained.[27] As mentioned earlier, Stalin was the only member to hold a position on the Politburo, the Orgburo and the Secretariat. This in itself would have allowed Stalin to acquire vast power, whatever his rivals might have thought.

Indeed, Stalin's accumulation of power soon came to be feared. His personality had long been a problem both in and outside the party. Stalin was even said to have beaten his son Iakov for smoking. (Iakov, who had been virtually abandoned by Stalin, came to Moscow in 1921 but was not accepted by Stalin. Iakov was gentle, 'peace-loving at heart', and 'couldn't have cared less about power'. Later in 1928, Iakov shot himself out of despair, but survived. Stalin made fun of him: 'Ha! He couldn't even shoot straight!' After this event Stalin effectively 'disowned' Iakov.)[28] According to Trotskii, Bukharin told him the following story: 'I have just come from seeing Koba. Do you know how he spends his time? He takes his year-old boy [Vasilii, born in 1921] from bed, fills his own mouth with smoke from his pipe, and blows it into the baby's face.' ' "It makes him stronger", Koba says. . . . "That's barbaric", I said. "You don't know Koba. He is like that – a little peculiar".'[29] Bukharin also noted of Stalin: 'He's gone mad. He thinks that he can do everything, only he can hold everything up, and everyone else is only a hindrance.' At another time, Bukharin fearfully said to Trotskii, 'Oh, you don't know Koba. Koba is capable of anything.'[30] According to Bazhanov, while Lenin was still alive, Stalin had the Kremlin wired so that he could tap the telephone conversations of all the Politburo members. A Czechoslovakian communist who installed the equipment was executed as a spy when the job was completed: Stalin had Genrikh Iagoda (of the secret police) shoot him without any evidence.[31] Most tellingly, Stalin was vindictive. One day at the beginning of the 1920s, several party leaders took a break and went on a picnic. Someone raised the question of what was the best thing in the world. Kamenev said, 'Books'; Radek, 'A woman, your woman'; Bukharin, 'Being one with the people'; Rykov, 'Cognac'; and Stalin, 'Revenge'. 'The sweetest thing', Stalin said, 'is to make a sound plan, wait, be on the watch, pounce and seize.' 'Only power – the terror it instills – rules, and one more thing – beastly cunning.'[32] Stalin's remarks have become so famous that there are many variations. One is, 'The best thing is to make a long and careful plan for revenge against an enemy, wait, get revenge, come home and drink.'[33] Another is 'The greatest delight is to mark one's enemy, prepare everything, avenge oneself thoroughly, and then go to sleep.'[34]

In December 1922 Lenin is said to have dictated a 'testament' that criticised Stalin (to be read at the forthcoming twelfth party congress): 'Comrade Stalin, having become General Secretary, has boundless power concentrated in his hands, and I am not sure whether he will always be capable of using that power with sufficient caution.' A few days later, he is said to have added that 'Stalin is too rude,' suggesting that 'comrades think about a way of removing Stalin from that post [General Secretaryship] and appointing another man in his stead who in all other respects differs from Comrade Stalin in having only one advantage, namely, that of being more tolerant, more loyal, more polite and more considerate for the comrades, less capricious, etc.'[35] Lenin's 'testament' may have been influenced by an altercation that is said to have taken place in December 1922 between Stalin and Lenin's wife, Krupskaia: Stalin rudely accused Krupskaia of allowing Lenin to work longer than his doctors had permitted. When this incident became known to Lenin, he is said to have written an ultimatum to Stalin on 5 March 1923: 'You had the rudeness to summon my wife to the telephone and swear at her. . . . I do not intend to forget so easily what has been done against me, and it goes without saying that I consider what is done against my wife to be done against me. . . . Therefore I ask you to consider whether to take back your words and apologise or to break off our relations.'[36] To this, Stalin is said to have responded on 7 March that he would take his words back for the sake of maintaining their relations. He added, however, that he failed to understand 'what the matter is, what my fault is and what in fact you want from me', because he and Krupskaia had agreed that the incident was a misunderstanding and not a rude insult against her or Lenin: he was just performing his duty to supervise Lenin's workload according to the advice of the doctors.[37]

If this story is true, it is consistent with Stalin's character: he behaved rudely, he failed to understand what the problem was and did not say that he would apologise. If this story (or at least Lenin's letter) has been doctored, then Stalin's puzzlement at Lenin's ultimatum makes sense. Upon receiving Lenin's letter, Stalin noted, 'This isn't Lenin speaking, it's his illness.'[38] According to another, Stalin said, '[Lenin] couldn't die as an honest leader'.[39] Whatever the case, according to his secretary, Bazhanov, Stalin was jubilant over Lenin's death while publicly putting on the mask of grief.[40]

'Lenin's testament' has been taken for granted by nearly all historians, but it has recently been the subject of scrutiny. The authenticity of the story (including Stalin's response) cannot be ascertained, as there are too many documentary and evidential inconsistencies. It is not even known whether Lenin received a response from Stalin, although it appears that Lenin did not break off relations with him. Ten days after the alleged incident, Lenin, who was in acute pain, asked Stalin for potassium cyanide. Lenin, however, was calmed by Stalin. If these documents (the 'testament' and the Lenin-Stalin exchange) were forged, then they were meant to be used against Stalin. In that case, who forged or at least doctored them? V.A. Sakharov, who has advanced the forgery interpretation, suspects Lenin's entourage (Krupskaia, Zinov'ev, Kamenev, Lenin's secretary L.A. Fot'eva) and Trotskii. Certainly Krupskaia and Stalin did not get along in the last years of Lenin's life. (Stalin asked Molotov why he should kowtow to Krupskaia: 'Sleeping with Lenin doesn't mean understanding Leninism!')[41] Whatever the case, even if the negative assessment of Stalin's personal character in 'Lenin's testament' was not Lenin's, it reflected the sentiment of the Politburo members who were not favourably disposed towards Stalin.[42]

'Lenin's testament' also includes a discussion of Trotskii: 'Comrade Trotsky, on the other hand, as his struggle against the CC on the question of the People's Commissariat for Communications has already proved, is distinguished not only by outstanding ability. He is personally perhaps the most capable man in the present CC, but he has displayed excessive self-assurance and shown excessive preoccupation with the purely administrative side of the work.' (Trotskii as the Commissar of Communications sought to merge the trade unions with the state apparatus, provoking a sharp conflict within the party.) 'These two qualities of the two outstanding leaders [Stalin and Trotskii] of the present CC can inadvertently lead to a split, and if our Party does not take steps to avert this, the split may come unexpectedly.'[43] Whether this assessment was Lenin's or not, Trotskii was feared and disliked by Stalin and others as 'the most capable man' in the party. (Krupskaia seemed to prefer Trotskii to Stalin, however.) Trotskii was not deferential towards Lenin. He was perhaps the only person that could call Lenin a 'hooligan' at a Politburo meeting. Naturally enough, Lenin was not in sympathy with Trotskii.[44] Referring to the post-Lenin period, Stalin once noted that Trotskii's mistake consisted in the fact that 'he has set himself up in opposition to the CC and imagines himself to be a superman standing above the CC, above its laws, above its decisions'. When told that CC members could not refuse to carry out CC decisions, Trotskii 'jumped up and left the meeting [of the CC]'. So the CC had to send a 'delegation' to Trotskii 'with the request that he return to the meeting', but he 'refused to comply with the request'.[45] Lenin was perhaps not mistaken when in 1921 he said of Trotskii, 'Trotsky is a temperamental man with military experience . . . as for politics, he hasn't got a clue.'[46]

Other leading figures of the party were subjected to a frank assessment in 'Lenin's testament'. Regarding the opposition of Kamenev and Zinov'ev to the October insurrection, the 'testament' noted that their action was, 'of course, no accident, but neither can the blame for it be laid upon them personally, any more than non-Bolshevism can upon Trotsky'. Bukharin, 'the favourite of the whole party', 'is a most valuable and major theorist of the Party, but his theoretical views can be classified as fully Marxist only with great reserve'. G.L. Piatakov, a Russian ruler of Ukraine, 'is unquestionably a man of outstanding will and outstanding ability, but shows too much zeal for administering . . . to be relied upon in a serious political matter'.[47] Like the assessments of Stalin and Trotskii, these remarks seem to reflect either sentiments felt by leading party figures or some fragments from Lenin's table talk.

Whatever the case, the 'testament', although apparently intended for the twelfth party congress to be held in spring 1923, did not surface until after the congress. The document 'The Question of Nationalities or "Autonomisation"', said to have been dictated by Lenin on 30 and 31 December 1922, did, however, surface on the eve of the congress by way of Trotskii and Fot'eva. (By that time, Lenin was entirely incapacitated.) This document, the authenticity of which is now also questioned, was critical of the centralised nature of the newly created Soviet Union and Stalin's 'haste' and 'malice' in dealing with the nationality question (Georgia in particular).[48] The document must have puzzled Stalin, because even though he may not have been the most subtle of politicians, he had reconciled all the issues he had had with Lenin (who in fact had been more centralist than Stalin was), and the Soviet Union was duly formed at the end of 1922 with the approval of Lenin.[49] By authorising the release of 'The Question of Nationalities' (along with the documents that explained the circumstances in which it surfaced) to the congress delegates, Stalin presented himself as a leader who took a politically principled position. He did, however, add a note that it was odd that even though Trotskii had received the document in March he did not inform the CC for more than a month,[50] a manoeuvre that was quintessentially Stalin: he tempered by cunning the politically principled position of authorising the release of Lenin's document unfavourable to himself. Trotskii later recalled how repellent he found Stalin – 'the narrowness of his interests, his empiricism, the coarseness of his psychological make-up, his peculiar cynicism of a provincial whom Marxism has freed from many prejudices without, however, replacing them with a philosophical outlook thoroughly thought out and mentally assimilated'.[51] Stalin repelled and outmanoeuvred Trotskii.

At the Twelfth Congress as well, Stalin presented himself as taking a principled, defensible position, as if unaffected by this strange document of Lenin's. Stalin stated to the congress that what he had done with regard to the non-Russian nationalities and the formation of the Soviet Union had been supported by Lenin himself, declaring that 'Lenin forgot that, he forgets much lately'.[52] Few if any were inclined to support or even recognise this strange volte-face of Lenin. Clearly, Stalin's authority as a nationality expert was accepted by the party. He had withstood the purported criticism by Lenin. The congress, which took place amid hyperinflation and workers' strikes, made Stalin's position more solid than ever.

Soon after the congress ended, in late May or early June 1923, Lenin's 'testament' became known to key party figures by way of Krupskaia. Trotskii voted for its publication, but others (including Stalin) vetoed it, and the 'testament' was not published. Meanwhile, sometime in the summer of 1923, an addendum to the 'testament' calling for Stalin's replacement as the party General Secretary became known to some party members (including Zinov'ev, Kamenev and Bukharin, but not Stalin). Zinov'ev, Bukharin and some others, using this 'testament of Lenin', sought to reorganise the party Secretariat, in order to curtail Stalin's power (the so-called 'cave conference').[53] It is said that Bukharin, fearing the consequences of the scheme, acted as a peacemaker. Informed of Lenin's call for his replacement and the 'cave conference' plan by Zinov'ev and Bukharin but without having read Lenin's note, Stalin humbly offered to step down because, he said, the position of General Secretary was not dear to him. In response to the implied criticism of his power by Zinov'ev and Bukharin, Stalin added that he never made any party decision alone. Zinov'ev and Bukharin responded, perhaps disingenuously, that they had decided for now not to show Stalin the addendum to 'Lenin's testament' so as 'not to make him nervous'.[54] Zinov'ev and Bukharin's scheme failed to gain the support of Kamenev or Trotskii. Zinov'ev is said to have gone so far as to propose an alliance to Trotskii who categorically rejected it, however. As a result, not much changed and Stalin remained the party General Secretary.

Trotskii was still better known to the public than Stalin and there was considerable support for Trotskii in the military and among the youth. (When Trotskii was ill and did not appear in public, rumour circulated that he had been put under house arrest by the Politburo.) After the failure of the Zinov'ev-Bukharin scheme, Trotskii and his supporters intensified their criticism of the party regime under Stalin's leadership, focusing on the lack of 'democracy'. Trotskii himself, however, appeared to other leading party members to behave like a 'superman', at once pledging to abide by the rules of the party and then acting against resolutions that he had supported. Stalin was probably right when in December 1923 he wrote to his friend and supporter Sergei Kirov (then head of the Communist Party of Azerbaijan) that Trotskii and his supporters had lost the battle for power 'on principled ground'.[55] At a party conference that took place just before Lenin died in January 1924 (Trotskii did not attend the conference owing to illness), the Trotskii opposition was routed. Stalin effectively depicted the opposition's demand for party democracy as 'a strategic move against the CC' motivated by factionalism. Radek, a brilliant writer and speaker given to wit and humour who strongly supported Trotskii, was characterised by Stalin as belonging to those peculiar people 'who are slaves of their tongue – their tongues manage them'. With Radek one could 'never know what and when' his tongue was 'liable to blurt out'.[56] Stalin would use this talent of Radek in one of the Moscow trials in the 1930s.

By the time Lenin died, Stalin's power, far from being endangered, appeared entrenched: 'Lenin's testament' had failed to dislodge him from his position at a time when no one wished to appear openly ambitious for power. In fact, Zinov'ev, Bukharin and others often feared Trotskii more than they did Stalin. They certainly came to Stalin's rescue at the time of his greatest crisis. Just before the thirteenth party congress met in late May 1924, Krupskaia delivered 'Lenin's testament' (calling for Stalin's replacement) to the CC. Bazhanov claimed that Stalin swore at Krupskaia and rushed to confer with Zinov'ev and Kamenev.[57] Upon reading 'Lenin's testament', according to someone present, Stalin uttered: 'He [Lenin] shit on himself and he shit on us!'[58] At the CC plenum on the eve of the congress, Kamenev read the 'testament'. It is said that, according to a prearranged scenario, Zinov'ev defended Stalin: 'We are happy to confirm that Il'ich's [Lenin's] fears have proved unfounded. We have all been witnesses to our work together in the last few months, and you, like myself, have been happy to see that what Il'ich feared has not happened. I mean [his remarks] about our General Secretary and the dangers of a split in the CC.' Zinov'ev proposed to re-elect Stalin as General Secretary while Trotskii stayed silent, expressing contempt for this comedy. Stalin was tense, just gazing out the windows. Because everyone was silent, Kamenev decided to solve the issue by taking a vote. Bazhanov counted hands. The majority of the CC members voted for Stalin to remain in his position, with a small group of Trotskii's supporters voting against (and a few abstentions).[59] At the congress, the delegates were 'shaken' by the 'testament'. Yet their sentiment echoed that of Zinov'ev: Lenin's fear that Stalin would abuse his power had proven unfounded and the CC, with the exception of Trotskii, had led the party correctly. No one voted for the publication of the 'testament', and everyone voted for Stalin to remain in his post. At the CC plenum after the congress, Stalin asked to be released from his positions in the Secretariat, the Politbuto and Orgburo and to be sent to Turkhansk, Iakutsk or overseas. Again Stalin received the unanimous support of the CC to stay in his positions.[60] Stalin had survived the most serious crisis in his rise to absolute power.

Considering the climate of the times, one must ask whether the fact that Trotskii was Jewish by origin affected the outcome of his struggle for power. In October 1923 Trotskii himself testified that his Jewish background made his position awkward, reminding the party how difficult it was for him, a Jewish leader of the Red Army, to staunch the anti-Semitic propaganda of the enemy forces during the Civil War. Lenin understood Trotskii's predicament well, even though he dismissed Trotskii's anxiety as 'rubbish'.[61] So Trotskii's Jewish background must have been one factor in the struggle for power. If so, it must also have been a factor for Zinov'ev and Kamenev (both Jewish by origin) but not for Stalin (formerly a Christian). Although Stalin is not known to have used anti-Semitism against his rivals at this stage, he was probably aware of his advantage.[62]

In the months following the thirteenth party congress Stalin let Zinov'ev and Kamenev attack Trotskii, though restraining them from expelling Trotskii from the Politburo. From August 1924 Trotskii was de facto removed from the Politburo, because an 'underground Politburo' without Trotskii had begun to operate,[63] and Trotskii was subsequently removed from his position as the People's Commissar of War. Meanwhile, Stalin was formulating his theory of 'socialism in one country'. Stalin had already begun to discuss the thesis in 1924, but it was not until 1925 and 1926 that he developed it fully, claiming that he was merely building on Lenin's theory. Stalin came to equate the final victory of socialism with a 'full guarantee against attempts at intervention, and hence against restoration'. For the final victory of socialism, therefore, 'the victory of workers in at least several countries' was needed. This did not mean that the 'victory of socialism' was impossible in the Soviet Union. What was impossible for bourgeois states was 'quite possible for the proletarian state'.[64] The victory of 'socialism in one country' meant, Stalin declared, 'the possibility of solving the contradictions between the proletariat and the peasantry by means of the internal forces of our country, the possibility of the proletariat seizing power and using that power to build a complete socialist society in our country'. Stalin even implied that it was a matter of faith:

> Without such a possibility, building socialism is building without prospects, building without being sure that socialism will be completely built. It is no use engaging in building socialism without being sure that we can build it completely, without being sure that the technical backwardness of our country is not an *insuperable* obstacle to the building of a complete socialist society. To deny such a possibility means disbelief in the cause of building socialism, departure from Leninism.

This is almost a religious catechism. Without believing in a second life in heaven, can one live in this world? 'To engage in building socialism *without the possibility* of completely building it, *knowing that it cannot be completely built*' – 'this is a mockery of the question, not a solution'. Stalin emphasised: 'the proletariat of the victorious country, having seized power, *can* and *must* . . . build a socialist society'.[65]

Stalin's theory of 'socialism in one country' was a direct rebuttal of Trotskii's internationalism. It also challenged Zinov'ev and Kamenev, two of the triumvirate against Trotskii. Even though Stalin insisted that his new theory was Lenin's by origin, it appeared to Zinov'ev and

Kamenev to deviate from what they considered Leninist internation-alism. Although they did not publicly accept Stalin's new platform, the issue did not immediately become divisive. Once they had politi-cally disarmed (or at least marginalised) Trotskii, however, the triumvi-rate began to collapse. Of course, the root cause was their struggle for power. Stalin did not let up on his attacks on Trotskii (and again he presented himself as taking a politically principled position in doing so),[66] but he was also wary of the intrigues of Zinov'ev and Kamenev, who ruled the party organisations in Leningrad (Petrograd was so re-named in 1924) and Moscow respectively. Zinov'ev and Kamenev, for their part, began to realise that the triumvirate had only led to a fur-ther entrenchment of Stalin's power. Zinov'ev and Kamenev found several issues on which to fight against Stalin. His alleged dictatorial use of power was one, and his theory 'socialism in one country' was an-other. Yet another was the extension of the NEP in 1925 in the form of considerable concessions to private economic activity in industry, agri-culture and trade. (This extension came in the wake of disturbances in the countryside, particularly several mass peasant uprisings in Georgia, prompting Stalin to express fears of the peasant disturbances spread-ing nationwide.)[67] Bukharin had gone so far as to proclaim to the peas-ants, 'Enrich Yourselves!', believing that the accumulation of wealth in the peasantry would ensure civil peace and ultimately help industrial-isation. Stalin distanced himself from this provocative slogan, but Zi-nov'ev and Kamenev seized the opportunity to awaken latent anti-NEP sentiments within the party. Their move drew Stalin and Bukharin closer, the 'duumvirate', whom the rest of the Politburo (save Trotskii, A.I. Rykov and M.P. Tomskii) supported.

The 'Leningrad Opposition' as the Zinov'ev-Kamenev opposition was called, was routed at the fourteenth party congress at the close of 1925. Trotskii sat through the congress without joining the fight. Krup-skaia's support of the opposition against Bukharin's interpretation of Lenin on the NEP was cut short. Lenin's sister Mariia, a good friend of Bukharin and Krupskaia's rival for Lenin's legacy, undercut her by stressing that as a sister of Lenin's she did not 'lay claim to a better un-derstanding and interpretation of Leninism than all other members of our party': 'I think that such a monopoly by Lenin's relatives . . . does not exist and cannot exist.'[68] When Zinov'ev and Kamenev attacked Stalin for his absolute power (and G.Ia. Sokol'nikov, People's Commis-sar for Finance, demanded Stalin's removal as General Secretary), the delegates suspected that the opposition's true concern was power, and not substantive policy issues. After their defeat, Stalin managed to elevate his own supporters, Voroshilov, Kalinin and Molotov to the

Politburo while relegating Kamenev to candidate status. (Kalinin had long been sceptical of Stalin, as was clear from his questioning of the award of the Order of the Red Banner during the Civil War. According to Trotskii, Kalinin was 'wont to say to his intimates', 'That horse [Stalin] will some day drag our wagon into a ditch,' but gradually and reluctantly Kalinin came to 'tie his own fate to Stalin's'.)[69] The leadership of the Leningrad and Moscow party organisations was taken away from Zinov'ev and Kamenev (Kirov took over Leningrad). When Zinov'ev, reminding Stalin of the 1924 CC plenum at which he and Kamenev rescued Stalin, asked him whether he knew what gratitude was, Stalin is said to have replied, pulling his pipe from his mouth: 'Why, surely, I know, I know very well, it's a dog's malady.'[70] Stalin was an unscrupulous politician. When Kamenev was concerned about political formality (such as winning a majority in the party), Stalin told him: 'You know what I believe. . . . Who votes how in the party is totally unimportant. What is extremely important is who counts the votes and how.'[71] Zinov'ev and Kamenev were no match for Stalin in politics. According to Bazhanov, Zinov'ev was capable of intrigue but no profound politician, while Kamenev, no coward, was poor at intrigue.[72]

Stalin methodically and relentlessly hounded his opponents. In the summer of 1926, for example, when an allegedly conspiratorial faction was uncovered in Moscow (the 'Lashevich affair'), Stalin insisted, against findings to the contrary, that this group, headed by the Old Bolshevik and Zinov'ev's supporter, M.M. Lashevich, was linked to Zinov'ev. Thus Zinov'ev was implicated in the 'conspiracy' and 'factionalism,' grave political offences.[73] The conspiracy charges marked a new stage in the political infighting of the party leaders. In the autumn of 1927, furthermore, the OGPU even tried to concoct a theory of military conspiracy linking alleged underground organisations of White Russian military men and Stalin's political opponents.[74] Clearly these incidents foreshadowed the methods Stalin would use in subsequent years in his terror against his political enemies. Meanwhile, by the autumn of 1926 the defeated three and erstwhile political foes, Trotskii, Zinov'ev and Kamenev, began to form a united front (the 'United Opposition') against Stalin and Bukharin. This was a hopeless bloc. Trotskii well knew how little support Zinov'ev and Kamenev had received at the congress in December 1925. Kamenev, according to Trotskii, said to him, 'It is enough for you and Zinov'ev to appear on the same platform, and the party will find its true Central Committee'. Trotskii 'could not laugh at such bureaucratic optimism'.[75] For all their joint effort, in the end they did not even come close to overthrowing Stalin.

There were many issues over which to fight. The question of intra-party democracy was one. Indeed, the party leadership, as seen in the case of the Lashevich affair in Leningrad, began to deal with the opposition in an extraordinarily high-handed manner, which the opposition declared to be political terror. Yet this was weak ground, on which they had been beaten already. The foreign policy issue was perhaps their strongest suit. The years 1926 and 1927 witnessed important events in Britain and China in particular. Stalin, unlike the image that 'socialism in one country' might conjure, keenly followed these affairs: the 1926 General Strike in Britain, for example, and the Soviet attempts to influence it; events leading up to Britain's severing of diplomatic ties with the Soviet Union in May 1927; the 1925–7 revolutionary development in China culminating in the massacre of Chinese communists by the Kuomintang. Serious errors of judgement on the part of the party leaders were evident. By then, however, the party proved unwilling to listen calmly to the argument of the opposition. Too much recrimination and insult had been exchanged. Emotions ran so high that, when the fight was over, the victorious demanded that the oppositionists renounce their views and repent openly and publicly. Politics had become a matter not of ideology and debate but of faith and loyalty. In October 1926 Zinov'ev was removed from the post of Chairman of the Comintern and Trotskii from the Politburo. In October 1927 they were expelled from the CC and in November from the party itself. In January 1928 Trotskii was exiled to Alma-Ata, Kazakhstan, and in February 1929 from the Soviet Union, settling for a while in Turkey. According to Trotskii, both Zinov'ev and Kamenev, who were not expelled, had been afraid of Stalin since their defeat in 1925. So Kamenev warned Trotskii: 'As soon as we [Kamenev and Zinov'ev] broke with him [Stalin], we made up something in the nature of a testament, in which we warned that in the event of our "accidental" death Stalin was to be held responsible for it. This document is kept in a reliable place. I advise you to do the same thing. You can expect anything from that Asiatic.'[76]

Stalin was more politically aware than the opposition. After Trotskii, Zinov'ev and Kamenev were ousted from the Politburo, Stalin said to Bukharin, 'You and I are the Himalayas; the others are nobodies.'[77] Privately, however, Stalin showed insecurity at times. On the eve of the fifteenth party congress, for example, it is said that Stalin begged Sokol'nikov to take pity on him and not to discuss 'Lenin's testament' at the congress.[78] At other times, he appeared overconfident. At a dinner with Leningrad colleagues to celebrate the defeat of the 'Leningrad Opposition', those present said that in the absence of Lenin 'the party should be governed by a collective'. Stalin responded, however, 'Don't forget we are living in Russia, the land of the tsars. The Russian people like to have one man standing at the head of the state.' Then he added, 'Of course, this man should carry out the will of the collective.'[79] Yet Stalin, unlike Trotskii, was astute enough to appear humble. In the July 1926 CC plenum, at which 'Lenin's testament' calling for Stalin's removal as General Secretary became an issue again, Stalin noted rightly that twice before in 1924 his resignation had been rejected by the party. He had to subordinate himself to the will of the party. 'I was obliged to take measures to correct my rudeness and mend my manners.'[80] At the December 1927 plenum, which took place after the 'United Opposition' had been defeated, Stalin again tendered his resignation: he had successfully performed his duty to keep the party from the danger of a split and he should now be relieved from duty. His disingenuous request was turned down a third time.[81]

The struggle for power was largely confined to the party – it did not involve open and democratic politics, and the population was largely left out of the government by the proletarian dictatorship, though it was still not the case that the population was in an antagonistic relationship to the Government. Prince L'vov, the first Prime Minister of the Provisional Government in 1917, wrote in 1923: 'The people support Soviet power. That does not mean they are happy with it. But at the same time as they feel their oppression they also see that their own type of people are entering into the apparatus, and this makes them feel that the regime is "their own".'[82] Stalin (but not Trotskii or Zinov'ev) might have appeared to the Soviet people as one of 'their own'. It was also Stalin's intention, as was clear from his Civil War experience, to staff the Soviet apparatus from within the people, and not from the hangovers from the old regime. If the NEP had slowed or even reversed this process, Stalin's 'revolution from above' was to make the apparatus decisively 'their own'.

Many of those deemed by Stalin's Government to be not one of 'their own' were liquidated. Terror did not cease. In the seven years from 1921 to 1927, as many as 20,423 people ('political criminals') were sentenced to death by the secret police (the Cheka and, from 1923, the OGPU).[83] In 1927, in conversation with the French writer Henri Barbusse, Stalin defended death sentences: no one wants to kill people, but the capitalists systematically send terrorists to the USSR, so it is impossible to do without capital punishment; in the Soviet Union only international considerations dictate death sentences.[84] His remarks were, of course, for foreign consumption. Obviously, all the people executed in the USSR could not have been spies and terrorists.

Possibly Stalin equated those people deemed not 'Soviet' with foreign spies and terrorists. The Stalin of the NEP era, as discussed earlier, was not yet the Stalin of the 1930s.

Historians have traditionally attributed the rise of Stalin to his cunning, political manipulation and intrigue. His rise, according to them, was somewhat accidental: to compensate for a mediocre intellect, Stalin played up to Lenin who, not realising Stalin's nature, made him the General Secretary. Meanwhile, Stalin's rivals vastly underestimated him as a politician. Stalin came to control the party by abusing power and appointing his own supporters to key positions. When Lenin realised the danger of Stalin, it was too late. All this may be true. Cunning, manipulation and intrigue are part and parcel of politics. (If Bazhanov's story is credible, Stalin abused his power by tapping his colleagues' telephone lines.) This interpretation of Stalin, however, calls for significant modification. Stalin was no blind follower of Lenin. He held to his own independent thought and argued against Lenin when necessary. Lenin saw Stalin as someone whose view of the Revolution most resembled his own. Unlike Trotskii, Stalin understood politics. Moreover, he was not loath to 'exert pressure' and not at all sentimental about it. Lenin knew that his character was potentially a serious problem (as he expressed during the Civil War). Still, Stalin could be humble (or cunning enough to appear humble) enough to tender his resignation thrice. Stalin played politics well. By contrast, while admiring Trotskii's talent and intellect, many party members (including his own supporters) saw, as Lenin did, that Trotskii was a poor and 'unbalanced' politician (and even 'stupid' and 'crazy').[85]

Nevertheless, Stalin harboured insecurity concerning his talent as a theorist. According to Bukharin, Stalin was 'consumed with a craving to become an acknowledged theoretician. He thinks that this is the only thing he lacks.' Avel' Enukidze, a fellow Georgian colleague of Stalin and the godfather of his wife Nadezhda, once confided to a friend: 'I am doing everything he [Stalin] has asked me to do, but it is not enough for him. He wants me to admit that he is a genius.'[86] All Bolshevik leaders had some intellectual pretence, but, unlike his rivals, Stalin did not let intellectual pretensions take precedence over politics. Whatever his anxiety, Stalin was proud of being a *praktik*.

Notes

[1] For this rebellion, see Oliver H. Radkey, *The Unknown Civil War in Soviet Russia: A Study of the Green Movement in the Tambov Region, 1920–1921* (Stanford, Calif., 1976).

[2]See Lars T. Lih, 'Bukharin's "Illusion": War Communism and the Meaning of NEP', *Russian History/Histoire Russe*, 27:4 (Winter 2000).

[3]Hiroaki Kuromiya, *Freedom and Terror in the Donbas: A Ukrainian–Russian Borderland, 1870s–1990s* (Cambridge, 1998), 122.

[4]Robert Himmer, 'The Transition from War Communism to the New Economic Policy: An Analysis of Stalin's Views', *Russian Review*, 53:4 (October 1994). Himmer exaggerates Stalin's 'anti-NEP' stance, however.

[5]Richard Day, *Leon Trotsky and the Politics of Economic Isolation* (Cambridge, 1973), 4, 6, 170.

[6]Eric van Ree, ' "Lenin's Last Struggle" Revisited', *Revolutionary Russia*, 14: 2 (December 2001); Jeremy Smith, *The Bolsheviks and the National Question, 1917–1923* (London, 1999), chs 7–8; and V.A. Sakharov, *'Politicheskoe zaveshchanie' Lenina. Real'nost' istorii i mify politiki* (Moscow, 2003). For the traditional view emphasising Lenin's 'last struggle against Stalin', see Moshe Lewin, *Lenin's Last Struggle* (New York, 1968).

[7]Sakharov, 129.

[8]Ibid., 194.

[9]*Izvestiia TsK KPSS*, 1989, no. 12, 197.

[10]Ibid., 199.

[11]Trotsky, *Stalin*, 375.

[12]Herbert J. Ellison, 'Stalin and His Biographers: The Lenin–Stalin Relationship', in Ralph Carter Elwood (ed.), *Reconsiderations on the Russian Revolution* (Cambridge, Mass., 1976), 260.

[13]Lidiia Shatunovskaia, *Zhizn' v Kremle* (New York, 1982), 36–7.

[14]Stalin, *Works*, 3:199–200.

[15]Ibid., 4:388–9.

[16]Lenin, *Collected Works*, 33:288, 424.

[17]Ibid., 33:480.

[18]Ibid., 33:468.

[19]Terry Martin, *The Affirmative Action Empire: Nations and Nationalism in the Soviet Union, 1923–1939* (Ithaca, New York, 2001).

[20]L.G. Babichenko, 'Politbiuro TsK RKP(b), Komintern i sobytiia v Germanii v 1923 g. Novye arkhivnye materialy', *Novaia i noveishaia istoriia*, 1994, no. 2.

[21]Iremaschwili, 64–82.

[22]Richard Pipes (ed.), *The Unknown Lenin: From the Secret Archive* (New Haven, Conn., 1996), 153.

[23]RGASPI, f. 558, op. 2, d. 27, l. 1.

[24]Smith, *The Bolsheviks*, 229–35.

[25]*Molotov Remembers*, 104.

[26]Boris Bazhanov, *Vospominaniia byvshego sekretaria Stalina* (Paris, 1980), 150–1.

[27]Sakharov, 173.

[28]Alliluyeva, *Twenty Letters*, 113, 168–9.

[29]Leon Trotsky, *Portraits: Political and Personal* (New York, 1977), 217.

[30]Lev Trotskii, *Portrety revoliutsionerov* (Benson, Vt., 1988), 106, 143.

[31]Bazhanov, 56–9.

[32]Mariia Ioffe, *Odna noch'. Povest' o pravde* (New York, 1978), 33–4.

[33]Galina Serebriakova, 'Oni delali chest' idee, kotoroi sluzhili', *Izvestiia*, 30 January 1989, 3.

[34] *Trotsky's Diary in Exile: 1935* (Cambridge, Mass, 1958), 64, or 'The best thing in life is to ferret out one's enemy, prepare the stroke carefully, revenge oneself mercilessly, and then lie down to sleep' in Emil Ludwig, *Stalin* (New York, 1942), 11.

[35]Robert C. Tucker (ed.), *The Lenin Anthology* (New York, 1975), 727–8.

[36]Ibid., 748.

[37] *Izvestiia TsK KPSS*, 1989, no. 12, 193.

[38]V.A. Kumanev and I.S. Kulikova, *Protivostoianie: Krupskaia – Stalin* (Moscow, 1994), 28.

[39]Serebriakova, 'Oni delali', 3.

[40]Bazhanov, 88.

[41] *Molotov Remembers* 133.

[42]Sakharov, 386–404, 564. For the controversial work of Sakharov, see the discussion by Russian specialists in *Otechestvennaia istoriia*, 2005, no. 2, 162–74.

[43]Tucker (ed.), 727.

[44]An account by Lenin's sister Mariia in *Izvestiia TsK KPSS*, 1989, no. 12, 197.

[45]Stalin, *Works*, 6:14, 39. Subsequently, in 1927, Stalin mocked Trotskii, who 'resembles an actor rather than a hero, and an actor should not be confused with a hero under any circumstances'. Ibid., 9:289.

[46] *The Unknown Lenin*, 124.

[47]Tucker (ed.), 727.

[48]Ibid., 719–24.

[49]Van Ree, ' "Lenin's Last Struggle" Revisited', 107–9.

[50]Sakharov, 517–18.

[51]Trotsky, *My Life*, 496.

[52] *Izvestiia TsK KPSS*, 1991, no. 4, 171.

[53]Sakharov, 549–66.

[54] *Izvestiia TsK KPSS*, 1991, no. 4, 203, 206, and *RKP(b). Vnutripartiinaia bor'ba v dvadtsatye gody* (Moscow, 2004), 137–41.

[55] *RKP(b)*, 350.

[56]Stalin, *Works*, 6:42.

[57]Bazhanov, 105.

[58]Trotskii's letter to Max Eastman, 7 June 1933, Trotskii Manuscripts, Lily Library, Indiana University, Bloomington, Ind. In his letter Trotskii used a euphemism ('soiled' [*ispachkhal*]), noting that Stalin in fact used a 'more "naturalistic" word to be found in the dictionary of [Vladimir] Dal' '. See also Robert D. Warth, *Leon Trotsky* (Boston, Mass., 1977), 137.

[59]Bazhanov, 106–7.

[60]Sakharov, 579–86, and *Rodina*, 1994, no. 7, 73.

[61] *Voprosy istorii KPSS*, 1990, no. 5, 36–7.

[62]Interestingly, after Lenin's death when it became known that Lenin's maternal grandfather was a Jew, Lenin's sister Anna twice asked Stalin to publish the fact. Stalin flatly refused her request, ordering her to 'keep absolutely quiet'. Yuri Slezkine, *The Jewish Century* (Princeton, NJ, 2004), 245–6.

[63]Lars T. Lih et al. (eds), *Stalin's Letters to Molotov, 1925–1936* (New Haven, Conn., 1995), 62.

[64] Stalin, *Works*, 7:16, 120, 202.

[65] Ibid., 8:69–70, 72, 73.

[66] Note Lars Lih's discussion of Stalin's dealing with the so-called 'Max Eastman Affair' (the leak of 'Lenin's testament' outside the USSR), in *Stalin's Letters to Molotov*, 18–24.

[67] Stalin, *Works*, 23.

[68] Stephen F. Cohen, *Bukharin and the Bolshevik Revolution: A Political Biography, 1888–1938* (New York, 1973), 227.

[69] Trotsky, *Stalin*, 388–9.

[70] Bazhanov, 107.

[71] Ibid., 80.

[72] Ibid., 175–7.

[73] *Stalin's Letters to Molotov*, 99–101, 115–17.

[74] Iu. Fel'shtinskii (comp.), *Kommunisticheskaia oppozitsiia v SSSR*, v. 4 (Benson, Vt., 1988), 189–201.

[75] Trotsky, *My Life*, 544.

[76] Trotsky, *Stalin*, 417.

[77] Quoted in Cohen, 225.

[78] Serebriakova, 'Oni delali', 3.

[79] Roy Medvedev, *Let History Judge* (New York, 1989), 586. For Stalin's view of himself being a new tsar in 1926, see also Ilizarov, 106.

[80] *Rodina*, 1994, no. 7, 73.

[81] Ibid., 1994, no. 1, 68.

[82] Figes, 816.

[83] V.P. Popov, 'Gosudarstvennyi terror v sovetskoi Rossii. 1923–1953 gg. (istochniki i ikh interpretatsiia)', *Otechestvennye arkhivy*, 1992, no. 2, 28.

[84] *Istochnik*, 1999, no. 1, 103.

[85] B.V. Sokolov, *Stalin. Vlast' i krov'* (Moscow, 2004), 383 (Iu.M. Steklov), 386 (K. Radek), 388 (Radek and A.G. Beloborodov).

[86] Trotsky, *Stalin*, 389.

Chapter 4

'Revolution from Above'

The NEP was short-lived. A grain-procurement crisis, which followed the fifteenth party congress in late 1927, led to the breakdown of the Stalin-Bukharin 'duumvirate' and the eventual demise of the NEP. From the grain crisis Stalin emerged victorious against Bukharin. This initiated the period of the so-called First Five-Year Plan (1928–32) characterised by rapid industrialisation, wholesale collectivisation and de-kulakisation as well as cultural transformation and social mobility. Subsequently, Stalin proudly referred to these events of the First Five-Year Plan as a 'revolution from above'. Indeed, the five years from 1928 to 1932 witnessed a great metamorphosis affecting all spheres, arguably the most important event in the history of the Soviet Union. What emerged from this 'revolution' was the Stalinist regime: a centrally planned economy that would successfully defeat the Nazi onslaught and in essence remain intact until the collapse of the Soviet Union itself in 1991. The 'cultural revolution' had a tremendous impact upon the education of an entire generation of people (the 'Brezhnev generation') who would run the country for three decades after Stalin's death. It was through the 'revolution' that Stalin eliminated all his major political rivals and established his dictatorship.

The Crisis of the NEP

In some respects the NEP had proved extraordinarily successful. In 1922, as discussed earlier, Lenin was already claiming that there was no reason to fear any resistance to the Soviet Government. By 1926–7 both agriculture and industry had managed to recover pre-war (1913) levels of production. As is often the case, success sowed the seeds of conflict. This was already apparent in 1925 in the debate between the duumvirate (Stalin and Bukharin) and the 'Leningrad Opposition' (Zinov'ev and Kamenev) regarding the extension of the NEP. While allying with Bukharin, Stalin was politically perspicacious enough to distance himself from Bukharin's slogan exhorting the peasants to 'Enrich Yourselves'. With widespread unemployment, poverty and a host of other economic problems, this slogan was too provocative.

In many respects the NEP was fraught with serious problems. The most significant was the difficulty of providing the peasantry with material incentives to part with their grain. This was not a new problem: the NEP had been introduced precisely in order to induce the peasants to sell their produce voluntarily. With the 1924 substitution of a money tax for tax in kind and the legalisation of a wide range of private trade, the peasants had more prima-facie incentive to do so, though several factors conspired to weaken that incentive. First, the 'goods famine', a shortage of manufactured goods for which the peasants were willing to sell their produce. Industry tended to lag behind agriculture in recovery, which created an imbalance between the prices for agricultural and industrial products (the 'scissors crisis' was particularly acute in 1923). Yet a reduction in the prices for industrial goods did not help much. Private traders ('NEPmen'), much more skilful at trade than the Soviet trade officials, simply profited by reselling goods from the state to the private sector. (Normally there were large gaps in prices between the state sector of trade and the private sector.) This did not create favourable market conditions for the peasantry. Second, agricultural marketing declined. Large-scale, market-oriented agriculture disappeared after the Revolution. The 'reduced level of taxation' and the elimination of land rents after the Revolution had relieved the burden on households. This meant that 'peasants who had marketed their produce before the war in order to meet these obligations now had less need to do so'.[1] The peasants consumed more of their own produce in the 1920s than before the Revolution, and more was reinvested in the village than before. For most of the NEP period the procurement of agricultural products in general and grain in particular remained a source of much anxiety and frustration for the Soviet Government.

When a serious grain-procurement shortage occurred in 1927–8, Stalin reacted violently. State collection of grain in November and December 1927 had fallen 'below half the level of the previous year'. In a panic, Stalin and his supporters resorted to 'extraordinary' or 'emergency' measures: 'the notorious Article 107 of the Criminal Code, which stipulated "deprivation of liberty" against speculators, was extensively applied to peasants holding or suspected of holding grain'.[2] Stalin took the matter seriously. Unlike the Stalin of later years who rarely left the Kremlin, the Stalin of 1928 took the trouble to head an expedition to Siberia, a key grain-producing area. In January 1928, at a time when his defeated rivals (Trotskii and others) had been exiled, Stalin travelled to inspect the grain-procurement activity in Siberia. On the day he departed for Siberia, he instructed his colleagues on similar expeditions to other grain-producing areas that 'the speculator and the kulak are the enemy of the Soviet power'.[3] Once in Siberia, Stalin stressed the danger of the grain deficit: 'You know, of course, what the effect of the deficit may be if it is not made good. The effect will be that our towns and industrial centres, as well as our Red Army, will be in grave difficulties; they will be poorly supplied and will be threatened with hunger. Obviously, we cannot allow that.' The deficit, Stalin asserted, was due entirely to the kulaks. 'If the kulaks are engaging in unbridled speculation on grain prices, why do you not prosecute them for speculation? Don't you know that there is a law against speculation – Article 107 of the Criminal Code. . . . Can it be that you are afraid to disturb the tranquillity of the kulak gentry?' Most importantly, the crisis threatened to jeopardise industrialisation: '[W]e cannot allow our industry to be dependent on the caprice of the kulaks'.[4]

Stalin's advocacy of 'emergency measures', however, was not greeted with enthusiasm by local officials, inasmuch as such steps were tantamount to the rejection of the NEP and threatened the newly won peace with the peasants. In Siberia Stalin was '[s]hocked and irritated by the repeated questioning and hostile reception' to his order to apply Article 107.[5] All the same, 'emergency measures' were taken and village markets were often closed. Inevitably, the measures led in some instances to arbitrary administrative 'excesses' and the 'infringement of revolutionary legality' such as illegal and house-to-house searches for grain, confiscation of grain and property, and beatings and arrests of traders and peasants (including well-off and poor peasants). When the procurement of grain increased and the 'emergency measures' were therefore halted in the summer, Stalin admitted that the measures had 'worsened the political situation in the country and created a threat to the *smychka* [alliance between workers and peasants, one of the cardinal themes of the NEP]'.[6]

There is evidence to suggest, however, that when faced with yet another grain crisis in December 1927, Stalin deemed the *smychka* based on the NEP doomed and decided to take decisive measures to end the vicious cycle of grain deficits once and for all. The 'United Opposition' had been defeated, and Bukharin appeared favourably and openly disposed towards the peasants, rich and poor alike. In Stalin's view, tolerant attitudes towards the rich peasants (kulaks) in particular appeared to have encouraged their 'speculation'. If this were true, then the position of Bukharin and his supporters appeared politically untenable.

Attacks on the kulaks would incur opposition from Bukharin, but it would be worth the fight for the extrication of the country from this vicious grain-procurement cycle. Indeed, Bukharin and his supporters blamed the crisis on the Soviet Government's poor price policies; more skilful negotiations with the peasants on the market would solve the problem. By contrast, Stalin and his supporters insisted that the crisis was a 'grain strike' by the kulaks and an 'expression of the first serious action, under the conditions of the NEP, undertaken by the capitalist elements of the countryside against the Soviet Government.'[7] In fact, the 1927–8 grain crisis was a result of Soviet economic policies (geared increasingly towards administrative control and planning that undermined the market's equilibrium) and a run on the markets caused by the diplomatic crisis of 1927 (Britain's abrogation of diplomatic relations with the Soviet Union).

On his expedition to Siberia, Stalin had already outlined his vision of what was to come – the collectivisation of agriculture. He maintained that the Soviet system could not persist on the heterogeneous foundations of socialised industry and '*individual* small-peasant economy based on *private* ownership of the means of production'. Therefore it was necessary for the country to 'pass from the socialisation of industry to the socialisation of the whole of agriculture'. This meant several important changes. Firstly, 'we must gradually, but unswervingly, unite the individual peasant farms which produce the smallest marketable surpluses into collective farms, *kolkhozes*, which produce the largest marketable surpluses'. Secondly, 'all areas of our country, without exception, must be covered with collective farms (and state farms) capable of replacing, as suppliers of grain to the state, not only the kulaks but the individual peasants as well'. Thirdly, this step implied 'doing away with all sources that engender capitalists and capitalism, and putting an end to the possibility of the restoration of capitalism'. Collectivisation would thus create a firm basis for food supply, ensure the 'necessary reserves for the state', 'create a single and firm socialist basis for the Soviet system' and 'ensure the victory of socialist construction in our country'.[8] How to go about implementing collectivisation was still far from clear, however.

What was clear was that Stalin and his supporters were galvanised to resolute action by the grain crisis. In January 1928 V.V. Kuibyshev, then head of Vesenkha (the Commissariat of Industry), stated that 'if there was a choice between the industrialisation programme and equilibrium in the market, the market must give way' and that the market situation might be 'one current', but a communist and Bolshevik had always been able to 'swim against the current.' What were important,

Kuibyshev emphasised, were the 'will and energy of the party': 'The will of the party can create miracles . . . and is creating and will create miracles despite all these market phenomena.' A few weeks later, Kuibyshev declared that 'the will of the state has smashed the market'.[9] There was a consensus among Stalin and his supporters that the voluntarist approach expressed in the 'emergency' measures had worked to break the 'grain strike' of the kulaks. In May 1928 Stalin exhorted the Komsomol to 'strengthen the readiness for action of the working class'. In July Kaganovich defended the use of the 'emergency measures' that had demonstrated a 'valuable thing': the party had 'demonstrated its fighting ability'. In 1929, when the 'emergency measures' were used again to secure grain procurements, Stalin defended the use of coercion:

> Point out even one political measure taken by the party that has not been accompanied by excesses of one kind or another. The conclusion to be drawn from this is that we must combat excesses. But can one *on these grounds* decry the line [of policy] itself, which is the only correct line?[10]

In a word, Stalin suggested that, in implementing policy, moderation was more dangerous than excess. Otherwise, the policy might be thwarted by bureaucracy, inertia and other hindrances. In the first few months of 1928 alone, several thousand communists were expelled from the party for their reluctance to apply the 'emergency measures'.[11]

Clearly Stalin had discarded the 'class-conciliatory' NEP in favour of a 'class-war' approach while at the same time denying that he was negating the NEP. Just as he persecuted the old military officers during the Civil War, during the 'revolution from above' Stalin persecuted both the 'commanders of agriculture', the kulaks, and the old, or 'bourgeois', commanders of industry – technicians and engineers. The industrial policy of the NEP, as Stalin summarised, was predicated on the following:

> Since Communists do not yet properly understand the technology of production; since they have yet to learn the art of management, let the old technicians and engineers – the experts – carry on production, and you, Communists, do not interfere with the technique of the business; but while not interfering, study technology, study the art of management tirelessly, in order later on, together with the experts who are loyal to us, to become true managers of production, true masters of the business.[12]

By early 1928, however, Stalin began to think that dependence on the 'bourgeois' experts whose political loyalty was doubtful should be ended sooner rather than later. The contradiction between 'Red' and 'expert' had to be resolved by educating the sons and daughters of workers and peasants deemed politically reliable to train as 'experts' and replace the old commanders. During the NEP this ultimate goal had appeared to fade into a distant future. There was reluctance on the part of educational authorities to focus narrowly on technical training at the cost of a well-rounded curriculum. Meanwhile, at a time when saving for industrialisation appeared imperative, expensive industrial investment appeared inordinately wasteful, particularly because communist managers poorly understood what their nominal subordinates (engineers and technicians) were doing with the running and planning of industry.

Stalin used the so-called 'Shakhty affair' to break through this industrial conundrum. Not without reason was Shakhty, located in the southern Ukrainian–Russian borderland of the Donbas coal and steel industrial centre, chosen as the target of Stalin's assault on the NEP. The Donbas had such an extraordinarily complex political history that Trotskii once despaired that one could not go there 'without a [political] gas mask'. 'Specialist-baiting' died hard in the Donbas, tempered by the memory of both the pre-war domination by foreign capital (served by many technicians and engineers) and a brutal Civil War (in which they served on the side of the anti-Bolshevik forces).

Stalin had been planning, probably since late 1927 or early 1928, to use the Donbas to discredit the old experts. He put his plan into practice in March 1928, more or less coinciding with his use of 'emergency measures' in the countryside. The Shakhty affair was the first major political show trial Stalin staged. Rykov, Bukharin and others intent on maintaining the NEP were initially sceptical of the charges of 'industrial wrecking' and 'economic counter-revolution'. So was Voroshilov, who hailed from the Donbas. Yet in the end everyone appeared to be convinced by the evidence presented. Trotskii, now in exile, also appeared to believe in the charges.[13]

The May–July 1928 trial of 53 defendants took place in Moscow, not in Shakhty. This fact alone testifies to the significance Stalin attached to the trial. Twenty defendants pleaded guilty to the charges, which included 'every possible detail ranging from the singing of the Tsar's anthem and rude treatment of workers' to 'intentional delays in the compilation of plans for capital constructions, constant revisions of already completed plans for no other reason than sabotaging economic planning, criminal waste of foreign currency, intentional flooding of mines, sabotage of equipment'. These 'wrecking activities' were said to be 'staged in cooperation with foreign powers and former mine owners living abroad to undermine the [Soviet] industrialisation drive that would have strengthened the dictatorship of the proletariat, thereby making a return to capitalism difficult'. Yet as many as 23 defendants maintained their innocence, and 10 pleaded only partial guilt. Four defendants, including 2 German citizens, were acquitted, but others were declared guilty. Ten were sentenced to death, and 5 of them (of whom 2 pleaded guilty, 1 partially guilty and 2 innocent at the trial) were actually executed four days after the sentencing when their appeal for clemency was rejected. A close examination of trial records suggests that the charges of 'economic counter-revolution' was almost certainly fabricated by the secret police.[14]

The attack on the experts, like the attack on the kulaks, made no economic sense. It was precisely these people who were sorely needed to run and develop industry. Stalin's class-war orientation, however, made political sense: he exploited explicit and implicit anti-NEP sentiments in the party and the population. The Shakhty affair, for example, discredited the class-conciliatory policy of the NEP in the eyes of the workers. The immediate impact was a vastly expanded and accelerated training programme of experts from among workers and peasants, supervised directly by industrial authorities. The old, meritocratic recruitment of students to higher education was replaced by a class-based 'affirmative action' explicitly favouring the students of proletarian origin. This proved highly popular among the workers. Unlike Mao Zedong's 'cultural revolution', which destroyed formal education in China, Stalin's 'cultural revolution' vastly expanded formal education.[15]

The class-war rhetoric and practice affected almost all spheres of life, including cultural areas: literature, film, science, history, law, the arts. During the NEP, the adherents of old, 'bourgeois' values and those advocating class-based values ('proletarian literature', 'Marxist history' and so on) bickered constantly, resulting in factionalism. From 1928 the party in the person of Stalin implicitly and sometimes explicitly intervened in the cultural life of the country in favour of class-based activity. This intervention from above invigorated those 'proletarian' activists who had been frustrated by the power and prestige of their 'bourgeois' rivals. Thus cultural life, too, assumed a decisively class-war tone.[16]

Stalin was aware of the conflict his new policy was bound to cause with Bukharin, Rykov and other proponents of the NEP. Unlike the previous struggles, this time the matter concerned concrete and pressing policy issues (not merely somewhat abstract matters such as party democracy) that affected the everyday life of the population and touched on the very essence of the NEP. The stakes were high. Both Stalin and his foes trod on politically delicate ground. Neither wanted to appear to have initiated a split within the party so soon after it appeared finally united when the 'Left Opposition' was defeated and expelled. Bukharin even wrote to Stalin in June 1928 to say that he would not and did not want to 'fight'.[17] Nevertheless, it was a deadly fight behind the scenes, at least for now. At a Politburo meeting in the summer of 1928, for example, Stalin began yelling at Bukharin, who then reminded him of his remark about the two Himalayas. Stalin retorted, 'A lie! You've made it up to set the members of the Politburo against me.'[18]

Stalin's class-war practice may have been popular to some degree among the working people. Donbas colliers inscribed on their trolleys 'Long Live the GPU [OGPU, the secret police]'. The workers of Shakhty, according to one account, appeared 'as if experiencing a second October 1917'.[19] Yet Stalin's new line of policy also caused serious everyday problems. Shortages of bread and other foodstuffs disquieted the urban population, and here and there rationing was introduced to alleviate the problem.[20] Extensive and detailed reports on 'famine' in the cities and the countryside flowed into the OGPU. So did information on a politically 'unsound' and 'anti-Soviet' political mood in the cities and the countryside. A similar mood among the Red Army soldiers, most of whom were peasants concerned about their home villages, was particularly worrisome.[21] Mass politics had virtually disappeared from the Soviet Union: under one-party dictatorship the voice of workers and peasants no longer meant much even though the party ruled in their name. Direct actions such as industrial strikes were dealt with harshly and decisively. How comfortable Stalin was with containing mass discontent with terror is not known. When N.A. Uglanov (Politburo candidate member and the head of the Moscow party organisation) told Stalin that there was no bread, that people were starving, and that the policy had to change, Stalin responded, 'This is hysteria.' Uglanov reminded Stalin of a Russian version of the Marie Antoinette story: 'Tsarina Mariia Fedorovna [wife of Alexander III] said, when told that the peasants had no bread, that they could eat sandwiches for now.' (Uglanov added that 'Stalin doesn't tolerate people who have their own opinions. He fights against them as his class enemies.')[22] Bukharin used the spectre of mass uprisings as his political trump card. In the summer of 1928, Bukharin spent two days in the OGPU examining its reports on 'peasant unrest' (he counted 150 small uprisings) and confronted Stalin. Stalin answered, however, that there was no need to draw conclusions: 'The GPU knows nothing. The GPU sows panic. Molotov himself toured around the country and saw nothing like that. Panic-mongers are everywhere. We know everything is calm in Shipke [probably in Siberia]. I shall dispel all trouble'. Later, Iagoda (of the secret police) was accused of supplying 'tendentious material' to Bukharin and his supporters.[23]

Although conciliatory in public, Stalin challenged Bukharin indirectly. At the July 1928 CC plenum, Stalin conceded to the demands of the Bukharin group: the 'emergency' measures were renounced and the procurement prices for grain were raised by the plenum. Yet Stalin also declared that, for the industrialisation of the country, it would be necessary, if 'unpleasant', to exact a sort of 'tribute' from the peasantry. (Bukharin later called this 'tribute' a 'military-feudal exploitation of the peasantry'.) Stalin added, in an allusion to the Bukharin group, that 'the advance to socialism cannot but cause the exploiting elements to resist the advance, and the resistance of the exploiters cannot but lead to the inevitable sharpening of the class struggle'.[24]

Bukharin correctly understood that Stalin's concessions were merely a cover. Even before the plenum ended, Bukharin sought a meeting with Kamenev through Sokol'nikov. Sokol'nikov informed Kamenev that Bukharin would rather have Zinov'ev and Kamenev than Stalin in the Politburo and sought a 'bloc for the removal of Stalin'. Aware that the OGPU were following him and Kamenev, Bukharin used a 'conspiratorial method' to visit Kamenev. Kamenev noted that Bukharin was 'shaken to the extreme and sometimes his lips trembled from nervousness', giving him the impression of a 'doomed person'. Bukharin told Kamenev, according to the memorandum Kamenev wrote down after the meeting, that the differences with Stalin were much more serious than the differences between themselves. Stalin was an 'unprincipled intriguer who subordinates everything to the preservation of his power'. Stalin's class-war line would lead to civil war and destroy the revolution and everything. Alongside Bukharin stood Rykov, Tomskii and Uglanov, as did A.A. Andreev, another Politburo candidate member. (Bukharin may have been wrong about Andreev, for Andreev remained a loyal Stalinist.) Voroshilov and Kalinin betrayed Bukharin at the last moment. According to Bukharin, Ordzhonikidze 'cursed Stalin', but he too betrayed Bukharin at a critical moment. Iagoda and M.A. Trilisser (both deputy heads of the OGPU) sided with Bukharin. Bukharin did not propose an anti-Stalin 'bloc' to Kamenev, but he did want Kamenev and Zinov'ev to understand what the issues within the party leadership were, especially because Stalin might approach them as well. Although Bukharin tried to convince Kamenev to conspire against Stalin, Bukharin was diffident, wondering whether he was indulging in a lonely battle and not knowing what to do with the 'Genghis Khan culture of the CC'. Stalin understood only one thing – revenge – and Bukharin recalled the story of Stalin's 'sweet revenge' (discussed in Chapter 3).[25] Bukharin met with Kamenev on three subsequent occasions.[26]

These meetings did not immediately become known to Stalin, but meanwhile, as expected, he ignored the concessions he had made at the July 1928 plenum and continued to attack Bukharin. Stalin noted privately in September 1928 that people thought that the removal of 'emergency measures' and the hike in grain-procurement prices signalled the end of the grain crisis, but these were 'empty hopes of empty liberals'.[27] Stalin also began to drop hints publicly of the existence and the danger of the 'rightist deviation' within the party. In November 1928 Bukharin had a six-hour meeting with Stalin, in which Bukharin remained defiant: he told Stalin that he did 'not wish to fight, because it will harm the party': 'If a fight starts, you'll declare us renegades from Leninism, but we'll call you organisers of famine.'[28]

Bukharin's July 1928 secret meeting with Kamenev, however, proved to be a fatal event. A copy of the memorandum Kamenev took of the meeting fell into the hands of Trotskii and his supporters, who in January 1929 published and circulated it, probably fearing a rapprochement between Stalin and Bukharin.[29] If so, Trotskii misunderstood the situation, for in late 1928 the 'emergency measures' were resumed and there was little ground for such a rapprochement. (Zinov'ev, for his part, feared that Stalin might ally with Trotskii or that Stalin might turn to the right after defeating Bukharin. Zinov'ev excluded the possibility of any alliance with Bukharin, hoping instead to secure a partnership with Stalin on his (Zinov'ev's) own terms, even though he was well aware of L.M. Kaganovich's words to the effect that because 'Zinov'ev and Kamenev hate Stalin', Kaganovich and other supporters of Stalin could not work with them.)[30] The publication of the memorandum was like manna from heaven for Stalin who had been waiting patiently for an opportunity to destroy Bukharin politically. In the memorandum, the authenticity of which neither Kamenev nor Bukharin disputed, Bukharin appeared to everyone as a conspirator. Kamenev was proved right: Bukharin was doomed. Bukharin denied ever trying to form a bloc with the former oppositionists, but Stalin asked why, if this were true, Bukharin hid his meeting with Kamenev from the CC – it was in fact a conspiracy.[31] Bukharin criticised Stalin's use of 'tributes' from the peasantry, his 'destruction of collective leadership' and his 'boundless power', which Lenin had criticised but which had since become more 'boundless'. Stalin 'humbly' admitted that he was indeed 'rude', as Lenin had said. Had he not tendered his resignation on several occasions? But, he asked (this time without feigning humility), who was it who had opposed his resignation? (Stalin did not mention Zinov'ev, Kamenev or Bukharin by name, but everyone knew who had.) The Trotskists had abused Lenin's testament, Stalin declared, and now so had Bukharin and his men. Stalin added that his resolute fight against the 'opportunists' and 'factionalists' in the party was not an expression of his 'rudeness'.[32] His confidence was evident. When he got a Russian proverb wrong in a speech in April 1929 ('An obliging bear is more dangerous than any enemy' rather than 'An obliging fool is more dangerous than any enemy', from Ivan Krylov's fable, 'The Bear and the Hermit'), Stalin was heckled by the floor, 'No, you got it wrong, you don't know Russian proverbs.' Stalin retorted to everyone's laughter, 'I know Russian proverbs, but I don't want to be "rude", dear comrades,' probably referring to his extensive knowledge of rude Russian proverbs.[33]

Bukharin and his 'rightist deviationists' were routed at the April 1929 plenum of the CC and the CCC (party Central Control Commission). Stalin attacked Bukharin furiously, branding him a 'liberal' opportunist who could not understand what 'class struggle' was. Stalin emphasised that only 'liberals', averse to the use of force, believed that the kulaks – the 'class enemy' – would voluntarily surrender to Soviet power. Unable to understand the 'rightists', Stalin went so far as to exclaim: 'You have gone mad!'[34] When Bukharin proposed importing grain to alleviate grain shortages, Ordzhonikidze responded by asking how he was going to 'solve the problem in the future'.[35] Impatience was everywhere. One of Bukharin's supporters criticised as 'fundamentally false' the assumption that the NEP agricultural policy was a 'policy of the [pro-peasant] SRs' and that only now, with the 'emergency measures', had they started to implement a 'truly Bolshevik peasant policy'.[36] But the assumption was evidently accepted by Stalin and his backers.

Stalin was still not strong enough to expel Bukharin and his men from the Politburo – in fact, he found it politically wiser to side with those who opposed their expulsion.[37] Nevertheless, he carefully and methodically prepared for their removal from influential political positions. In November 1929 Bukharin was removed from the Politburo, in July 1930 Tomskii and in December 1930 Rykov. Meanwhile, the harsh measures against the kulaks and NEPmen grew harsher still in an effort to secure grain, and the OGPU was mobilised to secure procurements and enforce penal measures (including execution for 'terrorist acts'). Stalin also worked from within the party, launching a campaign to purge the party and other organisations of unreliable elements. A

Soviet official used the absence of pluralism in the Soviet body politic to justify the purges:

> In the prerevolutionary period such wavering comrades left the Bolshevik party and found asylum in other opportunist parties. Now in the period of the dictatorship of the proletariat . . . the presence in the country of other political parties is impossible. Hence all who seek an active political life try to join the ranks of our party.[38]

The purges were also a calculated political move by Stalin to shake up and revitalise the party and government organisations for the immense task he was about to undertake. In April 1929 he stated that to put 25 million peasant households on a socialist footing meant 'raising the ocean'.[39] The purges were a political operation that made no sense from a purely administrative point of view: expelling knowledgeable and experienced experts and placing in their stead inexperienced and poorly educated people (workers and peasants) was detrimental to the smooth running of organisations. The real intent behind the purges was to strengthen the 'mobilisation readiness for the socialist offensive'. They were, as Stalin put it, 'necessary links in the single continuous chain which is called the offensive of socialism against the elements of capitalism'.[40]

Industrialisation and Collectivisation

Stalin did not say how or when he would 'raise the ocean'. In a narrowly political sense he had achieved influence and power. Once the 'rightists' were defeated, he was freer to exercise that power. Nevertheless, however impatient he may have been to put the countryside on a socialist footing, the socialisation or collectivisation of agriculture presupposed a strong industrial base for the mechanisation of large, collective agriculture. Stalin had naturally taken the grain crisis seriously because it had threatened to jeopardise industrialisation: 'We cannot allow our industry to be dependent on the caprice of the kulaks.' It was evident to both him and his supporters that agriculture had to serve the industrialisation drive. They never doubted the primacy of industrial interests over those of agriculture. The Soviet Union had to be industrialised and modernised, if only to survive in a hostile international climate. If the 1917 Revolution was a 'revolution against *Das Kapital*', the industrialisation drive was supposed to solve this painfully evident contradiction of the Revolution: the Soviet Union had to catch up and surpass the most advanced capitalist countries. In an oft-quoted speech of February 1931 Stalin spoke of Russian history as one of 'continual beatings owing to backwardness', beatings by the Mongol khans, the Swedish feudal lords, the Polish–Lithuanian pans, the Anglo-French capitalists and the Japanese barons, and declared: 'We are fifty to one hundred years behind the advanced countries. We must cover this distance in ten years. Either we do this, or they will crush us.'[41] Ten years later, the Soviet Union was almost crushed by Nazi Germany.

The crux of the problem was how to make agriculture serve industry without politically antagonising the bulk of the 25 million peasant households. The debate on industrialisation that took place during the NEP revolved around this intractable question. All the participants well understood that the Soviet Union, unlike its predecessors in industrialisation, could not exploit colonies. (The country did not own colonies, to begin with, although some argued that non-Russian areas were Russia's 'internal colonies'. Similarly, scholars now question whether colonies actually contributed significantly to industrialisation in Britain and elsewhere.) Unlike Sergei Vitte's (Witte's) industrialisation in the 1890s, they would not rely on foreign capital. They also knew that, given the hostile international environment, the country could not wait for ever (hence the importance of Stalin's February 1931 speech). The major source of capital had to be the agricultural sector in which the majority of the population was still engaged. Some theorists like Preobrazhenskii went so far as to advocate a 'primitive socialist accumulation' à la 'primitive capitalist accumulation', a phrase coined by Karl Marx in his *Das Kapital* to describe the long process of capital formation at the foundation of the industrial revolution in Britain. Bukharin and others rejected Preobrazhenskii's concept, which they claimed implied the 'exploitation' of peasants, and had attacked Stalin's use of 'tribute' for the same reason. The NEP had been expected to provide a market mechanism for pumping resources out of the agricultural sector and into industrialisation without breaking the civil peace with the peasantry. (This mechanism can be described as a 'peaceful exploitation of the peasantry' or a 'tribute' without civil war.) For Stalin the grain crisis signified a failure of the class-conciliatory NEP itself, whereas for Bukharin the blame lay with the Government, which had failed to operate the market in conjunction with the peasantry.

Almost all agreed that collectivisation was the ultimate solution, but none believed that wholesale collectivisation would be possible unless it was supported by appropriate technology, such as tractors. Despite Stalin's exhortation, the First Five-Year Plan, officially adopted in the spring of 1929 but retroactively effective from the autumn of 1928, did not envisage large-scale collectivisation: collective farms were to cover only approximately 10 per cent of the rural population by the close of the Five-Year Plan (1932–3).

For the production and distribution of grain alone, the 'emergency measures' might have sufficed even if they had had to be perpetuated or institutionalised. Indeed, in broad terms this was what actually happened, almost certainly against Stalin's intention. These measures would not solve the problem that Stalin had identified in the countryside: the danger of capitalist restoration inherent in the 'petit bourgeois' individual forms of agricultural production. Once he had defeated the Bukharin group, Stalin's interest in large-scale collectivisation as the ultimate solution grew immeasurably. It would both eliminate the danger of capitalist restoration and do away with the constant need for emergency measures. Collectivisation was neither pure improvisation nor a carefully planned measure. Stalin took the idea and implemented it in an extraordinarily brutal way.

Many local areas, sensing the way the wind was blowing from Moscow, had already begun collectivising their regions at an accelerated rate. Stalin followed the collectivisation drive in the Khoper *okrug* (county) in the lower Volga with special interest. He seemed to have found what he wanted in Khoper. In his letter to Molotov on 5 December 1929 he noted with apparent excitement:

> The collective farm movement is growing by leaps and bounds. Of course there are not enough machines and tractors – how could it be otherwise? – but simply pooling the peasant tools results in a colossal increase in sown acreage (in some regions by as much as 50 per cent!). In the lower Volga, 60 per cent of peasant farms have been transferred (already transferred!) to collective farms. The eyes of our rightists are popping out of their heads in amazement.[42]

The Khoper experience appeared to convince Stalin that, even without the immediate mechanisation of agriculture, collective farms were viable.

In a December 1929 speech Stalin used almost identical phrases to extol the Khoper experience, and posed (and answered) the question: 'How are these "dizzying" results to be explained? By the fact that the peasants, who were powerless under the conditions of individual labour, have been transformed into a mighty force once they have pooled their implements and have united in collective farms.' In this speech, Stalin also publicly sanctioned what had been practised in various parts of the country based to some extent on a Politburo directive: the 'elimination of the kulaks as a class' ('dekulakisation'). Stalin was confident that the kolkhozes would be able to replace the kulak output, so the elimination of the kulaks as a class became 'an integral part of the formation and development of the collective farms'.[43] His speech ignited a drive for all-out collectivisation and dekulakisation.

The frantic speed at which collectivisation and industrialisation proceeded engendered numerous problems. The real wages of workers declined, and the urban population went hungry. Many peasants also starved, having been deprived of their grain by the state. Yet in political terms Stalin had reason to be optimistic. The defeat of the rightists had made it finally possible to adopt an extremely ambitious Five-Year Plan of economic development. Economic equilibrium was dismissed as a non sequitur: Stalin's industrialisation was not just any kind of rapid industrialisation but one that also sought to supersede a market economy with a centrally planned economy. At a party conference in April 1929, one speaker noted, 'Every speaker from this platform ends with the conclusion: "Give us a power factory in the Urals, and to hell with the Rightists! [Laughter] Give us a power station, and to hell with the Rightists! [Laughter]".'[44] (Bukharin criticised this frenzy as the 'building of "present-day" factories with "future bricks"'.)[45] The Plan projected a 236 per cent increase in industrial output (at 1926/27 prices), a 100 per cent increase in labour productivity, a 35 per cent decline in industrial costs, and a more than 70 per cent increase in the real wages of industrial workers. Against the background of the Great Depression that gripped the Western capitalist world, Stalin's industrialisation assumed the tone of the heroic fight of Bolshevik 'consciousness' against market spontaneity.

Stalin's 'revolution from above' – rapid industrialisation and wholesale collectivisation coupled with dekulakisation – was welcomed by most former supporters of Trotskii who, having repented their past sins, had been readmitted to the party. At his trial in 1937 (at which he and other Trotskists were tried) Radek, for example, told the court that his return to the party in 1929 had been owing to his conviction in the rightness of Stalin's radical turn: 'the conviction that the accusation of Thermidorism we had made against the Central Committee of the Party was unfounded and that the programme of the Five-Year Plan was a programme for a great step forward'.[46] In October 1929 Piatakov, formerly a Trotskii supporter, referred to the industrialisation drive in an impassioned speech:

> In our work we must adopt the *rates of the Civil War*. Of course I am not saying we must adopt the methods of the Civil War, but that each of us . . . is obliged to work with the same tension with which we worked in the time of armed struggle with our class enemy. *The heroic period of our socialist construction has arrived.*[47]

This sort of spirit was widespread. An American who had witnessed

Stalin's revolution at first hand, later spoke of what 'a present-day observer can easily overlook, that is, the genuine upsurge of messianic hopes and revolutionary self-sacrifice' and 'a renewal of revolutionary spirit and a welcome release from the psychological doldrums of the NEP, with its undramatic goals and its petty bourgeois comfort. . . . The force of this emotion was great among many sons and daughters of previously underprivileged peasants and factory workers.' To them, 'the purpose of the revolution' was 'not merely to advance their own careers, but to create a new society, never known before, in which injustice and inherited social inequities would dissolve in a brotherhood of the proletariat and eventually of all people'.[48]

Stalin's industrialisation was not to be just any kind of rapid industrialisation, but one that represented his name *stal'* or steel, the symbol of modernity and power. At a very early stage of the industrialisation drive (May 1928) Stalin declared:

> Should we, perhaps, for the sake of greater 'caution', retard the development of heavy industry so as to make light industry, which produces chiefly for the peasant market, the basis of our industry? Not under any circumstances! That would be . . . suicidal; it would mean . . . transforming our country into an appendage of the world capitalist system of economics.[49]

More than ten years later, when Stalin proudly discussed his achievement, he noted:

> What is the main task of planning? The main task of planning is to ensure the independence of the socialist economy from capitalist encirclement. This is absolutely the most important task. It is a type of battle with world capitalism. The basis of planning is to reach the point where metal and machines are in our hands and we are not dependent on the capitalist economy. This is important.[50]

As was often said, one could fight a war not with cotton but with guns and tanks. A clear hierarchy emerged in which heavy industrial projects (such as steel mills) came at the top and light industry (such as cotton mills) below. Soviet youth in the 1930s 'found heroism in factories and on construction sites like Magnitogorsk and Kuznetsk [both major steel industrial centres], whereas working in the service sector as barbers, tailors, shoemakers, etc., did not attract them at all'.[51]

By this time Stalin appeared confident enough to have overcome whatever doubts he may have had about his lack of a role in the October 1917 Revolution. He certainly went out of his way to enhance his role in 1917, but he was also able to joke about it. On the eve of the July 1917 armed demonstration, Stalin received a telephone call from a 'sailor from the Kronstadt naval base who wanted Stalin's advice on a momentous question: should the sailors come armed to the demonstration in Petrograd then in preparation or should they come without weapons? Stalin thought for a moment, then gave an answer that reduced [the poet Dem'ian] Bedny [who published this story] to helpless laughter. "We scribblers", said Stalin, "always carry our weapons – our pens – with us wherever we go. As to your weapons, comrade, you can be the best judges of that".' This anecdote, probably apocryphal, appears to have been authorised by Stalin for circulation in late 1929.[52]

Stalin, however, did not rule by jokes or cunning or messianic hopes alone. He ruled by shock and awe. In late 1929 Ia.G. Bliumkin was executed. A former Left SR member and a participant in the July 1918 assassination of the German ambassador, Bliumkin joined the Communist Party in 1919 and served in the OGPU's foreign department. Following a visit to Trotskii in exile in Turkey, he was accused of treason. This was one of the first executions of communists for political treason at the hands of Stalin.[53] In a conversation with Ukrainian writers in February 1929, Stalin glorified the use of power. At the meeting, Ukrainian writers, frustrated by Mikhail Bulgakov's sympathetic treatment of the Whites during the Revolution and Civil War in *The White Guard* (aka *Days of the Turbins*), attacked the novel vehemently and persistently as anti-Soviet. Stalin defended it strongly and repeatedly, however. Stalin valued Bulgakov's novel because, he maintained, it demonstrated to the reader the 'all-conquering power of Bolshevism'.[54] In another note of February 1929 Stalin explained what this power meant: 'If even such people as the Turbins are compelled to lay down their arms and submit to the will of the people because they realise that their cause is definitely lost, then the Bolsheviks must be invincible and there is nothing to be done about it'. *Days of the Turbins* was 'a demonstration of the all-conquering power of Bolshevism'.[55] Stalin was so fond of *Days of the Turbins* that when it was staged he took the trouble to see the play at the Moscow Art Theatre no less than 15 times.[56]

Stalin used the 'all-conquering power of Bolshevism' to effect his 'revolution from above'. Just when all looked well, however, a crisis occurred. 'Raising the ocean' proved no easy matter. Stalin's December 1929 speech had created a political atmosphere in which provincial leaders competed for faster collectivisation and dekulakisation. They correctly read signals from Moscow that moderation was more dangerous than excess: no one wanted to be accused of 'right-wing deviation'. Collectivisation was a frontal onslaught on the traditional ways of life in the countryside. In practical terms, it entailed the closure of village markets, the confiscation of draught animals and other livestock, and the closure of village churches. Dekulakisation involved the dispossession of those deemed to be kulaks and their families, their deportation to far-off provinces (such as Siberia) or to other areas within their villages, districts or provinces, and sometimes their executions. This was not entirely unpopular, particularly with poorer peasants who often participated in the dispossession of the kulaks (whose clothes and shoes were sometimes taken directly from their bodies). The Soviet writer Mikhail Sholokhov describes these scenes in *Virgin Soil Upturned* (1932–59). The problem was that many poor peasants who opposed collectivisation were also dekulakised. So were other marginal people whose existence put the collective onus on the villagers. In order to help party and government officials carry out collectivisation and dekulakisation, tens of thousands of urban workers and the OGPU forces were mobilised, as were Red Army soldiers here and there. In the process, harsh coercion was used to force peasants into collective farms. The consequence for the countryside was utter chaos.[57]

If in October 1929 approximately 7.5 per cent of the peasant households were in collective farms, and by 20 February 1930 52.7 per cent were said to have been collectivised, by 1931 about 400,000 peasant families had been dekulakised; of them, more than 100,000 (more than half a million people) had been deported. Treated like livestock, they often died in transit because of cold, starvation, beatings in the convoys, and other miseries. Many resultant collective farms were farms on paper only. The peasants fought violently against the new regime that, introduced mainly by outside forces, appeared to them to be alien to their way of life. Peasant uprisings made the countryside unruly. The OGPU reported more than 13,000 peasant 'mass actions' (involving more than 3 million people) for the year of 1930, more than 70 per cent of which took place in the first four months of the year. Of the 993 uprisings that had to be quelled by the armed force of the police, special operation groups and Red Army units, 971 or 97 per cent took place in the same period. In these operations 147 (126 for the first four months) operatives were killed by the peasant rebels, bearing various slogans such as 'Down with Collectivisation', 'Down with the Soviet Government and Kolkhozes', 'Down with the Five-Year Plan', and 'Down with Stalin's Dictatorship'.[58] The year 1930 recorded 20,201 death sentences for 'political crimes', an almost ten-fold increase from 1929.[59] Undoubtedly, most of these were related to the upheaval in the countryside. The disquieting mood among the Red Army soldiers had also become politically worrisome. When forced to abandon their livestock to the collective farms, many peasants instead consumed their livestock. Sholokhov accurately described what happened in many villages:

> Both the peasants who had joined the collective farm and the individual farmers killed off their stock. They slaughtered oxen, sheep, pigs, even cows; they even slaughtered their breed animals. In two nights the head of cattle in Gremyachy was halved. . . . 'Kill, it's not ours now!' 'Kill, the state butchers will do it if we don't!' 'Kill, they won't give you meat to eat in the collective farm!' the insidious rumours spread around. And the villagers killed. They ate until they could eat no more. Young and old had the belly-ache.[60]

Stalin was forced to retreat and published an article 'Dizzy with success' in *Pravda* on 2 March 1930. Its reasoning was typical of Stalin. He declared that the collectivisation movement was a success and that even 'our enemies are forced to admit' it. Yet many 'distortions' of party policies have occurred. They have only led to 'strengthening our enemies and to discrediting the idea of the collective-farm movement': 'They could have arisen only as a result of the blockheaded belief of a section of our Party: "We can achieve anything ", "There's nothing we can't do!" They could have arisen only because some of our comrades have become dizzy with success and for the moment have lost clearness of mind and sobriety of vision.'[61] Stalin passed the blame on to those who worked in the localities. His evasion of responsibility did not endear him to many activists, however. There was a mass exodus of peasants from collective farms. Many collective farms collapsed almost overnight. Up to two-thirds of collective farms had thus disintegrated by the summer of 1930.

All the same, Stalin survived, helped by favourable climatic conditions that produced a bumper crop in 1930. The bumper crop made possible an increase in grain exports more than ten-fold from 1929, giving a breathing space. Once the situation had stabilised, Stalin launched a new offensive in the autumn of 1930, which was effected more carefully but equally forcefully. It made it virtually impossible for individual farmers to stay outside the collectives, inasmuch as they had to pay ten times as much tax as collective farmers. By the beginning of 1932 more than 60 per cent of households had been collectivised. The collective farm system was still not willingly accepted by many peasants, however, who called it a 'second serfdom', *vtoroe krepostnoe pravo*, whose acronym, VKP, was identical to that of the Communist Party (*Vsesoiuznaia Kommunisticheskaia Partiia*).[62] Moreover, dekulakisation was pursued relentlessly, especially in the spring and summer of 1931: in 1931 more than a quarter of a million additional peasant families were dekulakised. They formed the core of the forced-labour population in the country. They were often used in areas where few people were willing to work, and contributed much to the construction of such celebrated industrial centres as Magnitogorsk. Meanwhile, the decline in the number of livestock continued. From 1928 to 1933 the number of cattle in the country, for example, declined by as much as 45 per cent. In Kazakhstan, where a brutal campaign to settle nomadic people was staged, the decline was catastrophic: more than three quarters.[63]

Although Stalin appeared to have overcome the immediate crisis of spring 1930, he faced a new crisis in industry in the summer of the same year. The seemingly successful acceleration of industrialisation had led quickly to overambitious revisions of the plan targets. It began to appear possible to fulfil the already ambitious Five-Year Plan in four years. Running a planned economy was new to everyone, however, and the constant upward revisions of plans made planning difficult. The huge industrial expansion had caused a shortage of materials everywhere. The State Bank, in turn, issued currency in increasing volumes, precipitating inflation. Still, many revelled in the belief that they were finally released from the dictatorship of market forces and money that appeared to them to be obsolete in a planned economy. Indeed, such cumbersome concepts as debit, credit and cost-accounting were conveniently disregarded by managers. Freed from control by market forces, the economy appeared to become unhinged. Even labour had become scarce, prompting the Government to declare proudly in the autumn of 1930 that unemployment had been eliminated. The labour market had been transformed from a buyers' into a sellers' market, creating enormous new opportunities. This transformation also contributed to a huge increase in labour turnover, making the whole country appear to be in flux. The Government simply could not control the enormous movements of people. To complicate the matter, every sector of the country was hungry. The real wages of workers declined (in Moscow, for example, they declined almost 50 per cent from 1928 to 1932), and the consumption patterns of workers became increasingly 'vegetarian' owing to shortages of animal products. Consumption was severely curtailed for the sake of new construction. Several years later, when he was able to look back on these difficult years with some relief, Stalin said:

> If one wants to build a new house, one saves up money and cuts down consumption for a while. Otherwise the house would not be built. This is all the truer when it is a matter of building an entirely new human society. We had to cut down consumption for a time, collect the necessary

resources and strain every nerve. This is precisely what we did and we built a socialist society.[64]

Yet the level of capital investment was too high to allow optimal economic growth. In the summer of 1930 the economy was chaotic, disorganised and stalled. The mood of the workers was disquieting.

By the autumn of 1930 critical voices began to be heard from within the party and from among the supporters of Stalin. It is not known how many of these voices rose in criticism of his leadership, but at least one, the Rightist Martem'ian Riutin, appears to have questioned Stalin's leadership directly. Stalin wrote to Molotov on 13 September 1930 that 'it's impossible to limit ourselves to expelling him from the party': 'This counter-revolutionary scum should be completely disarmed.' Soon thereafter Riutin was arrested for 'counter-revolutionary agitation and propaganda'.[65]

The main thrust of Stalin's terror, however, was against 'wreckers' and 'class enemies'. Executions of suspected 'bourgeois' engineers and wreckers did not stop with the Shakhty affair. The economic crisis of summer 1930 led to more terror. In an August 1930 letter to Molotov, Stalin urged him to see that 'two or three dozen wreckers' from the finance and State Bank bureaucracy ('including several dozen common cashiers') be shot for such 'grave crimes' as the summer coin shortage. He also ordered, so as to 'solve' the meat shortage, that a 'whole group of wreckers in the meat industry must definitely be shot and their names published in the press'.[66] This was carried out literally. On 9 September the press announced that an 'organised group of wreckers and embezzlers' in a Moscow consumer cooperative had been uncovered and that six named 'wreckers' had been executed. A fortnight later the press reported that the OGPU had uncovered another 'counter-revolutionary' organisation and that 48 high officials of the People's Commissariat of Trade associated with food trade had been indicted for sabotaging food supplies. They were accused of attempting to 'organise famine' and of wrecking the plan to increase the real wages of workers, 'one of the most delicate and sensitive issues'. Three days later, all 48 named 'wreckers' were reported to have been shot.[67] In 1930–1 more than 10,000 former tsarist army officers (the 'All-Union Counter-revolutionary Organisation of Military Officers') were arrested, almost certainly on fabricated charges (Operation 'Spring') and at least 110 of them were executed.[68] Some of the arrested officers charged Tukhachevskii with complicity. Stalin took an interest in the matter, but Tukhachevskii successfully defended himself. Stalin, however, would remember this incident in 1937.[69]

Meanwhile, many 'bourgeois' and non-Bolshevik experts and specialists associated with industry, finance and trade were arrested in the summer and autumn of 1930, including V.G. Groman, an ex-Menshevik economist and the 'father of Soviet planning', and L.K. Ramzin, director of Vesenkha's Thermal Engineering Institute. In his letter to V.R. Menzhinskii, the OGPU chairman, Stalin instructed him to pay particular attention in his interrogations to a question of primary interest, the question of foreign intervention and its timing.[70] Ramzin and other 'bourgeois' experts (the 'Industrial Party') were tried in a show trial in November–December 1930. They were accused of 'intentionally creating economic troubles such as shortages of metals and the disorganisation of the supply system'. More importantly, they were accused of political terrorism and allegedly conspiring 'with foreign powers, especially France, for military intervention that would have coincided with the economic crisis' of 1930 and helped them to overthrow the Bolshevik Government. It was alleged that the strength of the Soviet Government forced them to postpone the planned intervention. Even Trotskii in exile abroad and his supporters in the country accepted all the charges against the defendants at the Industrial Party trial ('specialist wreckers . . . hired by foreign imperialists and émigré Russian *compradores*', in Trotskii's words).[71] The alleged terrorist plans of the Industrial Party prompted the Politburo to adopt a resolution cautioning Stalin to 'stop immediately walking around the town on foot'.[72] The Mensheviks were tried in early 1931 on similar charges. Some other specialists such as N.D. Kondrat'ev and A.V. Chaianov were not put on open show trials. None of these people were executed at the time, and some of them, whose expertise the Government needed, were allowed to return to their jobs or to continue their work in exile. However, these arrests and trials certainly intimidated the non-Bolshevik experts.

By mid-1931, it appears that Stalin had come to the conclusion that he had for now sufficiently intimidated the non-Bolshevik experts. The policy of class war had broken down their resistance to the socialist offensive. Stalin now saw little further political utility in disrupting production and administration by terrorising the experts. Thus by mid-1931 hints began to be dropped that some kind of 'normalisation' or restoration was in order. In June 1931 Stalin emphasised that the creation of new technical experts from the working class was well under way and that 'we have routed and are successfully overcoming the capitalist elements in town and country'. Therefore,

A large section of the old technical intelligentsia who formerly sympathised, in one way or another, with the wreckers have now made a turn

to the side of the Soviet regime . . . and the active wreckers have become
few in number, are isolated and will have to go deeply underground for
the time being. . . . It would be stupid and unwise to regard practically
every expert and engineer of the old school as an undetected criminal and
wrecker.[73]

Along with the rehabilitation of the 'bourgeois' experts came the introduction of correctives into the planned economy as it had emerged.
Freed from the control and punishment of the market, the economy
was in disorder. Financial discipline was therefore to be reimposed
through the restoration of 'control by the rouble'. Cost now had to be
accounted for by recording credit and debit. Money, once denounced
as an instrument of capitalism, was rehabilitated after a fashion and
was incorporated, albeit awkwardly, into the planned economy.

In agriculture, too, correctives were introduced. The most notable
was the legalisation of peasant markets in May 1932. This move was
forced by urban disturbances caused by food shortages in the spring of
1932.[74] The peasants (collective farmers and individual working peasants) were now allowed to engage in trade 'at prices formed on the
market' after they had delivered their due produce to the state. This
measure, reluctantly taken by the Soviet Government, was intended to
improve food supply through the markets and alleviate the food shortages in the cities.[75]

By 1932 more than 60 per cent of the peasant households and more
than 70 per cent of the crop area had been collectivised. It is not known
how Stalin meant to conclude his 'revolution from above', though it is
clear that much of what he considered to be the source of capitalist
restoration had been dealt a fatal blow and replaced by socialist collective farms. This point was emphasised repeatedly by Stalin as a
matter of the utmost significance. It was the defining event of the
epoch and was accordingly highlighted in the political primer *History
of the All-Union Communist Party: Short Course* (1938), which Stalin
personally edited in detail and in which he coined the term 'revolution
from above'. It therefore became a mortal offence to have opposed the
revolution. At any rate, the economic system that emerged in 1932 –
a centrally planned economy incorporating both money and collective-
farm trade – remained more or less intact until the very end of the
Soviet regime.

Stalin's 'revolution from above' was brutal. It squeezed the whole
nation for the sake of rapid industrialisation. It terrorised the 'class

enemies'. It completely changed the traditional way of life in the countryside. In the process, a very large segment of the population were
uprooted. Probably more than 3 million people were directly affected
by dekulakisation. From 1928 to 1932 'at least 10 million' peasants entered the wage- and salary-earning work force, and 'as many as three
out of every ten peasants migrating to town or entering the wage labour force' were 'probably departing wholly or essentially involuntar-
ily from the villages in connection with dekulakisation'.[76] Although the
infamous Gulag (forced-labour camp) system was born shortly after the
October Revolution, it was Stalin's 'revolution from above' that created
what the writer Aleksandr Solzhenitsyn called the 'Gulag Archipelago'.
Forced labour was used extensively on remote construction sites and
in the timber and mining industries where free labour was difficult to
recruit. In 1932 more than a quarter of a million people were working
in the Gulag Archipelago, and 1.3 million people were living as 'special
settlers' (mainly deported kulaks). In addition, hundreds of thousands
of people were confined to prison.[77] For many of these people, Stalin
was the anti-Christ.

Stalin's revolution created significant upward social mobility as
well. During the First Five-Year Plan as many as 150,000 workers and
communists were given higher education as part of the Soviet affirmative action programme.[78] Leonid Brezhnev (b. 1906) was one of them.
So were Nikita Khrushchev (b. 1894), Aleksei Kosygin (b. 1904), Andrei
Gromyko (b. 1909) and Nikolai Baibakov (b. 1911). For these people
of humble origin, it was the Soviet regime that had enabled them to
achieve their potential, and Stalin was its embodiment.

During the feverish upheaval of the time, in November 1930, the
American journalist Eugene Lyons was granted an interview with
Stalin. Lyons noted of the dictator responsible 'for the horrors in every GPU torture chamber': 'There was nothing remotely ogre-like in
his looks or conduct, nothing theatrical in his manner . . . "He's a
thoroughly likeable person," I remember thinking as we sat there, and
thinking it in astonishment.' Lyons, however, asked him squarely, 'Are
you a dictator?' Stalin replied: 'No, I am no dictator. Those who use
the word do not understand the Soviet system of government and the
methods of the Communist Party. No one man or group of men can
dictate. Decisions are made by the party and acted upon by its chosen
organs, the Central Committee and the Politburo.' Stalin the dictator
could not have been more disingenuous than he was in this statement.
Yet if Stalin believed that he personified the Central Committee and
the Politburo, he may not have been utterly hypocritical. Lyons noted:
'In his own fashion he [Stalin] possibly meant it too. He had identified

himself and the party, the "church" and its highest priest, so completely that he heard the party's voice issuing from his own mouth.'[79]

Notes

[1] R.W. Davies, *From Tsarism to the New Economic Policy* (Ithaca, New York, 1991), 17.

[2] This section draws substantially on Hiroaki Kuromiya, *Stalin's Industrial Revolution: Politics and Workers, 1928–1932* (Cambridge, 1988), 5ff. See also Roberta T. Manning, *The Rise and Fall of 'the Extraordinary Measures', January–June 1928: Toward a Reexamination of the Onset of the Stalin Revolution* (Pittsburgh, Pa.: Carl Beck Papers, no. 1504, 2001).

[3] *Tragediia sovetskoi derevni*, 1:147.

[4] Stalin, *Works*, 11:3, 5.

[5] James Hughes, *Stalin, Siberia and the Crisis of the New Economic Policy* (Cambridge, 1991), 141.

[6] Stalin, *Works*, 12:215.

[7] Kuromiya, *Stalin's Industrial Revolution*, 6.

[8] Stalin, *Works*, 11:8–9.

[9] Kuromiya *Stalin's Industrial Revolution*, 8.

[10] Stalin, *Works*, 12:97.

[11] *Kak lomali NEP*, 1:25.

[12] Stalin, *Works*, 13:38.

[13] For the Donbas, see Kuromiya, *Freedom and Terror in the Donbas*, and 'The Shakhty Affair', *South East European Monitor*, 4:2 (1997).

[14] Kuromiya, 'The Shakhty Affair'.

[15] Sheila Fitzpatrick, *Education and Social Mobility in the Soviet Union, 1921–1934* (Cambridge, 1979).

[16] Sheila Fitzpatrick (ed.), *Cultural Revolution in Russia, 1928–1931* (Bloomington, Ind., 1978).

[17] *Kak lomali NEP*, 4:187.

[18] Ibid., 4:563.

[19] Kuromiya, 'The Shakhty Affair', 51.

[20] E.A. Osokina, *Our Daily Bread: Socialist Distribution and the Art of Survival in Stalin's Russia, 1927–1941* (Armonk, New York, 2001).

[21] These reports were collected in *Tragediia sovetskoi derevni*, v. 1.

[22] *Kak lomali NEP*, 4:691. Probably this story, which may be apocryphal, refers to the 1891–2 famine.

[23] *Istoricheskii arkhiv*, 1997, no. 1, 164, *Kak lomali NEP*, 2:382 and *Genrikh Iagoda* (Kazan, 1997), 114–15.

[24] Stalin, *Works*, 11:167, 180.

[25] *Kak lomali NEP*, 4:559–63.

[26] Ibid., 4:689.

[27] V. Pribytkov, *Apparat* (Spb, 1995), 106, 108.

[28] *Kak lomali NEP*, 3:16.

[29] Ibid., 4:7, 558–63.

[30] Ibid., 4:696–7.

[31] Ibid., 4:497, 592, 679.

32 Ibid., 4:632.

33 Ibid., 4:465, 654.

34 Ibid., 4:654, 674.

35 Ibid., 4:180.

36 Ibid., 4:283.

37 Ibid., 4:682.

38 Kuromiya, *Stalin's Industrial Revolution*, 37.

39 *Kak lomali NEP*, 4:648.

40 Kuromiya, *Stalin's Industrial Revolution*, 38, and Stalin, *Works*, 12:15.

41 Stalin, *Works*, 13:41.

42 *Stalin's Letters to Molotov*, 40, 183.

43 Stalin, *Works*, 12:160–1, 176.

44 E.H. Carr and R.W. Davies, *Foundations of a Planned Economy, 1926–1929*, v. 1 (London, 1969), 893.

45 Cohen, 296.

46 Kuromiya, *Stalin's Industrial Revolution*, 112.

47 R.W. Davies, *The Socialist Offensive. The Collectivisation of Agriculture, 1929–1930* (Cambridge, Mass, 1980), 148.

48 Quoted in Kuromiya, *Stalin's Industrial Revolution*, 113–14.

49 Stalin, *Works*, 11:98.

50 Quoted in Ethan Pollock, *Conversations with Stalin on Questions of Political Economy* (Cold War International History Project Working Paper No. 33, Washington, DC, 2001), 19.

51 Kuromiya, *Stalin's Industrial Revolution*, 305–6.

52 Slusser, 155–6.

53 For Bliumkin, see O.B. Mozokhin, 'Ispoved' terrorista', *Voenno-istoricheskii arkhiv*, 2002, no. 6 (30).

54 Iu. I. Shapoval, *Ukraina XX stolittia. Osoby ta podii v konteksti vazhkoi istorii* (Kyiv, 2001), 107, 108, 122.

55 Stalin, *Works*, 11:343.

56 Vitalii Shentalinskii, *Raby svobody v literaturnykh arkhivakh KGB* (Moscow, 1995), 120.

57 See Davies, *The Socialist Offensive*.

58 *Tragediia sovetskoi derevni*, 2:790–1, 805. For peasants rebellions in general, see Lynne Viola, *Peasant Rebels under Stalin* (New York, 1996).

59 Popov, 28.

60 Mikhail Sholokhov, *Virgin Soil Upturned*, v. 1 (Moscow, 1957), 140–1.

61 Stalin, *Works*, 12:197–205.

62 For post-collectivisation farms, see Sheila Fitzpatrick, *Stalin's Peasants: Resistance and Survival in the Russian Village after Collectivization* (New York, 1994).

63 R.W. Davies and Stephen G. Wheatcroft, *The Years of Hunger: Soviet Agriculture, 1931–1933* (London, 2004), 451.

64 Kuromiya, *Stalin's Industrial Revolution*, 231.

65 *Stalin's Letters to Molotov*, 215.

66 Ibid., 200.

67 Kuromiya, *Stalin's Industrial Revolution*, 258.

68 Iaroslav Tinchenko, *Golgofa russkogo ofitserstva v SSSR. 1930–1931 gody* (Moscow, 2000).

[69] Lennart Samuelson, *Plans for Stalin's War Machine: Tukhachevskii and Military–Economic Planning, 1925–1941* (London, 2000), 113–14, 236,

[70] *Stalin's Letters to Molotov*, 195–6.

[71] Kuromiya, *Stalin's Industrial Revolution*, 167, 171.

[72] *Stalinskoe Politbiuro v 30-e gody* (Moscow, 1995), 99.

[73] Stalin, *Works*, 13:72–4.

[74] Jeffrey J. Rossman, 'The Teikovo Cotton Workers' Strike of April 1932: Class, Gender and Identity Politics in Stalin's Russia', *Russian Review*, 56:1 (January 1997).

[75] R.W. Davies, *Crisis and Progress in the Soviet Economy, 1931–1933* (London, 1996), 209–16.

[76] Sheila Fitzpatrick, 'The Great Departure: Rural-Urban Migration in the Soviet Union, 1929–1933,' in William G. Rosenberg and Lewis H. Siegelbaum (eds), *Social Dimensions of Soviet Industrialization* (Bloomington, Ind., 1993), 22, 25.

[77] For the Gulag, see Anne Applebaum, *Gulag: A History* (New York, 2003).

[78] Fitzpatrick, *Education and Social Mobility*, 187–8.

[79] Eugene Lyons, *Stalin: Czar of all the Russias* (Philadelphia, Pa., 1940), 200, 203.

Chapter 5

Famine and Terror

Stalin emerged from the 'revolution from above' as the creator and dictator of a newly ordered society. All his rivals had been politically defeated. Just when he had consolidated his position, however, he began to see even more enemies than before: the fact that open dissent had become impossible and all critical thought had been driven underground appeared only to breed and inflame his suspicion. The grave famine of 1932–3, which had resulted in the deaths of several million people, led some of Stalin's own supporters to doubt his leadership, although outside his entourage few if any challenged him politically. However, untold numbers of people appeared, at least to Stalin, to entertain doubts about him. This was far more menacing than open dissent in the view of a man with an extraordinarily suspicious nature. The famine coincided with a personal tragedy (the suicide of his wife Nadezhda) and with the rise of war threats both from the east (Japan) and from the west (Germany). Stalin took the threats seriously. In 1934 the Soviet Union entered the supremely bourgeois institution, the League of Nations. By 1935 Stalin had abandoned his theory of 'social fascism' and had adopted instead the united front against fascism. Meanwhile, he used the December 1934 assassination of the Leningrad party chief Kirov to exterminate potential internal enemies. This proved the beginning of a long and dangerous war against his own people. Up to one million were executed as 'enemies of the people' in the process. The Red Army was quite literally beheaded. Most of Stalin's erstwhile political rivals and collaborators, degraded as fascist collaborators and traitors at show trials, were put to death. All these seemed to be acts of madness, but in them Stalin saw the cold logic of politics: a means of ensuring the retention of his power and his regime.

Famine

The bumper crop of 1930 misled the Soviet Government. Apparently believing that the collective-farm system was working or at least would work to its advantage, the Government increased the state grain procurements, from 28.7 per cent of grain production in 1930 to 35.1 per cent in 1931; yet actual grain production declined from 73 million tons in 1930 to 57 million in 1931. The harvest of 1932, 55 million tons, was even lower than that of 1931.[1] The expectation that large, collective farming would be dramatically more productive than individual farming was dashed: tractors were few and far between, and even those delivered to farms often failed to work properly. The brutal and excessive seizure of grain demoralised the peasants. The future dissident Lev Kopelev, who participated in the grain-procurement campaign, remembers thinking that 'the famine was caused by the opposition of suicidally unconscious peasants' and that 'I mustn't give in to debilitating pity': 'We were realizing historical necessity. We were performing our revolutionary duty.' The collective farms, comparable to serfdom, became the symbol of inefficiency and poverty. As a 'kulak' *chastushka* (ditty) went,

> They've signed men up for the kolkhoz
> Now they lay plans
> Potatoes the men will eat
> Without butter, without cream[2]

In some areas famine conditions were already present in 1931. The famine became evident in 1932. Stalin mentioned in June 1932 that 'a number of *fertile* districts in Ukraine, despite a fairly good harvest, have found themselves in a state of *impoverishment* and *famine*'.[3] After touring Ukraine, Molotov reported to the Politburo in the summer of 1932 that 'we are indeed faced with the spectre of famine and in rich grain districts to boot'.[4] Undaunted by the spectre of famine, the Soviet Government continued to export grain in order to secure foreign currency and technology. In 1931 a record amount of grain (5.2 million tons of grain and flour) was exported. Even in the famine years of 1932 and 1933 1.8 million tons of grain and flour were exported. So were considerable amounts of animal products.[5]

The famine was devastating and the scenes of starvation horrific. One survivor recalled later that in the city of Enakievo in the Donbas, Ukraine, he

> saw the corpse of a young woman propped up against a plank fence. As we approached we saw there was a child on her breast who sucked the breast without realizing there was no milk left. A sanitary truck, whose job it was

to collect the dead bodies from the streets, pulled up as we watched. Two men jumped out of the truck, grabbed the body by the leg and dragged it up on top of the pile of bodies in the truck. Then they took the living child and threw it up with the dead bodies. My brother and I wept in pity for the child, but we realised that there was little that we or anyone else could do to help it, for we were all hungry.[6]

At a September 1940 meeting Stalin admitted, referring to the famine years, that '25–30 million people starved, there wasn't enough grain'.[7] How many people died in the famine has been a hotly contested issue, but it appears that the 1932–3 famine took somewhere between 7 and 8 million lives in the Soviet Union. Of these, at least 4 million died in Ukraine, the grain basket of Europe.[8] On his visit during the Second World War, Winston Churchill asked Stalin about the collectivisation of agriculture. Stalin said that he had had to deal with 10 million peasants and that it had been something 'fearful', lasting 4 years. Dealing with the kulaks was 'very bad and difficult – but necessary'.[9] If one adds the 3 million or so peasants who were dekulakised to the figures of death from the famine, one will reach 10 million or more.

Like most modern famines (the Irish potato famine, the Bengal famine and others), the 1932–3 famine was a man-made disaster, a product of inept and misguided politics and not of a deliberate policy aimed at famine or of absolute food shortages.[10] The economist Amartya Sen's famous thesis that no famine takes place under democracy also implies that politics is to blame for modern famines. The argument advanced by some scholars that there was not enough grain to feed the population is in all likelihood false in regard to the 1932–3 famine as well.[11] In 1936 grain production was even lower than in 1932, but the year 1936 did not witness widespread famine. Moscow was aware of famine conditions in various parts of the country. Several times in 1932 and 1933 (three times in the case of Ukraine, in August 1932, October 1932, and January 1933) Moscow curtailed grain-procurement plans in an apparent effort to alleviate the famine. In September 1931 Stalin opposed the increase in grain exports, and indeed grain exports were curtailed in the following years. Moscow even clandestinely purchased grain abroad to feed the hungry nation.[12] From April 1932 onwards, grain assistance (for sowing and food) was given to famine areas in the form of loans.[13] However, these measures were too late and too limited in scope to prevent widespread famine. If Moscow had terminated all grain export and released all 'untouchable' strategic grain reserves under optimal conditions of distribution, the available grain (some 2.6 million tons) might have saved up to 7.8 million lives, the approximate number of actual deaths from the famine (in fact, much grain was stolen or spoiled). Moscow did not do so even when faced with mass starvation. Unlike in 1921–2, the Soviet Government never publicly admitted that there was a famine in the country, and therefore no aid came from abroad.

Stalin faced the famine crisis in the midst of a diplomatic crisis. The 1931 Manchurian crisis and the 1932 foundation of Manchukuo, a Japanese puppet government in north-east China, dramatically increased the threat of war from the east. Japan's implicit goal appeared to be an eventual advancement into Soviet territory, and Moscow's offer of a non-aggression treaty with Japan did not get anywhere.[14] Meanwhile, Stalin sought hard to secure peace in the west. Stalin had long regarded Poland in particular as a dangerous aggressor. Poland under Józef Piłsudski, keen to protect its independence, had been endeavouring to undermine the Soviet Union (particularly Soviet Ukraine), and had placed secret-intelligence agents in various parts of the Soviet Union.[15] Nevertheless, Stalin sought a non-aggression pact with Poland. In August 1931, Stalin attacked the 'common narrow-minded mania of "anti-Polonism"'. He contended that although Litvinov (a Soviet diplomat) might yield to 'so-called "public opinion" and dismiss it as a trifle', the non-aggression pact was 'a very important matter, which almost determines the issue of peace (for the next two or three years)'.[16] Stalin may have seen in Piłsudski a political leader similar to himself, someone with whom he could deal. In any case, Stalin once said that 'Piłsudski – he is the entire Poland'.[17] Thus, by late 1932 Stalin concluded a non-aggression pact with Poland and her protector France.

Tellingly, soon after the rapprochement with Poland, Stalin 'uncovered' and liquidated the counter-revolutionary 'Polish Military Organisation' (POW), which operated allegedly 'in the service of Polish landowners and Ukrainian nationalists'. The real POW, originally created by Piłsudski in 1914, had long been dead. The purported existence of the POW was almost certainly fabricated by the OGPU with the aim of extirpating Polish agents and politically intimidating the ethnic Poles within the Soviet Union, particularly in Ukraine.[18] In February 1933 Stalin, exasperated by the reports of American journalists travelling to the famine-struck Kuban', north-east of the Black Sea, banned their free travel around the country: 'there already are many spies in the USSR'.[19]

In any case, the rapprochement with Poland and France alleviated whatever tension existed in the west. Hitler's rise to power in 1933, as is well known, did not immediately alarm Stalin, who then was preoccupied with the threat from the east. A very significant portion of industrial investment went to the defence industry at the cost of consumption, and armaments production expanded more rapidly than the rest of Soviet industrial production. In 1933, the 'published figure for expenditure for the People's Commissariat for Military and Naval Affairs' was '1,421 million roubles but the true figure was 4,299 million'![20]

The famine had created not merely an economic but a social and political crisis as well. The famine, combined with the labour shortage, had increased population mobility dramatically. To control the movement and to shield the cities from the mass influx of hungry peasants, an internal passport system was introduced in 1932–3. The passport was given only to urban residents, relegating rural residents to the status of second-class citizenship by fiat. Peasant uprisings broke out here and there, and workers struck demanding food. Armed 'bandits' roamed the countryside. One such group, allegedly composed of members of the former counter-revolutionary organisation 'The Sons of Offended Fathers', proclaimed that 'war was inevitable in Manchuria and that, come war, the government would collapse'. 'Insurgent armies', whose aims were said to be to arouse workers and soldiers for armed uprisings, were uncovered here and there. In Ukraine, peasants sang:

Lenin plays the accordion,
Stalin dances the hopak,
While Ukraine lives on
But one hundred grams [a day]

Stalin's responsibility was apparent to Ukrainian peasants, who sang: 'No cows,/No pigs,/Only Stalin on the wall'.[21] The poet Osip Mandel'shtam composed a poem that read, 'We live, deaf to the land beneath us,/Ten steps away no one hears our speeches,/All we hear is the Kremlin mountaineer,/The murderer and peasant-slayer'. For this 1933 poem he was arrested in 1934.[22]

The famine crisis adversely affected Stalin's reputation as a leader. At the seventeenth party conference Stalin hardly spoke, which raised among the party members the question of why he remained largely silent at a time of crisis. Moreover, Stalin gave no major public speech until 1933. His disappearance from the public scene suggested to many concerned with the state of affairs that it was symptomatic of Stalin's not acting properly as the leader. The so-called Riutin affair was of critical importance. In spring 1932, Martem'ian Riutin (who had got into trouble with Stalin in 1930) and his sympathisers began a secret but scathing attack on Stalin. They criticised his leadership in industrialisation, collectivisation and dekulakisation, as well as the lack of democracy within the party. They were alleged to have characterised Stalin as 'the gravedigger of the revolution' and called for his removal as the party's General Secretary. They were expelled from the party as 'enemies' and sentenced to various periods of imprisonment. Riutin received 10 years. Zinov'ev and Kamenev, accused of having been familiar with the Riutin 'conspiracy' but not informing the party of it, were expelled from the party again, though the accusation against Zinov'ev and Kamenev has not been proved.[23] Many similar groups were 'uncovered and liquidated' in various parts of the country. They were accused of 'counter-revolutionary' propaganda: 'The party is leading the country to destruction'; '[A]ll the grain has been exported abroad, and the people have been left to starve. The Soviet Government and the party have led the peasants to the point where they have no choice but to organise themselves into gangs [of plunderers].' Some were even accused of terrorism against Stalin.[24]

The political menace appeared serious. The rightists were made to admit in their 1938 show trial that the crisis was such that they had 'considered the seizure of power a foregone conclusion': they had sought to create 'several Kronstadts' (referring to the 1921 Kronstadt rebellion) and 'achieve corresponding political success'. This admission probably reflects not so much the hopes of the rightists as it does the concern (or fear) of Stalin and his supporters. Some of Bukharin's supporters were familiar with the Riutin document attacking Stalin. Suspecting their complicity, Stalin had for some time psychologically terrorised the rightists. At a party Maksim Gor'kii held in September 1933, for instance, Stalin turned to Bukharin, asking 'So you'll betray us soon?' Completely taken aback, Bukharin nevertheless rigorously denied ever thinking of anything of the sort. Stalin did not clink glasses with Bukharin; turning and clinking glasses with others, he returned to Bukharin, saying, this time more fiercely, 'Mind you, this'll come to a bad end.'[25]

In 1932, moreover, Trotskii attempted from abroad to form a bloc of former Zinov'evites and Trotskists within the Soviet Union. He succeeded, but the bloc quickly collapsed owing to the arrests of its major figures. Trotskii simultaneously pursued another strategy to return to power. He believed that the economic catastrophe was such that Moscow might be persuaded to accept him back because of the need to unite and mobilise the party. So in March 1933 he sent a secret letter to the Politburo offering his 'cooperation'. Trotskii had misread the situation completely: he appeared to Stalin as nothing more than an intriguer, and Trotskii completely failed in his scheme. Nevertheless, discontent within the party was widespread. In the minds of Stalin and others, discontent was tantamount to disloyalty and treason. In late 1932 and early 1933 another group, the N.B. Eismont–V.N. Tolmachev group, was thus accused of 'counter-revolutionary agitation' (to remove Stalin from his post) and 'terrorism' against the political leaders. Thirty-eight people, mainly adherents of Bukharin, were arrested and sentenced to various terms of incarceration. Their crime was that, while drunk, they had made some irreverent and critical remarks about Stalin and his policies. The tearing down of Stalin's portrait was deemed to be an act of terrorism. Stalin knew the nature of the group, which was declared 'counter-revolutionary'.[26]

The year 1932 was a tense and difficult time for Stalin. To make matters worse, his wife Nadezhda killed herself in the autumn of 1932. The end of his second marriage, like that of his first, was another devastating blow to Stalin, even though his marriage to Nadezhda had long been strained and troubled. Nadezhda hailed from a Bolshevik family and was herself a Bolshevik. She was independently minded and wished to pursue her own career, and it was a marriage her mother had never believed in, calling her a fool for marrying Stalin. As Stalin's daughter Svetlana testified, Nadezhda's 'spirit of independence irritated him':

> To have in his own home a modern, thinking woman, who stood up for her point of view on life, appeared to him as something unnatural. True enough, he quite often expressed himself in favor of the equality of women, when mass labor had to be encouraged. Such sayings of his as 'Women in the kolkhozes are a great power!' decorated all village clubs. But at home he expressed himself very differently. . . . In general my father never expressed any interest or sympathy toward educated women.[27]

Stalin's secretary Bazhanov noted that Stalin was a tyrant at home. Once Nadezhda complained to him, 'He has been silent for three days, speaks with no one, and doesn't respond when people call him.'[28] According to Svetlana, Stalin was

> callous and harsh and inconsiderate of her feelings, and that upset her terribly because she loved him very much. After a quarrel between them in 1926, when I was six months old, my mother took me and my brother and nurse and went up to Grandfather's in Leningrad intending to stay. She was planning to go to work and gradually build a life of her own. The quarrel was caused by some rudeness of my father's, something small in itself, but cumulative and of long standing. But my mother's anger passed.[29]

Stalin was known for being extraordinarily patient, but he was different at home, according to Svetlana:

My nurse said that my father had once thrown a boiled chicken out of a casement window in our apartment in the Kremlin. This was way back in the years when there were ration cards for food and famine reigned in the country – it must have been 1929 or 1930. . . . Mama had nothing for dinner but this chicken, but my father was fed up with the same 'menu'. For the rest of her life my nurse was unable to get over 'such valuable food being thrown away'.[30]

Nadezhda spent little time with her children, as Svetlana recalled: she was 'always off somewhere. She had a great deal of work and studying to do, jobs for the Party and all sorts of other things'.[31] Strained as their marriage was, Nadezhda exercised some influence: for example, she reported to Stalin very favourably on Khrushchev (who studied with her at the Industrial Academy in Moscow). Khrushchev's career was greatly helped by his acquaintance with Nadezhda. Towards the end of her life, according to Galina Kravchenko, Kamenev's daughter-in-law, Nadezhda 'turned more and more to God': 'Religion brought peace to her turbulent soul, and she started attending church.'[32]

The immediate cause for Nadezhda's suicide on the night of 7 November 1932, the fifteenth anniversary of the October Revolution, was Stalin's rude treatment of her at a dinner in the Kremlin. There Stalin had said to her, 'Hey, you. Have a drink!' She screamed, 'Don't you dare "hey" me!' Then she ran out. That night she shot herself in her bed.[33] Nadezhda is known to have suffered from various illnesses, both physical and mental, and her depression may have led to her suicide. She may also have long entertained serious doubts about the state of affairs in the country. She was said to have been opposed to collectivisation and its immorality. When Stalin ordered the arrests of her fellow students at the Academy (who witnessed and probably spoke about the famine in Ukraine), Stalin 'commanded his wife to stay away from the Academy for two months'. Anguished and disturbed, she told her friends that 'she had lost her love for life'. Nadezhda left a suicide note, but it is said to have been destroyed immediately after Stalin read it so as not to be politically exploited by his opponents. According to Svetlana, as narrated to Rosamond Richardson,

She wrote a dreadful letter. In it she poured out everything that she didn't like, in a final valedictory gesture. . . . She said that she was opposed to Stalin's policies, to the purges and everything that was going on. She really spoke out.

My father thought that she was probably on the side of the opposition, with Bukharin, supporting them against him. She had no doubt talked about these things many times with him. But she produced this sincere letter and left it for him to read: 'Now you have the truth: and I am killing myself.'[34]

This interpretation is interesting and, if true, extremely important, but it cannot be confirmed. Clearly, however, Stalin deemed it politically inexpedient to announce his wife's death as a suicide and had it officially declared a death from appendicitis. Svetlana learnt the true cause of her mother's death during the war from the foreign press.

There are also conflicting accounts of Stalin's reaction. According to Svetlana, at the funeral Stalin 'rejected the coffin saying, "She went away as an enemy" and walked away from it. He didn't go to the funeral and never visited the cemetery'.[35] However, according to Molotov, at the leave-taking Stalin approached the coffin, his eyes filled with tears, and said sadly, 'I didn't save her.' Molotov had never seen Stalin cry, but at Nadezhda's coffin he 'saw tears running down his cheeks'. He told Molotov that he 'was a bad husband': he 'had no time to take her to the movies'.[36] Kaganovich and others tend to support the Molotov account. Stalin genuinely mourned Nadezhda's death and frequently visited her grave.[37]

Whatever the case, Nadezhda's death devastated Stalin. Stalin, according to Svetlana,

> was terribly shaken . . . because he couldn't understand why it had happened. What did it mean? Why had such a terrible stab in the back been dealt to him, of all people? He was too intelligent not to know that people always commit suicide in order to punish someone. He saw that, but he couldn't understand why. What was he being punished for?'

Stalin asked whether he was indeed inconsiderate. After Nadezhda's death, Stalin said he 'didn't want to go on living either', so people around him were 'afraid to leave him alone'. He 'had sporadic fits of rage', and her death, emphasised Svetlana, 'destroyed his faith in his friends and people in general. He had always considered my mother his closest and most faithful friend. He viewed her death as a betrayal and a stab in the back.' Stalin began to avoid Nadezhda's family because they reminded him of this painful event. However, until the Second World War broke out, Stalin made an effort to be a good father, having dinner regularly with his children and looking after their homework. 'It wasn't easy with the kind of life he led, but he did his best,' according to Svetlana. Stalin later admitted that he had had to work day and night ('there were many enemies'!) and that there wasn't time left for children. After Nadezhda's death, Stalin lived almost exclusively among men. Svetlana insisted that this side of his life was neglected by his biographers. He lived isolated from 'any feminine

influence': 'the receptive, the intuitive, the yielding'. The lack of feminine influence, Svetlana believed, made his 'male qualities' take hold
of his personality, 'governed by a lust for power which made a deep-
seated link with his increasing paranoia'.[38]

Feminine influence or not, Stalin himself said that Nadezhda's
death 'crippled' him for life. Kaganovich noted that Stalin after 1932
was different from Stalin before 1932. He never forgot her, often asking the same question but fondly remembering her. After her death,
Stalin moved to a new flat in the Kremlin, had his favourite photograph of her enlarged and hung the enlargements in all the rooms of
his flat. In the photograph, according to Svetlana, she looked 'so happy
and radiant that looking at this picture you'd never guess what was to
happen to her later on'.[39]

Two months after Nadezhda's death, in January 1933, Stalin broke
a year-long silence. Addressing a CC plenum, he contended that the
country's enemies were becoming less visible and were thus becoming
more dangerous than before. It was a call for vigilance:

> [T]he last remnants of the moribund classes – private manufacturers and
> their servitors, private traders and their henchmen, former nobles and
> priests, kulaks and kulak agents, former White Guard officers and police
> officials, policemen and gendarmes, all sorts of bourgeois intellectuals of a
> chauvinist type, and all other anti-Soviet elements – have been tossed out.
>
> But tossed out and scattered over the whole face of the USSR, these
> 'have-beens' have wormed their way into our plants and factories, into our
> government offices and trading organisations, into our railway and wa-
> ter transport enterprises, and, principally, into the collective farms and
> state farms. They have crept into these places and taken cover there, don-
> ning the mask of 'workers' and 'peasants', and some have even managed
> to worm their way into the party.
>
> What did they carry with them into these places? They carried with
> them hatred for the Soviet regime, of course, burning enmity toward new
> forms of economy, life, and culture.

He went on to say:

> We must bear in mind that the growth of the power of the Soviet state
> will intensify the resistance of the last elements of the dying classes. It is
> precisely because they are dying and their days are numbered that they will
> go from one form of attack to another, sharper one, appealing to backward
> sections of the population and mobilising them against the Soviet regime.
> . . . This may provide fuel for a revival of the activities of defeated groups
> of the old counter-revolutionary parties: the SRs, the Mensheviks, and the
> bourgeois nationalists of the central and border regions . . . the Trotskists
> and right deviationists. . . .

This is why revolutionary vigilance is the quality most needed by the Bolsheviks at the present time.[40]

Three months later, at the Metro-Vickers espionage trial, the prosecutor Vyshinskii maintained that, having lost the battle, the enemy now resorted to 'methods known as quiet sapping' rather than direct frontal attack, and sought to conceal its wrecking acts with all sorts of 'objective reasons', 'defects' and the contention that the incidents did 'not seem to be caused by malicious human intent'. Therefore, Vyshinskii emphasised, the enemy 'becomes less detectable and hence it becomes less possible to isolate him'.[41] These statements almost implied that mass repression was inevitable.

Indeed, it was in 1933 that the concept of 'enemy' began to shift from 'class enemy' to the class-neutral 'enemy of the people'. This shift suggested that even party members were not immune from political terror. This was such a dangerous shift that even within the OGPU there was opposition to the vigilance campaign: 'Any talk of counter-revolutionaries is nonsense.'[42] Nevertheless, it was then that party members began to be arrested and even executed in substantial numbers as 'enemies with a party card in their pockets'. 'Ordinary people' were equally terrorised. The notorious, extraordinarily draconian 7 August 1932 law was applied extensively. This law made the death sentence generally mandatory (or ten years of imprisonment only in cases of extenuating circumstances) for stealing 'socialist property' (which included a watermelon in the kolkhoz field). The terror became so widespread and so threatening that in May 1933 Stalin had to retreat. He and Molotov sent out a secret circular condemning 'a saturnalia of arrests' and 'repression on an extraordinary scale' and calling for a halt to indiscriminate arrests.[43]

The famine crisis led to terror against many nationalities as well. Terror against ethnic Poles was discussed earlier, but the Poles were not unique. Stalin's nationality policy, embodied in the term 'indigenisation', had been premised on the assumption that, like the NEP, it would help to ensure civil peace with the numerous nationalities within the Soviet Union. In many respects 'indigenisation' outlived the NEP, even though political attacks against nationalities had already taken place in the late 1920s and early 1930s. It took the famine crisis of 1932–3 to effect a significant reassessment of the indigenisation policy. Ukraine became its focus.

As the largest non-Russian republic Ukraine was the most important. It was a problem republic, however. All peasants were suspect, but Ukrainian peasants were doubly suspect both for being peasants and for being Ukrainian, whereas Russian peasants were suspect only for being peasants. Indeed, from Moscow's point of view, the political record of Ukrainian peasants was not good. Ukrainian peasants had voted overwhelmingly for Ukrainian parties in the 1917–18 constituent assembly elections, and had fought obstinately against the Bolsheviks (and the Whites) during the Civil War. Nearly half of all peasant uprisings against collectivisation in 1930 took place in Ukraine. Stalin was so concerned about Ukraine that he wrote to Kaganovich on 11 August 1932 that

> Unless we begin to straighten out the situation in Ukraine, we may lose Ukraine. Keep in mind that Piłsudki is not daydreaming, and his agents in Ukraine are many times stronger than Redens [of the OGPU] or Kosior [the Ukrainian party leader] thinks. Keep in mind, too, that the Ukrainian Communist Party (500,000 members, ha-ha) has quite a lot (yes, quite a lot!) of rotten elements, conscious and unconscious Petliura [Ukrainian national leader during the Civil War] adherents, and, finally, direct agents of Piłsudski. As things get worse, these elements will waste no time opening a front inside (and outside) the party, *against* the party. The worst aspect is that the Ukraine leadership does *not* see these dangers.[44]

Probably for this reason, Ukraine and the northern Caucasus (where a significant section of the population was ethnic Ukrainian) were particularly hard hit by Moscow's terror. Extant evidence does not show that Stalin deliberately caused the famine, but the deepening crisis probably led him to conclude that the Ukrainian peasants, whose political loyalty Moscow had long courted through the policy of 'indigenisation' (or Ukrainisation in the case of Ukraine and the northern Caucasus), were more dangerous politically than ethnic Russian peasants in Russia proper. This conclusion led to harsher political and economic terror in Ukraine and the northern Caucasus than in Russia proper. The year 1933 witnessed an open attack on Ukrainian national communism culminating in the suicide of the man embodying it, Mykola Skrypnyk, and the uncovering of various 'counter-revolutionary' Ukrainian nationalist organisations. The indigenisation policy itself was not reversed, but it was no longer promoted in earnest after the famine crisis.

When the immediate crisis was overcome by 1934, a sense of elation emerged within the party. Indeed, a triumphal mood obtained at the seventeenth party congress which, took place in early 1934. One former oppositionist after another appeared and made repentant speeches, touting the victory of the party's 'general line' promoted by Stalin (thus this congress came to be known as the 'congress of victors'). In the mid-1930s, as the nation realised sizable returns on the capital investments of the five-year plans, its material life improved considerably, before war preparations began to squeeze national consumption again. Stalin may not have been entirely hypocritical when he declared in 1935 that 'Life has become better, comrades, life has become merrier.'[45] Although hunger persisted in the country, Stalin emphasised what he regarded as the chief achievement of his 'revolution from above': that the exploitation of man by man had been eliminated in the country. Of course, this point led Trotskii and others to discuss the emergence of a new exploitative class in the Soviet Union, but it allowed Stalin to adopt a new constitution (the 'Stalin constitution') in 1936 that he sold as the most advanced in the world. It indeed accorded (at least on paper) equal rights and civil liberties to all Soviet citizens. These rights included freedom of conscience, freedom of speech, freedom of the press and freedom of assembly as well as the right to employment, rest and leisure, education, maintenance in old age and free medical service for working people. The constitution also stipulated work as a 'duty and honour' for every able-bodied citizen ('He who does not work, neither shall he eat'). In a word, the constitution applied to the Soviet Union the principle of socialism: 'From each according to his ability, to each according to his work.'

Did Stalin come out of the famine crisis stronger or weaker? In all likelihood, paradoxically, both stronger and weaker. It appeared to many party members that only Stalin among the leaders was strong and determined enough to use brutal terror, if necessary, in order to overcome the grave famine crisis. Yet it also appeared to some members that it was Stalin who was responsible for the crisis to begin with and that it was Stalin who as the leader had used brutal terror and thus plunged the country further into the depth of despair with millions of lives lost. (The oft-quoted rumour, never confirmed, was that at the congress as many as 300 votes were cast against the re-election of Stalin to the party secretaryship, reflecting this negative sentiment against Stalin.) The lack of open politics makes any judgement provisional, but one of the reasons why it is difficult to know the strength of Stalin's position for certain is that these two conflicting sentiments about Stalin as the leader had developed within the party simultaneously. Almost certainly Stalin felt publicly flattered and privately disparaged. This only added to his suspicion of two-faced 'double-dealers'.

Great Terror

By the mid-1930s Stalin began to make serious preparations for war. Japan's threat from the east had not disappeared, and Hitler's rise to power in 1933 further complicated the international situation. Japan's expansionism in the Far East finally pushed Moscow and Washington together: in late 1933 the USSR and the USA resumed diplomatic relations. Stalin had to think hard about survival in an increasingly dangerous international environment. Initially, like many other leaders of the world, he underestimated Hitler's menace, but he soon came to understand the essence of a man who openly declared that Bolshevism was his life enemy. When Hitler brutally suppressed the German communists, Stalin did not even protest. In summer 1934 Stalin criticised Engels's supposed pro-German views of history and the contemporary application of Lenin's theory of 'revolutionary defeatism' to the Soviet Union in the face of the forthcoming war.[46] After Japan and Germany withdrew from the League of Nations, the Soviet Union entered this supremely bourgeois institute of world order in September 1934. In 1935 Stalin publicly abandoned the social fascism doctrine, shifting Comintern strategy to a united front against fascism and Nazism. In that year, with Nazi Germany in mind, the Soviet Government concluded cooperative treaties with France and Czechoslovakia. It would have been the height of political folly for Stalin to have assumed that certain groups of people in the country would not take a position of defeatism in the case of war. It was certainly clear to everyone that war presented an opportunity for change. At the time of the 1932–3 famine crisis, for example, Isaak Babel', in a conversation with Boris Souvarine in Paris, was pressed by Souvarine on the question of whether there was any possibility of change in the Soviet Union. Babel' answered bluntly: 'War.'[47]

Stalin was never averse to the use of terror for political purposes. He was also aware of the disruptive impact of terror and knew when to stop and retreat. His terror never completely stopped, however, and against the background of the threat of war, it soon intensified with a vengeance. Because of the threat from the west, non-Russian ethnic groups on the western borderlands, like their counterparts in the Far East, became politically suspect. Moscow had long suspected ethnic Poles, for example, as potential irredentists, but suspicion grew as the threat from the west increased. Already in 1933–4 many members of foreign communist parties (such as the Polish and Latvian) and foreign-born Soviet Communist Party members (such as the Galicians from western Ukraine under Polish rule) were executed. Many Korean refugees from Japanese colonial rule (including Korean communists working as Japanese-language instructors in the Soviet Union) were arrested and executed almost certainly as Japanese spies.[48] Ethnic Germans appeared to be particularly threatening because of their ethnicity and their suspected ties to Nazi Germany. In 1934 the Soviet

Government began to collect information secretly on ethnic Germans in the country, and by the end of 1934, according to one participant in the collection, the Government had gathered 'the most precise data on the numbers and occupations of all Germans living in the USSR. All the secret service work and the repressions carried out later were guided by the data we collected and arranged.'[49] In 1934, when a mentally unstable military person (one Nakhaev) was arrested for his allegedly counter-revolutionary agitation among soldiers, Stalin insisted that Nakhaev was 'of course (of course!) not alone. . . . He must be a Polish–German (or Japanese) agent.'[50] From 1935, ethnic Germans and Poles on the western borderland began to be deported to remote areas in the east.[51] In the industrial centre of the Donbas, numerous German 'counter-revolutionary' organisations were liquidated by the NKVD (the successor to the OGPU).[52]

Stalin, according to Anastas Mikoian, was captivated by Hitler's 'audacity' and 'persistence' in strengthening his power: in June–July 1934 Ernst Röhm, the head of Hitler's stormtroopers (SA), and other men of the SA were arrested ('the Night of the Long Knives') and then assassinated by the SS (*Schutzstaffel*) on Hitler's order. Hitler used this event to subordinate the SA to the army whose allegiance Hitler sought. Stalin, according to Mikoian, said with admiration, 'That was well done, wonderful. One has to be able to do that.' Stalin's remark left a terrible impression on Mikoian.[53] The December 1934 assassination of the Leningrad party chief Sergei Kirov eerily resembled the Röhm affair, coming so soon after it. Consequently, many people continue to believe that Stalin was a party to the Kirov murder. As in the John F. Kennedy assassination case, elaborate conspiracy theories are legion. Nevertheless, despite intensive study after the opening of the Soviet archives in the 1990s, no evidence of Stalin's involvement has been found (though this does not necessarily mean that Stalin was innocent).[54] In all likelihood, however, it was the act of a single assassin, a disgruntled former party member.[55] Because Kirov and Stalin had been close friends, Kirov's murder seems to have been a shattering blow to Stalin. Svetlana, Stalin's daughter, noted that 'maybe he [Stalin] never trusted people very much, but after their [Nadezhda's and Kirov's] deaths stopped trusting them at all'.[56]

Stalin's reaction to the Kirov murder was swift and violent. Immediately after the murder Stalin enacted by fiat a law legalising speedy execution of those accused of terrorism, and in December 1934 alone as many as 6,501 people were arrested under this law. Stalin travelled to Leningrad and personally interrogated the assassin, L.V. Nikolaev, who apparently idealised the pre-revolutionary political terrorist

A. Zheliabov. (Along with other members of the 'People's Will', Zheliabov organised the 1881 assassination of Tsar Alexander II. He was arrested, tried and hanged.) Many others who had nothing to do with Kirov's murder were implicated and, along with Nikolaev, were summarily executed. Nikolaev's own family was almost completely destroyed: his brother Petr, his wife Mil'da Draule, her sister Ol'ga Draule and Ol'ga's husband were executed, while his mother and Petr's wife were sentenced to four years in exile. Their subsequent fates are unknown. In 1935 Stalin told the French writer Romain Rolland that 100 people whom the Government sentenced to death did not have, from a juridical point of view, any direct connection with the murderers. Stalin added, however, that they were sent from Germany, Poland and Finland by enemies of the Soviet Union and were armed to commit terrorist acts against the leaders of the Soviet Government. In order to forestall their evil deeds, 'we had to assume the unpleasant duty of shooting these gentlemen. Such simply is the logic of power.'[57] Stalin insisted that the executions were necessary as a deterrent:

> It is very unpleasant for us to kill. This is a dirty business. Better to be out of politics and keep one's hands clean, but we don't have the right to stay out of politics if we want to liberate enslaved people. When you agree to engage in politics, then you do everything not for yourself but only for the state. The state demands that we are pitiless.

Stalin insisted to Rolland that capital punishment in general was important in order to instill a sense of terror even though the Soviet government would not admit it publicly.[58]

Stalin found in the Kirov murder a golden opportunity to remove his enemies once and for all: immediately after the incident Stalin concluded that the Zinov'evites were responsible for the murder in Leningrad, a former stronghold of Zinov'ev, and issued an order to find murderers among the Zinov'evites, even though no evidence existed to link the murder to them. When NKVD agents appeared reluctant to follow Stalin's orders, he called the head of the secret police, Iagoda, and warned him: 'Mind you, we'll slap you down.' In January 1935 Stalin circulated a closed letter to the party in which he linked the Zinov'evites to a German fascist agent, equated the former oppositionists with the White Guard, and called for punishment appropriate for counter-revolutionaries. Thus in January–February 1935, 843 former Zinov'evites were arrested by the NKVD. In the spring of 1935 A.G. Shliapnikov and other former members of the 'Workers' Opposition' (a 1920 party faction) were arrested for allegedly conducting underground anti-Soviet activities.[59] In summer 1935 Stalin acted to remove his own old friend and his wife's godfather, Avel' Enukidze, from the Kremlin. He was accused of helping former oppositionists (including Mensheviks and some former nobles) to find employment and even appointing some in the Kremlin. His alleged magnanimity and lack of vigilance had allowed some Kremlin staff to organise a 'terrorist' group within the Kremlin. Some 110 Kremlin employees (including Kamenev's brother) were arrested (hence the 'Kremlin affair'). Two, both of whom were party members, were sentenced to be shot.[60]

With Stalin's approval and urging, the NKVD intensified its enemy-hunting; numerous 'enemies' were thus uncovered and 'isolated' by the secret police. Untold numbers of people were accused of counter-revolutionary propaganda, agitation and terrorism, which were often no more than rumour, gossip and joke. In 1933, when Skrypnyk killed himself, one Donbas worker was said to have hoped that Stalin would follow suit: 'If Com. Skrypnyk has worked to the point of shooting himself, then now one may expect that perhaps Stalin, too, will shoot himself.'[61] The Kirov murder appeared to have led to the flourishing of black humour and ominous-sounding remarks. 'You have to respect Nikolaev, for he never crept round attics, but came to the place and did what he had to'; 'It's clear that not all Zheliabovs have disappeared in Russia, the struggle for freedom goes on'; 'Kirov was killed, it's not enough, Stalin has to be killed'; 'Kirov was killed. It's a pity that Stalin wasn't'; 'Kirov was killed – food rationing was abolished; if Stalin is killed – people will begin to live' (food rationing was abolished in early 1935 because of improved food supplies); 'Food rationing was abolished because they were scared after the Kirov murder; all the same the workers are eating rotten bread'; 'The more leaders were killed, the less school work we would have to do'.[62] It is not known whether these remarks indeed increased exponentially, or whether more of them were reported to the authorities, or whether the police fabricated them. Yet the mere mention of murder or assassination came to be interpreted as agitation for terrorism. The banning of a 1936 songbook containing the following innocent patriotic song suggests the political atmosphere of the time:

> We know how to shoot well,
> We're practising the machine-gun . . .
> We'll exchange books for a rifle.
> When [Marshal] Bliukher calls upon us.[63]

The censors apparently feared that this was a call to terrorism! In 1937, Stalin ordered the removal of Zheliabov from the film *The Great Citizen* on the Kirov assassination. He feared an analogy would be made between the 'revolutionary Zheliabov' and the alleged assassin of Kirov.[64] Even a discussion of Russian history with its rich history of political terrorism became dangerous. In 1937 Kaganovich attacked an article on the 1881 assassination of Alexander II, calling it a signal to the terrorists, the Trotskists, and the Zinov'evites.[65]

There may well have been assassination plans against Soviet leaders, for Russian émigré organisations were actively dreaming of subversion and terror against the Bolshevik regime, as well as other groups, such as Ukrainian and Georgian émigré organisations that would have been happy to see the Bolsheviks defeated. Foreign countries courted these organisations and encouraged them to infiltrate and subvert the Soviet Union. The Soviet Union, in turn, also courted many émigrés by appealing to their patriotism and nostalgia, while at the same time engaging in the kidnapping and killing of die-hard anti-Soviet émigré leaders and defectors: for example, Sergei Efron, the husband of the poet Marina Tsvetaeva, was recruited by the Soviet secret police in Europe, only to be executed after his return to the Soviet Union. Stalin suspected refugees (mainly communists) from foreign countries of being agents of Germany, Japan or Poland. In the summer of 1935, Nikolai Ezhov, soon to become Stalin's chief executioner as the head of the NKVD, reported to Stalin that '[a]gents of foreign intelligence services, disguised as political émigrés and members of sister parties' had penetrated the Soviet Communist Party, particularly Poles, Romanians, Germans, Finns and Czechs. Among others, Ezhov singled out the Polish Communist Party as 'one of the main suppliers of spies and agent provocateur elements in the USSR'.[66] A Russian historian has claimed, apparently based on Soviet secret police documents, that the German SD (security police) sent an assassin (a West Ukrainian communist) to the seventh Comintern congress in Moscow (August–September 1935). The poor assassin could not muster the courage to perform the difficult task and feigned illness.[67] Because many organisations were infiltrated by Soviet agents and double agents, however, one should not necessarily take such stories at face value. Indeed, at the first Moscow show trial in 1936, Fritz David and K.B. Berman-Iurin were wrongly accused of attempting, allegedly on Trotskii's orders, to assassinate Stalin at the seventh Comintern congress, and were executed.[68]

It was evident that the prospect of war intensified the international battle of the intelligence services. In his 1935 conversation with Romain Rolland, Stalin maintained that 'Our enemies from the capitalist circles are tireless. They infiltrate everywhere.'[69] Stalin used the spectre of war and terror to disarm his political enemies. As Stalin and Vyshinskii had made clear, the enemy had become increasingly invisible, and so the hunt for enemies was bound to become massive and extensive. In March 1937, Stalin contended that:

> To win a battle in war, several corps of Red Army soldiers may be needed, but to ruin the victory at the front a few spies will suffice somewhere in army headquarters or even in the division headquarters who can steal an operation plan and pass it to the enemy.[70]

For this reason alone, in Stalin's mind, intelligence had to play a key role. He emphasised in June 1937 that, whereas the Soviet government had defeated the international bourgeoisie, the bourgeoisie had beaten the Soviet government effortlessly in the area of intelligence operations. In his view, if only 5 per cent of the alleged enemies were indeed enemies, it was a 'big deal', to be taken extremely seriously.[71] Similarly, according to Khrushchev, he used to say that 'if a report [denunciation] was 10 per cent true, we should regard the entire report as fact'.[72] Everyone understood that Stalin was willing to imprison or exile thousands of innocent people in order to catch one spy. According to Molotov, the 1935 expulsion of some 30,000 'social aliens' (former nobles, tsarist officials, and their families among others) from Leningrad in the wake of the Kirov murder, was because of both the city's proximity to the international border and the complex international situation.[73] This was a pre-emptive strike. In late 1935 and early 1936 Bukharin prophesied that within two years Koba would 'shoot us all', and Sokol'nikov told his wife: 'In case of war intra-party terror will start. This may prove much more terrible than [that of] 1793 in France. At the time only 14,000 were guillotined, but our scale is different. Hundreds of thousands, a million innocent victims.'[74] Bukharin and Sokol'nikov's prophesies would prove to be correct, except that the terror Sokol'nikov anticipated took place before war broke out.

The threat of war had dramatically increased by the spring of 1936. As Adam B. Ulam noted 30 or so years ago, the advance of Hitler's armed forces into the Rhineland on 7 March 1936, a blatant violation of the Versailles treaty, gave a clear signal to the world that Hitler was bent on waging war in Europe. As Ulam put it, it was 'foolish to imagine that all those Zinovievs, Bukharins, and Radeks might not secretly feel the same way now' as Lenin and others had felt towards the tsarist government during the First World War. Stalin appeared to be intent on physically destroying them.[75]

Earlier, he had manipulated the 1927 war scare to discredit Trotskii and his supporters. Trotskii denied Stalin's accusations of defeatism, but promised to continue his fight, just as Georges Clemenceau did in France during the First World War:

> At the beginning of the imperialist war the French bourgeoisie had at its head a government without a sail or rudder. The Clemenceau group was in

opposition to that government. Notwithstanding the war and the military censorship, notwithstanding even the fact that the Germans were eighty kilometres from Paris (Clemenceau said: 'precisely because of it'), he conducted a fierce struggle against petty-bourgeois flabbiness and irresolution and for imperialist ferocity and ruthlessness. Clemenceau was not a traitor to his class, the bourgeoisie; on the contrary, he served it more loyally, more resolutely and more shrewdly than [René] Viviani, [Paul] Painlevé and Co. The subsequent course of events proved that. The Clemenceau group came into power, and its more consistent, more predatory imperialist policy ensured victory for the French bourgeoisie.[76]

Trotskii implied that he would not be a traitor to his class, the working class, by fighting against Stalin. At the August 1927 CC plenum, however, Stalin used this remark to defeat Trotskii. In 1936, unlike 1927, the threat of war became real. Stalin meant not so much to isolate as physically to destroy the suspected defeatists.

Since 1934, Stalin had suspected that Zinov'ev was secretly advocating defeatism, and Kamenev appeared to Stalin to be still engaged in indirect criticism. In 1934, for example, Kamenev published a Russian translation of Machiavelli's *The Prince* for which he provided a preface. If Stalin was an aficionado of Machiavelli, then he must have read it. In the preface, Kamenev wrote:

> A master of political aphorism and a brilliant dialectician who from his observations had formed the firm opinion that all concepts and all criteria of good and evil, of the permissible and impermissible, of the lawful and criminal were relative. Machiavelli made from his treatise an astonishingly sharp and expressive catalogue of the rules by which the ruler of his time was to be guided in order to win power, to hold it and to withstand victoriously any attacks upon it. This is far from being the *sociology* of power, but from this prescription there magnificently stand out the *bestial* features of the struggle for power in the society of slave owners based on the rule of the rich minority over the toiling majority. Thus, this secretary of the Florentine bankers and their ambassadors at the Pope's Court, by accident or design, created a shell of tremendous explosive force which disturbed the minds of rulers for centuries.[77]

It is not difficult to imagine Stalin reading this passage as a veiled criticism of his rule and suspecting Kamenev of justifying his clandestine struggle for power. In fact, this passage was quoted *in toto* at his trial in August 1936 by Stalin's prosecutor, Vyshinskii.[78] In June 1936 Stalin ordered the trial of Zinov'ev and Kamenev. He did not trust the people around him. In the summer of 1936, according to Aleksandr Svanidze, Stalin's brother-in-law, Stalin constantly complained that there were no 'devoted people' around him and that 'honest people' were in short supply.[79]

It is often rumoured that Stalin had promised Zinov'ev and Kamenev that he would save their lives in exchange for an admission of terrorism and treason. Whatever led Zinov'ev, Kamenev and their co-defendants to confess to ghastly crimes, Stalin did not save their lives: they were executed. Their public admission that they had degenerated into terrorists and fascists served Stalin's purpose of discrediting his enemies in the most damning fashion. At the trial Trotskii was depicted as the linchpin of an international conspiracy against the Soviet Union. Even Bukharin and his supporters were hinted to have been party to it. In 1936 Trotskii completed a new book *The Revolution Betrayed.* Stalin probably remembered the speech that, according to Bazhanov, Trotskii gave to Stalin's supporters in November 1927:

> You are a band of talentless bureaucrats. If the question arises on the fate of the country and if war breaks out, you'll be utterly incapable of organising the defence of the country and of achieving victory. When the enemy closes in to a hundred kilometres of Moscow, we will do what Clemenceau did in his time: we will overthrow the incompetent government, with one difference that while Clemenceau was content to take power, we will additionally shoot this dull band of worthless bureaucrats who have betrayed the revolution. Yes, we'll do it. You'd want to shoot us, too, but you won't dare. We dare do it, because it will be an entirely necessary condition for victory.[80]

If Bazhanov is right, Trotskii underestimated Stalin. Stalin was willing to shoot Trotskii and everyone else if necessary. In 1937 Stalin called Trotskii an *ober-shpion* (supreme spy).[81]

The year 1936 proved to be important in another respect: the Spanish Civil War began in which the Soviet Union, Italy and Germany intervened. The Soviet Politburo decision to intervene in Spain on 29 September 1936 coincided with the appointment of Nikolai Ezhov as chief of the NKVD and with whose name Stalin's Great Terror is often associated. As Oleg Khlevniuk has convincingly shown, the Spanish Civil War (which Stalin closely followed) demonstrated to him that 'the situation in Spain itself, the acute contradictions between the different political forces, including those between the Communists and Trotsky's adherents, provided Stalin with the best-possible confirmation of the need for a policy of repression as a means of strengthening the USSR's capacity for defence'. As Soviet military dispatches from Spain in 1936 and 1937 made clear, the war was characterised by 'anarchy, partisan and subversive and divisionist [*sic*, diversionist] movements, relative erosion of the frontiers between front and rear, betrayals'. 'The events in Spain were for Stalin direct proof that there existed, and very obviously, just such a threat from within.'[82] The very term 'fifth column' (enemy spies), famously originated in the Spanish Civil War. Interestingly, at the 1945 Potsdam Conference, Stalin confided to Truman: 'To enable an army to win and advance, it must have a quiet rear. It fights well if the rear is quiet, and better if the rear is friendly.'[83]

Stalin had hoped that his support of the Spanish Republicans would help to draw the major Western powers (Britain and France) and the Soviet Union closer together against Hitler's Germany. Frustrated by the Franco-British reluctance (or inability) to oppose Germany, in 1936-7 (when he was executing many Soviet citizens as German spies) Stalin apparently sent out feelers to Germany for a possible rapprochement.[84] Stalin's remark concerning the alleged betrayal by Trotskii, Zinov'ev and Kamenev that '[T]here is nothing surprising in human life' surely applied equally to him as well.[85] Stalin's plan for Germany did not bear fruit at the time, but in August 1937 the Soviet government concluded a non-aggression treaty with China against Japan.

Stalin's Great Terror took place in this context of desperate efforts to secure the country against the menace of war. In early 1937 the second Moscow trial against Piatakov and other former Trotskii supporters (such as Sokol'nikov and Radek) took place. Like Zinov'ev and Kamenev, they confessed to terrorism, espionage and treason, and most of them were executed. At the trial Radek provided the most incriminating testimony upon which the testimony of all the other defendants rested. Radek knew what he was doing when he declared to the court that he was 'fighting not for my honour, which I have lost', but 'for the recognition of the truth of the testimony I have given, the truth in the eyes not of this Court, not of the Public Prosecutor and the judges, who know us stripped to the soul, but of the far wider circle of people who have known me for thirty years and who cannot understand how I have sunk so low'.[86] The eloquence of the man whom Stalin described as being managed by his tongue appeared to clinch the case against the Trotskists. Yet Trotskii thought it absurd: 'Who will believe that I placed at the head of a grandiose plot an individual whose tongue controls his head and who is in consequence capable of expressing serious ideas only "by accident"?'[87]

Stalin was clearly very busy destroying his 'enemies'. When in May 1937 his mother died in Georgia, he did not attend the funeral, and from 1937 until after the war ended Stalin did not take a summer (or autumn) break from work, a long-established custom.

Stalin was obsessed with spies, seeing them everywhere. He began to decimate the party elite as traitors and terrorists even though no evidence existed in virtually any of the cases. Numerous artists, writers and intellectuals, in addition to party and government officials, were terrorised. As if giving proof to his suspicions, Stalin sanctioned torture, rhetorically asking why a socialist government ought to be more lenient with foreign agents than capitalist regimes were with the representatives of the proletariat.[88] Bukharin and his former supporters were tried at the third and last Moscow show trial in 1938 and then executed. Once, in the company of Molotov, while reviewing a list of people to be executed, 'Stalin muttered to no one in particular: "Who's going to remember all this riff-raff in ten or twenty years time? No one. Who remembers the names now of the boyars Ivan the Terrible got rid of? No one. . . . The people had to know he was getting rid of all his enemies. In the end, they all got what they deserved." "The people understand, Iosif Vissarionovich, they understand and they support you," Molotov replied automatically.'[89] Of the 139 CC members elected at the 1934 'congress of victors', 97 or 69 per cent were killed or imprisoned, 5 killed themselves and another 5 were executed for the 'violation of socialist legality'. Ten years later, after the war, Stalin indirectly defended the executions of the pre-war years:

> One of Ivan the Terrible's errors was that he failed to knife through five large feudal families. Had he wiped out these five families, there would have been no Time of Troubles. But Ivan the Terrible executed someone and then he felt sorry and prayed for a long time. God hindered him in this matter. Tsar Ivan should have been even more resolute.[90]

Without God hindering him, Stalin was more resolute than Ivan, killing off almost all his rivals. Despite Ivan's shortcomings, Stalin declared that he was much greater ('in the tenth circle of heaven') than the French King Louis XI 'who prepared for the absolutism of Louis XIV'.[91] Stalin's philosophy probably followed that of Genghis Khan: 'The deaths of the conquered are necessary for the conquerors' peace of mind.' Stalin was more than a victor, however. To Ezhov he was God. Ezhov used to quote the saying 'God's will – the Tsar's trial', meaning that Ezhov (the Tsar) executed God's (Stalin's) will.[92] Stalin even turned to English history to justify his ruthlessness: 'Was the English [Queen] Elizabeth really less cruel when she fought to consolidate absolutism in England? How many heads rolled during her reign? She didn't spare even her cousin Mary Stuart. But the English are not stupid people and honour her by calling her great.'[93]

Like the party elite, the Red Army elite also disquieted Stalin, who saw invisible links between them and the former oppositionists (including Trotskii). Stalin suspected that some military leaders had inherently Bonapartist tendencies and were not reliable in an emergency. In April 1937, the Red Army's intelligence unit published seven articles on foreign intelligence in the central press, almost certainly on Stalin's orders. Then, on 4 May 1937, *Pravda* published the article 'Some insidious methods of recruitment by foreign intelligence services', this time explicitly following Stalin's instructions.[94] At the same time, a number of books by foreign intelligence operatives (including Georg Wald, *Im Dienst der Weltkrieg-Spionage* [1930] and Franz von Rinteln, *The Dark Invader* [1933]) were translated into Russian, and Stalin read and commented on them.[95] These were probably signs of what was to come. In April–May 1937 a number of top military leaders (Tukhachevskii, I.E. Iakir, I.P. Uborevich and others) were arrested, tortured, tried in camera in June, sentenced to death, and immediately executed. In the waves of terror that followed, the Red Army high command was literally beheaded: two out of five marshals (Tukhachevskii and Egorov) were executed, another marshal (V.K. Bliukher) died in prison, all commanders of the first and second ranks were executed except for one who returned alive from prison, all corps commanders were arrested (the majority executed). In all, from 1937 to 1941, of the 767 members of the 1936 high command (brigade commanders and above), 412 were executed, 29 died in prison, 3 committed suicide, and 59 were eventually released from incarceration. In other words, 65.6 percent were crushed.[96]

In a speech he gave to military leaders after the Tukhachevskii affair, Stalin emphasised that it was their absolute political loyalty that mattered: 'We are against the neutrality of the army.' He contended that of the five marshals, A.I. Egorov, from an officer family, deserved the rank least (apart from Tukhachevskii who was from a noble family). Tukhachevskii was shot in 1937 and Egorov in 1938. (Egorov was said to have complained to his colleagues that Stalin, who was his political commissar in Ukraine during the Civil War, had claimed his, Egorov's, military feats as his, Stalin's, own.) Only Voroshilov, Bliukher, and S.M. Budennyi deserved the rank, because they were promoted during the Civil War 'from the people'. If they went against the policy of the party and the government, however, they would be 'swept away by the people'.[97] Bliukher died in prison in 1938.

The brunt of Stalin's terror, however, was directed against 'the people': the majority of its victims were ordinary workers, peasants, soldiers, socially marginalised (such as unemployed) people and other 'small people'. In many cases, their prior political convictions, ethnic origins or foreign connections doomed them. 'Foreign connections' included exposure to anti-Soviet radio broadcasts from Manchukuo, Germany, Poland, Finland and elsewhere.[98] Thus, by a series of mass operations directed against former kulaks, criminals and certain ethnic groups (Poles, Germans, Greeks, Koreans, Finns and others), very large numbers of people were imprisoned as 'spies', 'defeatists' and 'fifth columnists'. They were deemed to pose a serious internal threat in case of war. Thus in the two years of terror, 1937 and 1938, more than 1.3 million people were arrested for political crimes. Of them, more than 680,000 were sentenced to death. (In fact, these official numbers were almost certainly underestimated. The actual number of deaths is probably about 1 million.)[99] Death sentences accounted for 44.66 and 59.29 per cent of all those convicted of political crimes in 1937 and 1938 respectively. Nearly three-quarters of those arrested through the national purge were sentenced to death. Almost all (with a few exceptions) were executed. These two years were extraordinary. The closest peak year of death sentences for political crimes had been 1930, the year of collectivisation and dekulakisation, with 'only' 20,201 deaths; 1937 and 1938 alone accounted for about 91 per cent of all death sentences for political crimes between 1921 and 1940 and 84 per cent of the 1921–53 period.[100]

As was the case with collectivisation and dekulakisation, the Great Terror was a momentous operation and all resources had to be mobilised. Moderation was viewed by the people involved as more dangerous than excess. Indeed, Ezhov told his subordinates that 'in such a large-scale operation mistakes are inevitable' and that 'if during this operation an extra thousand people will be shot, that is not such a big deal': 'better too far than not far enough'.[101] Ezhov told NKVD executives that 'a war with fascism' was imminent, and that therefore the NKVD had to 'destroy all the nests of fascists in the country'. 'Of course,' Ezhov declared,

> there will be some innocent victims in this fight against fascist agents. We are launching a major attack on the enemy; let there be no resentment if we bump someone with an elbow. Better that ten innocent people should suffer than one spy get away. When you cut down the forest, woodchips fly.[102]

When the terror threatened to spin out of his control, however, Stalin had to stop. He may have concluded that the nation had been sufficiently intimidated or that he had overfulfilled the plan of eliminating 'foreign agents.' In any case, he had 'cut down the forest'. By 1938 the Gulag population had expanded to close to two million. Stalin blamed Ezhov ('a scoundrel') and others for all the 'excesses', and removed him from his position in the autumn of 1938. He was executed as a foreign spy in 1940.

The Great Terror has appeared and still appears to many observers as an act of madness. Stalin's daughter Svetlana later noted that at the time she didn't even understand what was going on.[103] Yet Stalin and his supporters and victims saw it as, in its own morbid way, a politically 'rational' preparation for war. In June 1938 Kaganovich justified the terror operations in his address to the Donbas party organisations: it was the threat of war that mattered, according to Kaganovich. Had the numerous kulaks, enemies and spies not been annihilated, 'perhaps we would be at war already'. Ruthless operations without fear of criticism, declared Kaganovich, had ensured the delay of war.[104]

Equally revealing is Stalin's own statement to the eighteenth party congress in March 1939. Rebutting the 'prattle' of the foreign press that the Soviet Union had been weakened by the recent executions of Zinov'ev, Kamenev, Bukharin, Tukhachevskii and many others, Stalin emphasised that the country had in fact been strengthened precisely because it was 'cleansed' of the 'murderers', 'wreckers' and 'spies'. This is demonstrated, Stalin declared, by the Soviet victory at the battle of Lake Khasan against the Japanese–Kwantung Army in the summer of 1938.[105] As will be discussed later, Stalin may not have been so sure in 1940 when the Soviet Army performed poorly in the war against Finland and in 1941 when the Soviet Union was almost crushed by Nazi Germany. All the same the Soviet Union won in the end. According to Akakii Mgeladze, after the Second World War Stalin admitted to him that 'mistakes' were made in 1937 and that 'many honest people' suffered. Nevertheless, he insisted that the 'fifth columns' had basically been eliminated by the terror, without which the Soviet Union, like France, would have been crushed from without and from within.[106]

Both Molotov and Kaganovich used the war threat to explain and defend the terror, repeating it consistently and passionately until their deaths in the 1980s and 1990s respectively. Stalin suspected, according to Kaganovich, that those enemies, lying in wait, would stab him and his Government in the back in the case of war. According to Kaganovich, former opponents of Stalin such as Trotskii, Bukharin, Zinov'ev and Kamenev were 'engaged in underground activity and conspiracy, considering themselves the [Soviet] government and believing that they had the right to fight [against Stalin's government]'. 'Maybe they were not foreign spies, but they considered it possible to enter into agreement with a foreign government against the [Soviet] people.' The Soviet leaders had made mistakes to which Stalin would admit were he alive: 'We were to blame for overdoing it.' Yet the Great Terror was correct, they felt, because there were fifth columns, and had they not been eliminated the Soviet Union would have been beaten by the Nazis.[107]

Molotov concurred. By the terror 'Stalin played it safe'. There was no hard evidence of, for example, Tukhachevskii being a German agent, but he was 'dangerous' because 'we were not sure whether he would stay firmly on our side at a difficult moment'. (Molotov probably meant that in case of war Tukhachevskii and others, as social democrats had done during the First World War, might betray the cause of socialism.) Evidence was not very important, Molotov said in Stalin's defence, because 'there is no smoke without fire'. Stalin let 'an extra head fall' so that there would be 'no vacillation at the time of war and after the war'. The terror against the 'enemies of the people' was justified for the survival of Stalin's Soviet Government, he argued: 'if only to hold on to power'.[108]

Stalin's victims, too, understood the terror in the same way. Bukharin, for example, whose political capitulation to Stalin appears to have been final and complete after 1932, openly echoed Stalin in December 1936:

> I am happy that this entire business [of destroying our enemies] has been brought to light before war breaks out and that our [NKVD] organs have been in a position to expose all of this rot before the war so that we can come out of war victorious. Because if all of this had not been revealed before the war but during it, it would have brought about absolutely extraordinary and grievous defeats for the cause of socialism.[109]

In the wake of the executions of Zinov'ev, Kamenev and others, Bukharin almost certainly knew that his life, too, was doomed. Arthur Koestler proved more or less right in his famous *Darkness at Noon* (1940) which used this same logic to explain the self-indictment of his protagonist (modelled partially on Bukharin). Whereas Bukharin, unlike Zinov'ev and Kamenev, drew the line at admitting to charges of foreign espionage and terrorism, he did plead 'guilty' to forming an 'anti-Soviet bloc' with Trotskii against Stalin and declared to the court that Stalin 'is the hope of the world'. What disarmed him completely, according to his own words, was 'everything positive that glistens in the Soviet Union'. 'The monstrosity of my crimes is immeasurable especially in the new stage of the struggle of the USSR'.[110] By his confession of guilt, Bukharin 'implored discontent[ed] Soviet citizens to forsake "a defeatist orientation" and defend the Soviet Union, even a Stalinist one, as "a great and mighty factor" against German fascism'.[111] In essence, when it came to the survival of the Soviet Union, Bukharin's position was not different from that of Trotskii whom Bukharin demonised at the trial as a fascist agent. While declaring that Stalin had betrayed the Bolshevik revolution, Trotskii publicly defended the Soviet Union as a workers' state (albeit a bureaucratic and degenerate one).

It is noteworthy that Pavel Miliukov, a former Kadet leader and an avowed enemy of Bolshevism, was politically disarmed in similar fashion. Unlike Petr Struve (a former Marxist and founding member of the Russian Social Democratic Workers' Party), in the latter half of the 1930s Miliukov came to terms with Stalin's Soviet Union, almost accepting the rationale for his Great Terror because of the foreign threat to the survival of 'Russia' (not the Soviet Union).[112]

The Great Terror was a pre-emptive strike in preparation for war. Using the threat of war Stalin destroyed potential traitors and disarmed the sceptics so as to gain internal security. In his view, the mere isolation and confinement of those whose loyalty he suspected did not suffice, but their physical destruction did. He demanded absolute security: 'Death solves all problems. No man, no problem'. At the height of the terror, in January 1938, Stalin explained his policy by referring to a Russian proverb (which was also Lenin's favourite): 'God save us from our "friends", from our enemies we shall save ourselves.'[113] Subsequently, during the Second World War, Stalin intimated to Churchill: '[W]e like a downright enemy better than a pretending friend'.[114] Obviously, however, Stalin could not have liked the following precept of Machiavelli: 'It cannot be called virtue to kill one's fellow-citizens, betray one's friends, be without faith, without pity, and without religion; by these methods one may indeed gain power, but not glory.' At the same time, Machiavelli also said: 'A prince, therefore, must not mind incurring the charge of cruelty for the purpose of keeping his subjects united and faithful; for, with a very few examples, he will be more merciful than those who, from excess of tenderness, allow disorders to arise, from whence spring bloodshed and rapine; for these as a rule injure the whole community, while the executions carried out by the prince injure only individuals.'[115] Stalin would have liked Machiavelli if he had considered a million executions 'a very few examples'. Afterwards he may have realised that he overdid it, but he never regretted it.

Notes

1. R.W. Davies and Stephen G. Wheatcroft, *The Years of Hunger: Soviet Agriculture, 1931–1933* (London, 2004), 448–9.
2. Kuromiya, *Freedom and Terror in the Donbas*, 166, 317.
3. R.W. Davies et al. (eds), *The Stalin-Kaganovich Correspondence 1931–1936* (New Haven, Conn., 2003), 138.

[4]N.A. Ivnitskii, *Kollektivizatsiia i raskulachivanie (nachalo 30-kh godov)* (Moscow, 1994), 203.

[5]Kuromiya, *Freedom and Terror in the Donbas*, 167.

[6]*Second Interim Report of Meetings and Hearings of and before the Commission on the Ukraine Famine Held in 1987* (Washington, DC, 1988), 20–1.

[7]*Surovaia drama naroda* (Moscow, 1989), 503.

[8]For the famine, see Ivnitskii, op. cit., and Davies and Wheatcroft, *The Years of Hunger.*

[9]Winston S. Churchill, *The Hinge of Fate* (Boston, Mass., 1950), 498.

[10]For a view emphasising the famine as an ethnic genocide, see Robert Conquest, *The Harvest of Sorrow: Soviet Collectivization and the Terror-Famine* (Oxford, 1986).

[11]For a view emphasising natural disaster, see Mark B. Tauger, *Natural Disaster and Human Actions in the Soviet Famine of 1931–1933* (Pittsburgh, Pa.: Carl Beck Papers, no. 1506, 2001).

[12]*The Stalin–Kaganovich Correspondence*, 71, and *Voprosy istorii*, 1999, no. 10, 124, 126.

[13]For these measures, see *Tragediia sovteskoi derevni*, 3:862.

[14]For Soviet diplomatic relations for these years, see Jonathan Haslam, *Soviet Foreign Policy 1930–33: The Impact of the Depression* (New York, 1983).

[15]Andzej Pepłoński, *Wywiad polski na ZSRR 1921–1939* (Warsaw, 1996) and Marcin Kwiecień and Grzegorz Mazur, 'Działalność prometejska i dywersja na wschodzie', *Zeszyty Historyczne*, v. 140 (2002). See also Timothy Snyder, *Sketches from a Secret War: A Polish Artist's Mission to Liberate Soviet Ukraine* (New Haven, Conn., 2005).

[16]*The Stalin-Kaganovich Correspondence*, 68.

[17]Oleg Ken, *Moskva i pakt o nenapadenii s Pol'shei (1930–1932 gg.)* (Spb, 2003), 110.

[18]Mikołaj Iwanow, *Pierwszy naród ukarany* (Warsaw, 1991), 141–5.

[19]*Stalin i Kaganovich. Perepiska. 1931–1936 gg.* (Moscow, 2001), 307.

[20]Mark Harrison and R.W. Davies, 'The Soviet Military–Economic Effort during the Second Five-Year Plan (1933–1937)', *Europe-Asia Studies*, 49:3 (1997), 369.

[21]Kuromiya, *Freedom and Terror in the Donbas*, 176, 189–90, 200.

[22]Quoted in Nadezhda Mandelstam, *Hope against Hope* (London, 1970), 13.

[23]Martem'ian Riutin, *Na koleni ne vstanu* (Moscow, 1992). See also Catherine Merridale, *Moscow Politics and the Rise of Stalin: The Communist Party in the Capital* (London, 1990), 83–6.

[24]Kuromiya, *Freedom and Terror in the Donbas*, 177–8.

[25]*Istochnik*, 2003, no. 5, 60.

[26]Kuromiya, *Stalin's Industrial Revolution*, 313–14; Pierre Broué, 'Trotsky et bloc des oppositions de 1932', *Cahiers Leon Trotsky*, 5 (January–March 1980); J. Arch Getty, 'Trotsky in Exile', *Soviet Studies*, 38:1 (January 1986); and *Sovertskoe rukovodstvo. Perepiska. 1928–1941 gg.* (Moscow, 1999), 196.

[27]Svetlana Alliluyeva, *Only One Year* (New York, 1969), 381.

[28]Bazhanov, 154.

[29]Alliluyeva, *Twenty Letters*, 115.

[30]Alliluyeva, *Only One Year*, 365.

[31]Alliluyeva, *Twenty Letters*, 110.

[32] Larissa Vasilieva, *Kremlin Wives* (New York, 1994), 69.

[33] Ibid., 119. There is a much fuller account of this event in Simon Sebag Montefiore, *Stalin: The Court of the Red Tsar* (London, 2003), 1–18. Others suspect that Nadezhda was jealous of women with whom Stalin was said to have flirted.

[34] Richardson, 124. See also Alliluyeva, *Twenty Letters*, 124.

[35] Richardson, 126. See also Alliluyeva, *Twenty Letters*, 125.

[36] *Molotov Remembers*, 173–4.

[37] Galina Serebriakova, 'Smerch', *Pod"em*, 1988, no. 7, 24.

[38] Alliluyeva, *Twenty Letters*, 124, 133, 147–8, Richardson, 205 and Akakii Mgeladze, *Stalin. Kakim ia ego znal* (n.p, 2001), 118.

[39] *Iosif Stalin v ob'iatiiakh sem'i* (Moscow, 1993), 177; Feliks Chuev, *Tak govoril Kaganovich* (Moscow, 1992), 154; and Alliluyeva, *Twenty Letters*, 114.

[40] Stalin, *Works*, 13:211, 216.

[41] Kuromiya, *Stalin's Industrial Revolution*, p. 318.

[42] O.V. Khlevniuk, *1937-i: Stalin, NKVD i sovetskoe obshchestvo* (Moscow, 1992), 24.

[43] Kuromiya, *Freedom and Terror in the Donbas*, 102.

[44] *The Stalin–Kaganovich Correspondence*, 180. See also Terry Martin, *The Affirmative Action Empire: Nations and Nationalism in the Soviet Union, 1923–1939* (Ithaca, New York, 2001), 208.

[45] Stalin, *Sochineniia*, 1 (13): 89.

[46] See 'I.V. Stalin – "O stat'e Engel'sa 'Vneshniaia politika russkogo tsarizma"' – ideologicheskaia podgotovka k mirovoi voine', *Voprosy istorii*, 2002, no. 7.

[47] Boris Souvarine, 'Derniers entretiens avec Babel', *Contrepoint* (Paris), 30 (summer 1979), 79. This section of the chapter relies to an extent on my essay 'Accounting for the Great Terror', *Jahrbücher für Geschichte Osteuropas*, 53:1 (2005).

[48] See *Rasstrel'nye spiski*, 2 vols. (Moscow, 1993–5).

[49] Quoted in Ingeborg Fleischauer and Benjamin Pinkus, *The Soviet Germans: Past and Present* (New York, 1986), 34, 91.

[50] *The Stalin-Kaganovich Correspondence*, 241–2, 248.

[51] Martin, 329–32.

[52] Kuromiya, *Freedom and Terror in the Donbas*, 208.

[53] Anastas Ivanovich Mikoian, *Tak bylo. Razmyshleniia o minuvshem* (Moscow, 1999), 534.

[54] See Amy Knight, *Who Killed Kirov?: The Kremlin's Greatest Mystery* (New York, 1999).

[55] For the most recent examination of the murder, see 'Gibel' Kirova. Fakty i versii,' *Rodina*, 2005, no. 3.

[56] Alliluyeva, *Twenty Letters to A Friend*, 88–9.

[57] *Istochnik*, 1996, no. 1, 147. No evidence has been found to implicate them in espionage or terrorism.

[58] *Voprosy literatury*, 1989, no. 3, 221–2. See also *Cahiers Romain Rolland. 29. Voyage a Moscou (juin-juillet 1935)* (Paris, 1992), 130–1.

[59] Kuromiya, *Freedom and Terror in the Donbas*, 203–4.

[60] J. Arch Getty and Oleg V. Naumov, *The Road to Terror: Stalin and the Self-Destruction of the Bolsheviks, 1932–1939* (New Haven, Conn., 1999), 160–79.

[61] Kuromiya, *Freedom and terror in the Donbas*, 199.

[62]Sarah Davies, *Popular Opinion in Stalin's Russia. Terror, Propaganda and Dissent, 1934–1941* (Cambridge, 1997), 51, 94, 117, 176–7; Leslie A. Rimmel, 'Another Kind of Fear: The Kirov Murder and the End of Bread Rationing in Leningrad', *Slavic Review*, 56:3 (Autumn 1997), 484; and Kuromiya, *Freedom and Terror in the Donbas*, 216.

[63]Arlen Blium, *Zapreshchennye knigi russkikh pisatelei i literaturovedov, 1917–1991* (Spb., 2003), 273.

[64]Mar'iamov, 34.

[65]*Voprosy istorii*, 1992, no. 10, 34.

[66]Marc Jansen and Nikita Petrov, *Stalin's Loyal Executioner: People's Commissar Nikolai Ezhov, 1895–1940* (Stanford, Calif., 2002), 40–1.

[67]Lev Sotskov, *Neizvestnyi separatizm na sluzhbe SD i Abvera* (Moscow, 2003), 80–1.

[68]*Report of Court Proceedings in the Case of Trotskyite-Zinovievite Terrorist Centre* (Moscow, 1936), 27, 96, 115. The Soviet secret police recorded several earlier attempts (including one allegedly made by a British agent in November 1931). See *Istochnik*, 1996, no. 3, 161–2 and Oleg Mozokhin, *VChK-OGPU. Karaiushchii mech diktatury proletariata* (Moscow, 2004), 337–44.

[69]*Voprosy literatury*, 1989, no. 3, 221.

[70]Stalin, *Sochineniia*, 1 (14):219.

[71]*Istochnik*, 1994, no. 3, 79–80.

[72]*Khrushchev Remembers*, 283.

[73]*Stranitsy istorii KPSS*, v. 2 (Moscow, 1989), 650.

[74]Serebriakova, 'Oni delali chest' idee'.

[75]Adam B. Ulam, *Stalin: The Man and His Era* (New York, 1973), 404–5.

[76]Quoted in Stalin, *Works*, 10:56.

[77]Reproduced in *Nikkolo Makiavelli: pro et contra* (Spb, 2002), 503–4.

[78]*Report of Court Proceedings in the Case of Trotskyite–Zinovievite Terrorist Centre*, 138–9. For a more detailed account of Kamenev's use of Machiavelli, see E.A. Rees, *Political Thought from Machiavelli to Stalin* (Basingstoke, 2004), 200–5.

[79]Serebriakova, 'Smerch', 25.

[80]Bazhanov, 160.

[81]*Istochnik*, 1994, no. 3, 75.

[82]Oleg Khlevniuk, 'The Objectives of the Great Terror, 1937–1938' in Julian Cooper et al. (eds), *Soviet History, 1917–53: Essays in Honour of R.W. Davies* (London, 1995), and 'The Reasons for the 'Great Terror': The Foreign Political Aspect', *Annali* (della Fondazione Giangiacomo Feltrinelli), 1998, 163, 165.

[83]*Memoirs by Harry S. Truman*, v. 1 (New York, 1955), 368.

[84]Silvio Pons, *Stalin and the Inevitable War, 1936–1941* (London, 2002), 9, 66–7, 95. In November 1936 the 'anti-Comintern' pact was signed by Germany, Italy, and Japan, following the Ethiopian crisis.

[85]*Voprosy istorii*, 1992, nos. 4-5, 36.

[86]*Report of Court Proceedings in the Case of the Anti-Soviet Trotskyite Centre* (Moscow, 1937), 543–4.

[87]*The Case of Leon Trotsky: Report of Hearings on the Charges Made Against Him in the Moscow Trials* (New York, 1937), 524.

[88]Oleg Mikhailov, 'Limit na rasstrel', *Sovershenno sekretno*, 1993, no. 7, 5.

89 Volkogonov, 210.

90 *Moscow News*, 1988, no. 32, 8. Here and elsewhere on Stalin and Ivan, see also Maureen Perrie, *The Cult of Ivan the Terrible in Stalin's Russia* (Basingstoke, 2001).

91 G. Mar'iamov, *Kremlevskii tsenzor: Stalin smotrit kino* (Moscow, 1992), 85.

92 Jansen and Petrov, 174.

93 Mar'iamov, 92.

94 For Stalin's instruction, see RGASPI, f. 558, op. 1, d. 1594, l. 1.

95 Ibid., d. 1595, 1596, 1597, 1598. It appears that the English translation rather than the German original of von Rinteln was used.

96 O.F. Suvenirov, *Tragediia RKKA, 1937–1938* (Moscow, 1998), 315.

97 *Istochnik*, 2002, no. 3, 73–5.

98 In August 1937 Ezhov noted that the 'agitation' of foreign radio stations would pose a serious threat in the event of war and urged Stalin to take counter-measures. *Istochnik*, 1999, no. 1, 111–2.

99 Michael Ellman, 'Soviet Repression Statistics: Some Comments', *Europe–Asia Studies*, 54:7 (November 2002).

100 For this, see Kuromiya 'Accounting for the Great Terror', 88.

101 Jansen and Petrov, 89, 131, 201.

102 Medvedev, *Let History Judge*, 603.

103 Alliluyeva, *Twenty Letters*, 151.

104 RGASPI, f. 81, op. 3, d. 231, ll. 73, 79.

105 Stalin, *Sochineniia*, 1 (14):368–9. For the battle at Lake Khasan, see p. 134.

106 Mgeladze, 167–8, 172, 173, 211.

107 Kuromiya, 'Accounting for the Great Terror', 96.

108 Ibid.

109 Getty and Naumov, 309.

110 *Report on Court Proceedings in the Case of the Anti-Soviet 'Bloc of Rights and the Trotskyites'* (Moscow, 1938), 777–9.

111 Stephen F. Cohen, *Bukharin and the Bolshevik Revolution: A Political Biography, 1888–1938* (New York, 1971), 378–9.

112 Jens Petter Nielsen, *Miliukov i Stalin. O politicheskoi evoliutsii Miliukova v emigratsii (1918–1943)* (Oslo, 1983).

113 Nevezhin, 180.

114 Churchill, *The Hinge of Fate*, 493.

115 Niccolò Machiavelli, *The Prince and the Discourses* (Modern Library College Editions) (New York, 1950), 32, 60 (chs VIII, XVII).

Chapter 6

War

Stalin emerged from the Great Terror stronger than ever. Whatever danger he had perceived from real or imagined challengers to his power was now gone, but even though he ruled the country dictatorially, he could not control the international situation as he wished. No one, including Stalin, knew when and how war would begin, though nearly everyone in the Soviet Union, including Stalin, knew for sure that war would come. In the end Stalin struck a 'Faustian bargain' with Hitler. Stalin knew that the deal merely postponed a forthcoming showdown. For a few months leading up to June 1941 many sources warned Stalin of Hitler's resolve to attack the Soviet Union in violation of the deal that had been struck, but Stalin still got it wrong. Hitler's blitzkrieg almost crushed the Soviet Union, exactly 10 years after Stalin's famous speech warning of the risk of being crushed by advanced capitalist countries unless the gaps between them and the Soviet Union were closed in 10 years. It was probably the most dangerous and humiliating point in Stalin's life. He lost heart temporarily but soon rallied and eventually led the country to victory. It was a stunning victory, which impressed even those most sceptical of Stalin's rule, but for many it was also a deeply hollow victory wrought at staggering human and material costs. Stalin and his regime survived, but the war also marked the end of an era.

Struggle for Survival

As Stalin terrorised the country, the threat of war became more apparent. In July 1937 the Sino-Japanese war broke out. In March 1938 Hitler annexed Austria. In September 1938, when Hitler threatened to grab the Sudetenland, Britain and France acquiesced (the Munich accord), and Hitler soon took the area from Czechoslovakia. In July–August 1938 the Soviet army clashed with the Japanese–Kwantung

Army on the Soviet–Manchukuo border (Lake Khasan). In May–August 1939 the Soviet Army and the Japanese–Kwantung Army clashed again (the Khalkin Gol or Nomonhan incident). Nearly 7,000 Red Army soldiers were killed in action, but the Soviet Army emerged victorious. Stalin was pleased with the performance of the Red Army, mentioning 'with almost sadistic glee' that 'twenty thousand Japanese had been killed' on that occasion and boasting of the lesson that 'Soviet troops had dealt the Japanese': 'That is the only language these Asiatics understand. After all, I am an Asiatic, too, so I ought to know.'[1]

Stalin meant to survive whatever war might come and by whatever means. On the twentieth anniversary of the October Revolution, 7 November 1937, Stalin told his close associates at a private banquet that the Russian tsars 'did a great deal that was bad', but

> they did one thing that was good – they amassed an enormous state, all the way to Kamchatka. We have inherited that state. And for the first time, we, the Bolsheviks, have consolidated and strengthened that state as a united and indivisible state, not in the interests of landowners and capitalists, but for the benefit of the workers, of all the peoples that make up that state. We have united the state in such a way that if any part were isolated from the common socialist state, it would not only inflict harm on the latter but would be unable to exist independently and would inevitably fall under foreign subjugation. Therefore, whoever attempts to destroy that unity of the socialist sate, whoever seeks the separation of any of its parts or nationalities – that man is an enemy, a sworn enemy of the state and of the peoples of the USSR. And we will destroy each and every enemy even if he was an old Bolshevik; we will destroy all his kin, his family. We will mercilessly destroy anyone who, by his deeds or his thoughts – yes, his thoughts – threatens the unity of the socialist state. To the complete destruction of all enemies, themselves and their kin![2]

Indeed, Stalin had repressed almost all the members of the Trotskii kin, for example, who stayed in the Soviet Union: his older brother Aleksandr, his sister Ol'ga, his first wife A.L. Sokolovskaia, and his son Sergei Sedov were all shot. Another son, Lev Sedov, died in suspicious circumstances in Paris in 1938.[3] (Earlier Stalin had destroyed the kin of Nikolaev, Kirov's assassin.) Stalin's destruction of the families of Nikolaev, Trotskii and numerous others went much further than Machiavelli had advocated: 'to preserve the newly recovered liberty in Rome, it was necessary that the sons of Brutus should have been executed'.[4]

Even though his family was destroyed, Trotskii himself, the only remaining serious challenger to Stalin's power, stayed alive in Mexico. Stalin's 1937 order to kill him did not bear fruit. According to Pavel Sudoplatov, a Soviet master spy, Stalin told him in 1939 to 'finish' Trotskii: 'There are no important political figures in the Trotskist movement except Trotsky himself. If Trotsky is finished the threat will be eliminated.' 'Trotsky', Stalin said,

> should be eliminated within a year, before war inevitably breaks out. Without the elimination of Trotsky, as the Spanish experience shows, when the imperialists attack the Soviet Union we cannot rely on our allies in the international Communist movement. They will face great difficulties in fulfilling their international duty to destabilise the rear of our enemies by sabotage operations and guerrilla warfare if they have to deal with treacherous infiltrations by Trotskyites in their ranks.[5]

Sudoplatov performed Stalin's order faithfully: in 1940 Stalin succeeded in having his arch-enemy murdered in Mexico.

Yet just as his rapid industrialisation was not just any kind of rapid industrialisation, his survival was to be not just any kind of survival. Stalin meant to preserve his power and the socialist regime he had created: in 1936 he had declared that socialism had been successfully built in the Soviet Union. He was defending not merely 'Russia' (substituting for the Soviet Union), as is claimed by some historians, but the Soviet system he had built (in opposition to his 'enemies'). In 1936, instructing Kaganovich on how to present the significance of the Zinov'ev–Kamenev trial in *Pravda*, Stalin emphasised that a struggle against himself and other leaders was a struggle against collectivisation and industrialisation and for the restoration of capitalism: Stalin and the other leaders were 'the personification of the efforts of workers, peasants, and the working intelligentsia for the defeat of capitalism and the triumph of socialism' and 'the personification of all the victories of socialism in the USSR'.[6]

In October 1938, just before he put an end to the Great Terror, Stalin addressed a Politburo meeting on the propaganda of the just-released *History of the All-Union Communist Party: Short Course*. Stalin had been involved intimately in the drafting and editing of the book that was to serve as the political primer of the Soviet people. It was in essence an 'autobiography' of Stalin and as such an explication of his political rule.[7] At any rate, in the meeting, Stalin noted that Bukharin had had 'ten, fifteen, twenty thousand' supporters, and that there were as many, possibly more, Trotskists. Then he maintained that their opposition to his 'revolution from above' was their mortal sin:

> Well, were they all spies? Of course, not. Whatever happened to them? They were cadres who could not stomach the sharp turn toward collective farms and could not make sense of this turn, because they were not trained politically, did not know the laws of social development, the laws of economic development, the laws of political development . . . How to

explain that some of them became spies and intelligence agents? . . . It turns out that they were not well-grounded politically and not well-grounded theoretically. They turned out to be people who did not know the laws of political development, and therefore they could not stomach the sharp turn.[8]

Even though Stalin did not say that neither Trotskii nor Bukharin was a foreign spy, this was a very revealing speech. Stalin knew that the spy charges hurled against the supporters of Bukharin and Trotskii were in large part untrue, but he believed in what he did: he followed what he trusted to be the laws of history. His opponents were wrong because they did not know or believe in them. Their true crime was that they had lost faith in the rightness of the party. Stalin emphasised this point when helping Vyshinskii to prepare for the second Moscow trial in 1937.[9]

Speaking to Soviet economists in 1952, Stalin made an equally revealing comment: 'You can't transform the laws of nature and society. If you can transform a law, that means you can abolish it. If you can transform and abolish a law of science this means that we are all for nothing.'[10] Instead of succumbing to the law of history, the Bukharinists and Trotskists had succumbed to their own emotion. As Stalin told Georgi Dimitrov, the Comintern's General Secretary,

> they could never stomach *collectivisation* (when cuts had to be made across the living body of the kulak), and they went *underground*. Powerless themselves, they linked up with external enemies, promised Ukraine to the Germans, Belorussia to the Poles, the Far East to the Japanese. They hoped for war and were especially insistent that the German fascists launch a war against the USSR as soon as possible.

Stalin believed that his strength stemmed from his theoretical knowledge, a belief in the laws of development, and that his critics were weak because they did not believe in the laws or did not truly understand them. Stalin contended that his opponents had planned to attack the Politburo and the Kremlin in 1937, but that they had 'lost their nerve'.[11]

The kolkhoz system, for all its defects, had become a prominent item of Stalinist pride. In November 1937 Stalin boasted that the collectivisation of the countryside was 'a completely novel, historically unprecedented event'.[12] It was *his* great achievement. Just as he was aware that many oppositionists were not spies, he may have been utterly hypocritical when he declared that 'Freedom and hunger are incompatible.'[13] Yet clearly when he compared the old serfdom with the kolkhoz system, he insisted that the latter (which many peasants called the 'second serfdom') was superior. In all likelihood Stalin was very proud of the new society he had created. Although Sidney and Beatrice Webb have rightly been criticised for their naïve and uncritical discussion of the Soviet Union in their *Soviet Communism: A New Civilisation?* (1935), Stephen Kotkin has argued that Stalin's Soviet Union was indeed a serious attempt at creating a new, socialist civilisation.[14]

To doubt the success of his creation was tantamount to treason, in Stalin's view. Indeed, he was fond of saying that 'an enemy of the people is not only one who undertakes sabotage, but one who doubts the rightness of the party line. And of those there are a lot among us, and we must liquidate them.'[15] As Stalin made clear to military leaders after the Tukhachevskii affair, it was absolute loyalty to the party and the Government that mattered to him. The Great Terror marked the beginning of a solution to the problem of 'Red' versus 'expert' by placing in elite positions those from humble origins (workers and peasants) who had acquired education. The new elite came to be known as the 'men of 1937'.[16] Indeed, in October 1938, Stalin declared that at some point, the Soviet power would make all workers and peasants educated. 'Then we shall be invincible.'[17]

Stalin's identification of himself (the leader) with the party, the Government and the Soviet Union was such that he often referred to himself in the third person singular as 'Stalin'. He went even further. According to Artem Sergeev, Stalin's adopted son, Stalin told his son Vasilii that he was not a 'Stalin': 'You're not Stalin and I'm not Stalin. Stalin is Soviet power. Stalin is what he is in the newspapers and the portraits, not you, no, not even me!'[18] In 1937 Stalin banned the making of a film on Pavlik Morozov, a boy 'martyr' said to have been murdered in 1932 by his family for denouncing his own father. Presumably Stalin objected to the representation of the boy as a cult figure. Stalin is said to have denounced the enterprise with 'We can't allow any small boy to act as though he were Soviet power itself.'[19] That prerogative belonged to Stalin alone.

Stalin thought that the people needed to believe in the party. 'People used to have faith – they believed in God, now we have deprived the people of this faith, saying that there is no God. They are confused. It's necessary that one still believes in something, believes in someone.' Stalin's answer was that the party should replace God, but he also said that it was still not easy for people to believe in such an 'abstract concept'.[20] So 'the people need a tsar'.[21] As Stalin explained to his mother in 1935, it was he who was the new tsar. Later, in 1946, while discussing a book on Western philosophy, Stalin declared that

'Marxism is the religion of the [working] class, its symbol of faith.'[22] Stalin may, however, have entertained some doubts about whether Marxism could replace religion altogether. According to Iurii Zhdanov, Stalin said, 'Here an old woman has domestic trouble or is suffering some family misfortune. Where to go? Not to the district party committee. We need Soviet priests.'[23] Stalin clearly believed in the strength of faith: if everyone believed in Marxism and became educated, the country would be truly invincible. With his tacit encouragement, the cult of Stalin the Leader soon attained a grotesque and absurd level.[24]

Stalin said in 1937, 'Leaders come and go, but the people stay. Only the people are immortal. Everything else is ephemeral.'[25] Did Stalin realise that he was also ephemeral? Or did he mean that as the Soviet power, he, like the people, was immortal? In any case, both Stalin the leader and Stalin the Soviet power faced the mortal danger of war. Stalin sought to deal with the question of war within the Marxist framework of a fluid world. Yet, as his reference to the Russian tsars demonstrates, he was also keenly aware of the national (not class or international) interests of the Soviet state. In this regard, Stalin, the self-acknowledged 'new tsar', suggested that the national interests of the Soviet state were in fact identical to the international interests of the working class. In 1941, criticising Trotskii's internationalism, Stalin asked, 'The victory of socialism in the USSR, the victory of revolution in the USSR – is it a national affair or an international affair? Of course, it's an international affair. Therefore talk of the contradictions between the "national interests" of the USSR and the interests of the world proletariat is *counter-revolutionary*'.[26] Indeed, Stalin pursued *Realpolitik* in defending the interests of the Soviet Union. On the one hand, he courted Western democracies as a counterweight to Germany and Japan. He even had a new, 'democratic' constitution drafted and promulgated in 1936 in part to make the country more acceptable to the Western democracies. (The 'Stalin Constitution' remained largely a constitution on paper only.) On the other hand, Stalin did not exclude appeasement and a rapprochement with Germany and Japan.

Whatever his ideology and phraseology may have been, Stalin's insistence that he was defending the national interests of the country prevailed upon his erstwhile enemies and émigrés (like Miliukov, Nikolai Ustrialov and other Eurasianists whose main concern was the defence of Russia as a world power) to come to terms with the Soviet Government. Miliukov did not return to the Soviet Union, but Ustrialov did. Ustrialov was nevertheless executed by Stalin in 1937 on charges of 'espionage' and 'anti-Soviet agitation'.[27]

Far from everyone believed that Stalin, like the European politicians, was merely pursuing the security of the country through balance-of-power policies. Britain in particular never discarded suspicions that Stalin's ultimate goal was the export of revolution, with which the Comintern, based in Moscow, was associated. Stalin's own remarks were open to different interpretations. In October 1938, for example, he addressed party propagandists:

> The Bolsheviks are no mere pacifists who yearn for peace and only later take up arms when they are attacked. This is wrong. There are cases when the Bolsheviks themselves will attack; if the war is just, if the situation is right, if the conditions are favourable, then the Bolsheviks will attack. They are not at all against an offensive, against any war. What we are screaming about defence now is a veil, a veil. All states camouflage themselves: 'If you live with wolves, you have to howl like wolves.'[28]

True, Stalin did not reject war in general. Ever since the Civil War period, Stalin had worn military tunics and high boots instead of suits and shoes, projecting himself as a soldier of the Revolution. As in the First World War, Stalin surely hoped that a new war would lead to socialist revolution in at least some of the imperialist states and especially in states bordering on the Soviet Union. This was an ideal and a matter of strategy and future possibilities, but not an immediate policy question. He could not project how the international situation would develop, and his first priority was to safeguard the Soviet Union.

Later, in 1942, when Churchill visited Moscow during the war, he intimated to Stalin, perhaps disingenuously, that at the beginning of 1938 he had had a 'plan for a League of three Great Democracies: Great Britain, USA and USSR, which between them could lead the world. There were no antagonistic interests between them.' Stalin responded that he 'had always hoped for something of that nature, only under Mr Chamberlain's government such a plan would have been impossible'. Stalin recalled for Churchill the 1939 visit to Moscow of the British delegation: 'No talks with them were possible.' When asked what forces could be put up against Germany, the British had said 3 divisions (in contrast to the French response of 80 divisions). Stalin 'had the impression that the talks were insincere and only for the purpose of intimidating Hitler, with whom the Western Powers would later come to terms'. Churchill said that 'he had not been in the Government for 11 years', but agreed that 'the Delegations in 1939 had no weight behind them'.[29] In fact, Stalin had correctly suspected at the time that the ideal scenario for Britain and France would be for Germany to expand eastwards, and in that case they would have been willing to strike a deal with Hitler. The 1938 Munich agreement, from which the

Soviet Union was excluded, appeared to Stalin to encourage Germany's historical *Drang nach Osten* (drive to the east) and away from Western Europe.[30] Stalin's ideal scenario, on the other hand, was for Germany, France and Britain to fight and destroy (or at least weaken) each other and, if circumstances allowed, for the Soviet Union to intervene at the most favourable moment to reap the most favourable political harvest. Stalin almost certainly knew that this best-case scenario was a pipe dream.

Whatever the future was to hold, Stalin prepared for war. The rapid industrialisation drive had markedly strengthened Soviet industry. In the mid-1930s the country began to see a noticeable return on vast investments made during the First Five-Year Plan. Against the backdrop of residual effects of the Great Depression, the Soviet Union increased its industrial production quite remarkably. Even discounting overstatements inherent in the official statistics of the Soviet Union and the poor quality of the products, Soviet industrial production more than quadrupled from 1929 to 1938 (at 1926–7 values). The defence industry's growth was far more impressive: its gross output more than tripled from 1930 to 1933 and grew by more than 1,600 per cent between 1933 and 1940![31] The size of the Soviet armed forces jumped from 1.3 million in 1935–6 to more than 5 million by June 1941. In 1935 the titles of ranks, abhorred by the rank and file and abolished during the Revolution, were formally reintroduced into the Red Army to ensure discipline. Stalin also prepared the country psychologically for war. In 1938, for example, he had the brilliant Soviet film director Sergei Eizenshtein (known for his *Battleship Potemkin*) release a patriotic film *Aleksandr Nevskii* about the thirteenth-century victorious battle of Prince Nevskii and his people against the Teutonic Knights. Stalin also rehabilitated famous Russian military commanders such as M.I. Kutuzov (saviour of Moscow during the 1812 Napoleonic War).

For all the preparations for war, Stalin believed, according to Molotov, that 'only in 1943 would we be able to meet the Germans as equals'.[32] Accordingly, he sought to postpone war at least until then. Many observers, including the German General Staff, suspected that the impact of the Great Terror on the Red Army had been so devastating that the army was unequipped to fight a total war. Stalin had reason to delay war as long as he could, whereas, paradoxically, Hitler was frustrated by the Munich accord which delayed war because the British and French, as Hitler later put it, accepted all the demands he made in Munich.[33]

It is not known exactly when Stalin decided to come to an agreement with Hitler. By May 1939, however, Stalin was leaning towards

Germany. Some suspect that Stalin's speech at the eighteenth party congress in March 1939, criticising France and Britain, was a signal to Germany. In any event, in May Stalin replaced Maksim Litvinov (a Jew married to an English woman and a long-time Soviet diplomat who had pursued the aim of collective security with Britain and France) with Molotov as People's Commissar of Foreign Affairs. Upon appointing Molotov, Stalin ordered him to '[r]emove Jews from the People's Commissariat'.[34] Stalin's apparent change of course was related almost certainly to the March 1939 guarantee given to Poland by Britain. This unilateral guarantee of armed support in the event of attack, given by Neville Chamberlain against the advice of the British Chiefs of Staff, was precipitated by Hitler's seizure of Prague in contravention of the Munich agreement. Chamberlain may have hoped that the guarantee would deter Hitler from invading Poland. In case Hitler invaded Poland, however, he would be forced to secure the neutrality of the Soviet Union in order to fight against Britain and France and avoid a war on two fronts. In turn, it was imperative for Britain and France to secure Soviet military cooperation. To complicate the matter, Poland refused to join any agreement with the Soviet Union for fear of provoking Germany. Britain and France, distrustful of the communist regime, did not promise Stalin reciprocal aid while asking for a unilateral commitment to the defence of Poland. For Stalin, after the 1935 death of Piłsudski, whom he had called 'the entire Poland', Poland may have ceased to exist. In 1937–8 Stalin dissolved the Polish Communist Party (along with the Western Ukrainian and Western Belarusan Communist Parties) on the grounds that they were saturated with 'spies and provocateurs'.[35] The fact that neither Britain nor France had intervened to save Czechoslovakia in March 1939 further heightened Stalin's suspicion that the ultimate goal of the two countries was to strike a bargain with Hitler against the Soviet Union. Moreover, since the Red Army had been fighting the Japanese-Kwantung Army at Khalkin Gol from May, a rapprochement with Germany had become a more attractive option for avoiding war on a new front, at least for the time being.

This was the background for the infamous Molotov–Ribbentrop (or Soviet–German) non-aggression pact signed on 24 August 1939, a marriage of convenience between two enemies. When asked by the German Foreign Minister how this pact squared with the 1935 Franco–Soviet treaty (which 'provided for consultation in the event of agreements with third states'), Stalin replied that Russian interests come before everything'.[36] The Western world was taken aback by this new development. It threw the united front against fascism into disarray all over the world. In the Soviet Union anti-Nazi propaganda disappeared almost overnight. Nevertheless, no one in the Soviet U-nion believed that war had been averted for good. Neither the defence industry nor the Red Army ceased to prepare for war. Consumption was squeezed for war preparations. The Soviet people, according to one account, took the new turn of events stoically: 'Stalin did it. . . . He knows what he is doing'.[37] According to another, some were deeply perplexed but there also was 'widespread chuckling among many Russians about the punishment meted out to England and France "after all their dirty tricks" '.[38]

Stalin's remark that 'there is nothing surprising in human life' applied to his 'Faustian' pact with Hitler as well. Stalin seems not to have sold his 'Marxist soul' to Nazism, however. He had a mischievous sense. He proposed to toast himself, 'the new anti-Cominternist – Stalin'.[39] (According to another account, it was Ribbentrop who recounted a joke making the rounds in Berlin that Stalin would join the Anti-Comintern Pact.)[40] After signing the pact, Stalin took the trouble to toast his close associate Kaganovich, a Jew, forcing the German Minister of Foreign Affairs Joachim von Ribbentrop to walk up to Kaganovich and clink glasses. After the banquet, Stalin told Kaganovich: 'We have to gain time.'[41] When Ribbentrop suggested a joint communiqué the text of which 'praised the newly formed German–Soviet friendship in flowery and bombastic terms', Stalin objected that after many years of 'pouring buckets of slops over each other's heads', 'now all of a sudden are we to make our peoples believe that all is forgotten and forgiven?' So a 'more moderately worded communiqué' was adopted.[42]

Stalin chose to see the pact in the most favourable terms. He believed that by signing it he was turning the cage of tigers (Nazis) around to face Britain (a 'professional enemy of peace and collective security').[43] Stalin intimated to Dimitrov on 7 September 1939 that 'We are the masters of our own house' and that '[w]e can manoeuvre, pit one side against the other to set them fighting with each other as fiercely as possible'. Admitting that the pact helped Germany, Stalin said to Dimitrov, *'Next time we'll urge on the other side.'*[44] Khrushchev similarly recalled the August 1939 pact: 'I heard with my own ears how Stalin said, "Of course it's all a game to see who can fool whom. I know what Hitler's up to. He thinks he's outsmarted me, but actually it's I who have tricked him!" Stalin told Voroshilov, Beria, myself, and some other members of the Politbureau that because of this treaty the war would pass us by for a while longer. We would be able to stay neutral and save our strength. Then we would see what happened.'[45]

Stalin regarded (and presented) the entire affair from a Marxist perspective of the contradictions among imperialist powers, but it was also the case that Stalin, like the tsars, was not free from imperialist ambitions. The pact was supplemented by an infamous secret protocol that divided eastern Europe into German and Soviet 'spheres of influence'. This secret protocol was such an embarrassing imperialist document for the Soviet leaders that its Soviet signatory Molotov denied its very existence until his death in 1986. Nor did the Soviet Government officially acknowledge its existence until 1990 when it finally released the original secret protocol for publication.

Uncertainty

Having secured the neutrality of the Soviet Union, on 1 September 1939 Hitler invaded Poland, in accord with the secret protocol that had given Germany control of much of it. Hitler knew he had to go to war with Britain and France because these two countries had guaranteed Poland's security. Two days later, Britain and France declared war on Germany. According to the agreement with Germany, the Soviet Army advanced into eastern Poland on 17 September 1939 and occupied it. Based on yet another secret protocol signed in late September, the Soviet Union placed western Ukraine and western Belarus, as well as all the Baltic republics under its sphere of influence. Poland was partitioned. Stalin saw no problem with this. He told Dimitrov that formerly 'the Polish state was a nat[ional] state. Therefore, revolutionaries defended it against partition and enslavement,' but now Poland had become a *'fascist state, oppressing Ukrainians, Belorussians, and so forth'*: the 'annihilation of that state under current conditions would mean one fewer bourgeois fascist state to contend with!'[46] Western Ukraine and western Belarus were quickly incorporated into the Soviet Union. The population was terrorised and intimidated, and many so-called 'bourgeois' elements were deported to Central Asia, Siberia and elsewhere. (In the famous Katyn massacre, more than 20,000 Polish officers were executed.) Based on rigged 'popular elections' the new territories became part of the Soviet Union. The Baltic states fared better for the moment, merely being forced to sign pacts of 'mutual assistance' (which in fact meant surrendering much of their sovereignty). To intimidate Estonia, a nation much smaller than Poland, Stalin told the Estonians that what happened to Poland could happen to them: 'Poland was a great country. Where is Poland now? Where are Mosicki, Rydz-Smigly and Beck?' To the Lithuanians, whose country was larger than Estonia, Stalin said, 'You argue too much.' Insisting that the

Soviet action was not imperialist, Molotov said that any imperialist country would have simply occupied Lithuania and 'that would be that. Unlike us. We wouldn't be Bolsheviks if we didn't search for new ways.' To the Lithuanian protest that the Soviet demand was tantamount to the occupation of the country, Stalin insisted that the Soviet Union was in fact assisting Lithuania.[47]

In destroying Poland with Germany, Stalin now feared attack from Britain and France. They did not declare war on the Soviet Union immediately, but at the beginning of October Stalin thought that they might.[48] Fortunately, they never did. In fact, as Hitler had expected, they did very little to save Poland which, to Stalin's surprise, collapsed almost overnight. Stalin hoped for a 'war of attrition,' which would weaken the imperialist powers in Europe. In September 1939 Stalin told Dimitrov that before the war opposing a democratic regime to a fascist one was 'entirely correct', but that now, in the midst of 'war between the imperialist powers that [proposition] is incorrect': 'The division of capitalist states into fascist and democratic no longer makes sense.' Again Stalin attacked Britain and France: 'We preferred agreements with the so-called democratic countries,' but 'the English and the French wanted us for farmhands and at no cost! We, of course, would not go for being farmhands, still less for getting nothing in return.' Stalin hoped in Leninist fashion that war would undermine the old order in Europe: 'Under [the] conditions of an imperialist war, the prospect of the annihilation of slavery arises!' There are also some indications that Stalin expected that the war would weaken or undermine the Nazi regime. Speaking to Dimitrov in November 1939, Stalin said, 'In Germany, the petty-bourgeois nationalists are capable of a sharp turn – they are flexible – not tied to capitalist traditions, unlike bourgeois leaders like Chamberlain and his ilk.'[49]

For the time being, Stalin managed to stay out of the European war, which in practice meant helping Germany. According to the Soviet–German agreements, enormous amounts of economic aid from the Soviet Union poured into Germany which, at war, needed them sorely. Germany was also able to transport vital minerals such as manganese from Asia through the Soviet Union, but proved less than willing to honour the mutual economic assistance agreements. In other respects, however, Stalin drew the line, refusing to help Germany, and condemned the defeatism of the European countries: in October 1939 Stalin said to Dimitrov, *There must be no copying now of the positions the Bolsheviks held then* [during the First World War]'.[50]

According to the pacts with Germany, Stalin sought to place Finland under the Soviet sphere of influence, but, unlike the small Baltic states, Finland would not give in. So 30 November 1939 the Red Army invaded Finland. For this act of aggression, the Soviet Union was expelled from the League of Nations, although the League retained very little prestige or power by then. When, however, Britain and France hovered on the brink of declaring war, the Soviet Union hastened to conclude a peace treaty with Finland. The Soviet Union secured some territorial gain. After the Finnish–Soviet war (or the 'Winter War') ended in March 1940, Stalin declared that making the Soviet Union more secure by territorial expansion had been the goal of the war:

> We had to protect Leningrad because its safety is the safety of our Fatherland. Not only because 30–35 per cent of our defence industry is concentrated there, but Leningrad's safety is all-important for the country's destiny. Besides, the city is the second capital. A breakthrough to Leningrad and the formation there of, say, a bourgeois White Guard government would [have] provide[d] a serious basis for a civil war inside the country against the Soviet government.

Stalin added that he could not have waited. When 'the three biggest powers' in the West (Britain, France and Germany) were 'locked in deadly combat' was 'the most opportune moment to settle the Leningrad problem'. 'To miss the moment would have been great stupidity and political shortsightedness. . . . A delay of a couple of months would have meant a delay of 20 years, because you can't predict political development. They may have been fighting there, but the war was too vague: one couldn't tell if they were fighting or playing cards.' Stalin was afraid of 'a sudden peace', thereby missing the favourable moment.[51] If the three powers were playing games and concluded a 'sudden peace', not only would Stalin have missed out on the territorial issue but the Soviet Union might have faced a Germany turned eastwards.

The Finnish-Soviet war exposed a multitude of problems in the Red Army, even though the Soviets eventually won and Finland was forced to make considerable territorial concessions. The Soviet performance was so embarrassingly weak that it alarmed even the political leadership. Soviet deaths, more than 80,000, were much higher than the number of Finnish dead. Khrushchev admitted that 'A victory at such a cost was actually a moral defeat.' Stalin was angry with the military commanders, and Khrushchev recalled a meeting at Stalin's dacha:

> Stalin jumped up in a white-hot rage and started to berate Voroshilov. Voroshilov was also boiling mad. He leaped up, turned red, and hurled Stalin's accusations back into his face. 'You have yourself to blame for all this!' shouted Voroshilov. 'You're the one who annihilated the Old Guard of the army; you had our best generals killed!' Stalin rebuffed him, and

at that, Voroshilov picked up a platter with a roast suckling pig on it and smashed it on the table.[52]

After the Finnish defeat, the leaders had to review seriously the fighting preparedness of the army and to reform it. To begin with, the soldiers were poorly armed, ill clad, poorly shod and poorly fed. Stalin brushed aside the apologia offered by Soviet military commanders that the army's fighting capacity was at an ebb in wintertime: 'All the Russian army's major victories were won in wintertime. Alexander Nevsky against the Swedes, Peter I against the Swedes in Finland, Alexander I's victory over Napoleon. *We are a northern country*.'[53] The commanders complained that their authority, severely undermined in 1937, had to be enhanced, subtly criticising the Great Terror and the continuing interference of the secret police. Stalin brushed aside such complaints as well. He also subjected some of his old comrades to severe criticism. Voroshilov, for example, who had already been replaced by Marshal S.K. Timoshenko in January 1940, humbled himself before Stalin, who then disingenuously praised him, 'it does not often happen around here that a People's Commissar speaks so openly about his own shortcomings'.[54] At a meeting devoted to a discussion of the problems of the army in April 1940, Stalin intervened constantly in the speech made by the Army Commander Second Rank M.P. Kovalev:

> Comrade Kovalev, you are a fine man, one of the rare Civil War commanders, but you haven't readjusted yourself to the modern ways. . . . All our commanders, who had some Civil War experience, have readjusted themselves. [V.A.] Frolov has readjusted himself quite well, while you and [V.I.] Chuikov will not readjust yourselves, no matter what. This is the first conclusion. You are an able man and a brave one, you know your job, but you fight the old way, the way when there was no artillery, no aviation, no tanks, when only men could be sent to fight the enemy. This is an old method. You are an able man, but you have some hidden pride that will not let you adjust yourself. Accept your drawbacks and readjust yourself, then things will get going.

Kovalev only responded with 'Yes, Comrade Stalin.'[55] Both Kovalev and Chuikov outlived Stalin, retiring from the army with distinguished service records.

Stalin participated in the April 1940 meeting energetically, attending every session and responding to almost all the speeches. He made suggestions even on subjects such as dry foods, biscuits and felt boots, subjects that Stalin suspected were neglected by the military. Stalin's participation underlined the seriousness of the matter, and he was serious about reforming the military. He excoriated complacency within the army, contending that the Red Army was terribly spoilt by the 1939

Polish campaign, which was 'merely a military stroll, not a war'. The skirmishes with the Japanese in 1938 and 1939 were 'trifles, not a war'. It had taken the army a while to realise that the Finnish war was a real war. There had been 'a lot of bragging that our army was invincible'. 'We have to drive home the fact that there has not been and will never be an invincible army.' Stalin attacked the commanders' 'cult of traditions and experience of the Civil War', urging them to work in 'a really new way' appropriate to the modern war of artillery, aviation, tanks and mortars. The old way was like 'the Red Indians in America' fighting 'against rifles with clubs'. 'Those who believe them [the traditions and experience of the Civil War] adequate will certainly perish'. Stalin also insisted that 'political workers, staunch politically and well versed in military matters', were needed. 'It is not enough for a political worker to pay lip service to the Party of Lenin and Stalin, never mind all the hallelujahs'. Stalin ended his concluding speech on a positive note, however. It was good that the Red Army had the chance to get the experience of modern war 'not from German aviation but in Finland, with God's help'. 'The main thing in our victory is that we have destroyed the equipment, tactics and strategy of the advanced states of Europe, who were the Finn's teachers.' Stalin specifically named Britain, France and Germany as these advanced states.[56]

Hitler and the German General Staff reached a different conclusion from the Winter War, however. Influenced by their view of the Slavs as an inferior race, they willingly saw the Soviet 'mass' (not even an army) as no match for the superior German army and its leadership. The war made them overconfident.

The German advance to western Europe in April and May 1940 and the unexpectedly swift German occupation of Paris in June upset Stalin deeply. According to Khrushchev, 'Stalin's nerve cracked when he learned about the fall of France. He cursed the governments of England and France. "Couldn't they put up any resistance at all?" he asked despairingly.' Stalin 'let fly with some choice Russian curses and said that now Hitler was sure to beat our brains in'. After the fall of France, Hitler asked Stalin to help him to put down the resistance against the Germans led by the French Communist Party, but Stalin drew the line at this – Khrushchev recalled that he was indignant.[57] The turn of events in Europe did not encourage his hope for a 'war of attrition', dramatically increasing as it did the possibility of Germany turning eastwards. Yet Stalin also believed that Hitler, having learnt the lessons of history, would not risk a war on two fronts. Clearly, however, Stalin began to think about the possibility of a German attack. Thus in the summer of 1940 he ordered studies of methods for repelling a German attack. It was then that the Soviet Union incorporated the Baltic states into the Soviet Union and increased its military presence there. It also took Bessarabia and northern Bukovyna (the latter, not stipulated in the Soviet–German agreements, was a somewhat provocative act). In the summer of 1940 Hitler decided to wage war on the Soviet Union, a decision that was almost certainly known to Stalin through intelligence.

really? [handwritten marginal note]

Stalin still hoped that he could negotiate a deal with Hitler for the remainder of Europe, the Balkans and Turkey in particular, and stay out of the European war. He did not believe that Britain would fall quickly and feared the possibility of Britain and Germany coming to a peace accord in opposition to the Soviet Union. Stalin rejected British overtures (through the ambassador Stafford Cripps) for a dialogue regarding the German threat, premised on the preservation of the Versailles agreements of 1919.

Stalin was deeply worried. On 7 November 1940, after the anniversary celebration of the October Revolution Stalin, irritated by the military state of affairs, severely criticised his close colleagues. He discussed the weaknesses of the Soviet Army, particularly in aviation and anti-aircraft defence.

> I am busy at this every day now, meeting with designers and other specialists. . . . But I am the *only* one dealing with all these problems. None of you could be bothered with them. I am out there *by myself* . . . Look at me: I am capable of learning, reading, keeping up with things every day – why can you not do this? You do not like to learn; you are happy just going along the way you are, complacent. You are squandering Lenin's legacy. . . . People are thoughtless, do not want to learn and relearn. *They will hear me out and then go on just as before.* But I will show you, if I ever lose my patience. (You know very well how I can do that.) I shall hit the fatsos so hard that you will hear the crack for miles a round.

'Everyone stood straight', according to Dimitrov who witnessed this scene, 'and listened quietly; clearly no one ever expected J.V. [Stalin] to come out with such scolding. There were tears in Voroshilov's eyes.' It was as if a father were scolding his prodigal sons. Dimitrov added in his diary: 'Have never seen and never heard J.V. [Stalin] the way he was that night – a memorable one.'[58]

When invited to join the September 1940 tripartite pact of Germany, Italy and Japan (the Axis powers), Stalin considered the invitation seriously but with certain conditions (which included the withdrawal of German troops from Finland, a guarantee of Soviet security through a mutual aid pact between the Soviet Union and Bulgaria, the creation of Soviet military bases in the Bosphorus and Dardanelles straits and recognition of Soviet rights to the south of Batumi and Baku in the direction of the Persian Gulf). Through Molotov's trip to Berlin in November 1940, Stalin sought to clarify Germany's position towards Finland, Romania, the Balkans, Turkey, Persia and Asia. Germany's disregard of the pact concerning Finland and Romania disquieted Stalin, but Hitler did not take the matter seriously, promising nothing certain or concrete to the Soviet Union. Still Stalin offered to join the Axis powers provided that his conditions were met,[59] but Hitler never responded. Instead, fearing that Stalin might forestall him, he ordered Operation Barbarossa on 18 December 1940, an attack on the Soviet Union. Meanwhile, two neighbouring countries, Hungary and Romania, joined the Axis in November 1940, and in April 1941 Germany invaded Greece and Yugoslavia, a blatant violation of the non-aggression pact. Stalin managed to secure the east, however, by concluding in April 1941 a neutrality pact with Japan, which would advance to the south and attack British, Dutch and American interests. Soviet and other intelligence reports from London, Berlin, Tokyo and elsewhere indicated that Hitler was preparing for war against the Soviet Union.

All the same, Stalin adhered to his illusion, or perhaps he was even overconfident. Before the Russian edition of Otto von Bismarck's memoirs was published in late 1940 by the order of Molotov, Stalin edited out several passages in the introduction by the historian A.S. Ierusalimskii, including 'Bismarck's repeated warnings against involvement in a war with Russia'. When Ierusalimskii timidly defended his passage, Stalin said, 'But why do you frighten them? Let them try.'[60] On the eve of the German invasion of Yugoslavia, Stalin had meetings with the Yugoslav delegates. Stalin told them that the Germans had tried to intimidate the Soviets, too, but 'we are not afraid of them'. When the Yugoslavs asked Stalin whether he knew of rumours of Hitler's attack scheduled to begin in May [1941], Stalin responded, 'Let him. Our nerves are strong. We don't want war, and so we concluded a non-aggression pact with Hitler. But how is he carrying it out? Do you know what kind of forces the Germans have moved to our borders?'[61]

Stalin was probably bluffing. He still appeared to believe that Germany would not wage war against the Soviet Union and that he could continue to live with Hitler at least for a time. No fundamental rethinking of strategy and diplomacy took place in 1941. In May 1941 Stalin, who 'relied on personal contacts with Hitler and was confident he could convince Hitler not to launch the war', assumed the chairmanship of Sovnarkom (the cabinet), signalling that he was 'ready for negotiations and that this time he would lead them directly'.[62] Some historians argue that Stalin was in fact planning a pre-emptive strike against the Reich in 1941.[63] They draw in particular on Stalin's 5 May 1941 speech to the graduates of the Red Army Academy in the Kremlin in which Stalin declared: 'Now we have to move from defence to offence . . . the Red Army is a modern army, and a modern army is an army of offence'.[64] Yet Stalin appeared to speak of offence in general to boost the morale of the graduates and alert them to possible dangers to come. Following Stalin's speech, the military drew up a strategic plan, but Stalin grew agitated and strongly reprimanded Georgii Zhukov, the Chief of the General Staff, 'What, did you go mad, do you want to provoke the Germans?' Stalin assured Zhukov and Timoshenko that his speech had been meant to counter the view that the German army was invincible: 'Germany will never fight on her own against Russia.'[65] Despite the vast deployment of the Wehrmacht forces on the Soviet western borders, Stalin maintained the illusion that it was a war of nerves, confident that his nerves were stronger than Hitler's. Stalin considered British warnings about German war preparations a ruse to embroil the Soviet Union in the war. On 17 June 1941, five days before Operation Barbarossa began, Stalin received a dire warning of German war preparations based on a German source from the Soviet security organ. Stalin rejected the missive, however, returning it with a note to V.N. Merkulov, the chief of state security: 'You can tell your "source" in the Ger[man] air force staff to go f[uck] his mother. He's not an "informer" but a "disinformer".'[66] As it turned out, Stalin made a colossal misjudgement.

War

The Wehrmacht invaded the Soviet Union at 4 a.m. on Sunday, 22 June 1941, in violation of the August 1939 non-aggression pact. The invasion began one hour after the Politburo dispersed, having ended a discussion of the situation on the western borders. When awoken and informed of a massive German attack shortly after 4 o'clock in the morning, Stalin did not believe it had happened. Suspecting that the attack was only a provocation by the Wehrmacht without the sanction of the Chancellor of the Reich, Stalin gave orders not to fire back. Only at 5.30 a.m. when the German ambassador read a declaration of war to Molotov in his Kremlin office, did it become clear that what Stalin had dreaded had actually happened. The critical initial hours of defence had been lost, and the Wehrmacht's blitzkrieg continued in full force. 'In just a few hours (to noon, 22 June), the western districts lost 528 planes on the ground and 210 in the air.'[67] Stalin realised that he had made the mistake of his life.

When the leaders of the country met, and Stalin was asked to address the nation, he refused, saying, 'Let Molotov speak.' Everyone objected, insisting that the people would not understand why at such an important moment Stalin did not speak. Still he refused, saying that he could not do it; he would speak another time.[68] So Molotov addressed the nation on the radio at 12.15 p.m., calling on the people to fight the Nazi invaders: 'Our cause is just, the enemy will be obliterated, victory will be ours.'

However, the war did not go well for the Red Army, which had not been put on alert to begin with. It suffered one crushing defeat after another. On 29 June, the seventh day of the war, Minsk, the capital of Belarus, fell. This presented a grave danger: the loss of Minsk opened a direct assault route to Moscow. Contact with the Belarusan front was lost, and the Commissariat of Defence was left in the dark about the situation there. So Stalin, Molotov, G.M. Malenkov (a party CC member), Mikoian and L.P. Beriia (who had replaced Ezhov as the chief of the secret police in 1938) decided to go to the Commissariat to learn more. Zhukov reported that he was trying to resume contact, but could not tell when that would happen. After half an hour of calm discussion, Stalin exploded: 'What kind of General Staff is this? What sort of Chief of Staff are you who on the first day of the war gets flustered, loses contact with the troops, represents no one and commands no one?' Zhukov, who had done his best to prepare for the German invasion and had alerted Stalin repeatedly to the ominous signs on the borders before the invasion, could not take Stalin's insult. This otherwise 'courageous soldier', according to Mikoian, 'literally burst into tears' and ran out of the room. Everyone was despondent. Molotov went after Zhukov, and five or ten minutes later both returned, Zhukov with red eyes. When Stalin and the others left the commissariat, Stalin said, 'Lenin left us a great legacy, but we, his heirs, have shit it out our asses.'[69] According to other accounts, Stalin said, 'Lenin founded our state, and we've fucked it up!' or 'Lenin left us a state and we've turned it to shit.'[70]

This time, unlike, say, in 1930, Stalin could not easily shift the blame to others even though he tried to do so. He well knew how gravely he had miscalculated, and that was why he could not muster the courage to speak to the nation on 22 June. Appropriate intelligence information had been available, but, what decision to take based on it was a matter of politics. As G.I. Kulik, Deputy People's Commissar of Defence, said, 'This is big politics. It's not our business.'[71] Somewhat surprisingly, Stalin and his supporters, who had relied so much on the secret police, also entertained much suspicion of their intelligence,

particularly when it came to foreign intelligence. Molotov later recalled
that every day he used to spend half a day reading intelligence reports,
but insisted that it was impossible to rely on spies, who 'could push
you into such a dangerous position that you would never get out of it':
'You have to listen to them, but you also have to verify their information.'[72] According to a former NKVD official, 'Stalin, who was his own
intelligence boss and who liked to take a personal part in the cloak and
dagger business, warned his intelligence chiefs time and again to keep
away from hypotheses and "equations with many unknowns". . . . He
used to say: "An intelligence hypothesis may become your hobby horse
on which you will ride straight into a self-made trap" ', and he often interjected during his conferences with intelligence chiefs, 'Don't tell me
what you think, give me the facts and the sources!'[73] Stalin indeed
appeared to have ridden 'straight into a self-made trap'.

It is often said that at the beginning of the war Stalin was paralysed
by his mistake. In fact, he was not, and he at first worked energetically
in his office, though undeniably the incident with Zhukov seemed to
throw him into the depths of despair. He lost interest in everything,
took no initiatives and was generally in a poor state. His own supporters were forced to act without him. A day or two after the Zhukov
incident, Molotov, Malenkov, Voroshilov and Beriia decided to set up a
State Committee of Defence (GKO) to which all the powers of the Government and the party would be transferred. Stalin was to be its chair.
Then they went to Stalin's dacha with the proposal, but when he saw
them he appeared to sink back into his armchair. Then he asked, 'What
did you come for?' with a strange, suspicious look. His question was
even more strange, for it was he who should have summoned them.
Mikoian had no doubt that Stalin had decided that they had come to
arrest him.[74]

Relieved from the uncertainty that had nagged him and realising
that everyone stood behind him, Stalin rallied. Finally on 3 July, 11
days after the war had broken out, Stalin spoke to the nation by radio.
To the surprise of everyone, Stalin opened his speech with 'Comrades!
Citizens! Brothers and sisters! Fighters of our army and navy! I am
speaking to you, my friends!' 'Brothers and sisters', an expression used
by the church, was now employed by the head of an atheist government. Stalin denounced the perfidious attack by Hitler, but defended
the 1939 pact, a pact which 'no peace-loving nation could have rejected' with a neighbouring state even if 'such monsters and cannibals
as Hitler and Ribbentrop stood at its head'. Stalin asked whether the
German troops were invincible, and declared 'Of course not!' No army
in history has been invincible. Napoleon's army, Kaiser Wilhelm II's

army, both considered invincible in their time, were defeated. This was a 'war for the freedom of our fatherland' and against the enslavement of the Soviet peoples by the German fascists.[75] Given the Nazi ideology, which regarded the Slavs as 'subhumans', Stalin's speech must have made some sense to the population. The war came to be known in the Soviet Union as the Great Patriotic War, after the Patriotic War against Napoleon's army. Alexander Werth, a British journalist who spent the war years in the Soviet Union, wrote how important this speech, 'addressed to a nervous, and often frightened people', proved to be. Until then, there was 'something artificial in the adulation of Stalin', but the speech made the Soviet people 'feel that they had a leader to look to . . . It was a great pull-yourselves-together speech, with Churchill's post-Dunkirk speech as its only parallel'.[76] Khrushchev later noted that Stalin 'had pulled himself together, straightened up, and was acting like a real soldier. He had also begun to think of himself as a great military strategist, which made it harder than ever to argue with him. He exhibited all the strong-willed determination of a heroic leader.'[77]

A week later Stalin assumed the post of Supreme Commander of the Armed Forces, and shortly thereafter Stalin replaced Timoshenko as People's Commissar for Defence. Stalin thus became the head of the party, the Government and the armed forces. He formally became an omnipotent dictator.

Khrushchev, based in Kyiv (Kiev) when the war began, stated that 'during the German advance on Kiev, there was a great awakening of patriotism among the people'.[78] There was also much panic and confusion all over the country, however. For the initial debacle of the military, Stalin had a number of commanders (most notably Major General D.G. Pavlov, Chief of Staff of the Western Front) executed. Remarks by civilians such as 'The Germans will win' or 'they have technology and we haven't' and 'they've got abundance, we've got a pittance' were recorded carefully by various organisations.[79] So were popular doubts about Stalin's leadership and remarks that were explicitly anti-Soviet and anti-Semitic. As the Soviet troops retreated and the population evacuated, the Soviet authorities summarily executed many people whom they considered politically suspect.[80] Official statistics show that the number of death sentences against political criminals rose sharply from 1,649 in 1940 to 8,011 in 1941 and to 23,278 in 1942. When the authorities found it difficult to evacuate prisoners, they executed them as well. (Thus the former head of the Left SRs, Mariia Spiridonova, was executed in Orel in September 1941. Also executed was Stalin's own brother-in-law, Aleksandr Svanidze. Stalin instructed V.N. Merkulov, Beriia's deputy, to pardon Svanidze if he asked for forgiveness, but Svanidze refused on account of his innocence. Svanidze spat in the face of Merkulov, saying 'This is my answer to him.' Stalin's reaction was to comment that Svanidze had 'noble pride'. His wife Mariia was executed in 1942.)[81] In L'viv, Ukraine, for example, according to a Ukrainian émigré study, well over 10,000 were said to have been murdered by the Soviet authorities before their evacuation. Similar atrocities were committed everywhere, and brutal treatment was certainly not confined to civilians. Between 22 June and 10 October 1941, 657,364 military servicemen were detained by the NKVD for desertion. Most deserters were sent back to the front, but 25,875 were arrested on charges of espionage, diversion, treachery and other crimes. Of them, as many as 10,201 were executed by the Soviet authorities, 3,321 in front of their comrades.[82]

Soviet terror was overshadowed by Nazi terror. Approximately one third of the six million or so Jews killed in the Holocaust lived in the Soviet Union. In addition, untold numbers of Soviet soldiers and civilians were murdered by the occupiers whose racist ideology barbarised the war in the extreme.[83]

Even the Gulag population appeared to be patriotic. One inmate in Kolyma, 13,000 kilometres to the east of Moscow, recalled the reaction of the camp population to the news of war: 'We, its rejected children, now trembled for our fatherland. Some of us had managed to lay hands on scraps of paper to trace a message with a stubby pencil: "I ask to be sent to the most dangerous sector of the front. I have been a member of the Communist Party since the age of sixteen. . . . "'[84] Thus during the war almost one million prisoners, condemned for espionage, counterrevolutionary propaganda and other political crimes, were transferred to the Red Army. (After the war, as will be discussed, Stalin admitted that he had imprisoned and killed too many Soviet citizens for nothing.) The productivity of labour in the camps increased dramatically during the war. Except for a few cases, the Gulag remained largely peaceful and no serious uprisings took place within or outside it.[85]

By October 1941 German troops approached the suburbs of Moscow. There was panic in the city. Some government offices were evacuated to Kuibyshev (formerly Samara) on the Volga. Stalin called the western front. According to its commander, I.S. Konev, Stalin, in a hysterical tone, referred to himself in the third person: 'Comrade Stalin is not a betrayer, Comrade Stalin is not a traitor, Comrade Stalin is an honest man, his only mistake is that he trusted the cavalrymen [such as Voroshilov and S.M. Budennyi] too much, Comrade Stalin will do everything in his power to correct the situation.'[86] At that time Stalin may have tried to negotiate a deal with Hitler for a 'second Brest-Litovsk' treaty (as Lenin did in 1918), whereby peace and territorial concessions would be exchanged. If such an attempt, which has not yet been proved, was made at all, it miscarried. The Bulgarian mediator, Ivan Stamenov, appeared more confident: 'Even if you retreat to the Urals, you'll still win in the end.'[87] At that time, Japan, too, made a secret gesture to mediate peace between the Soviet Union and Germany, to no avail.[88] Meanwhile, Konev's failure to prevent the German troops from threatening Moscow (Konev had lost 500,000 of his men taken prisoner) prompted Stalin to hold him (like Pavlov) accountable. Yet Zhukov, now entrusted with the defence of Moscow, defended him on the grounds that he needed Konev as his deputy. Stalin acquiesced with a threat that 'If you surrender Moscow, *both* your heads will roll.' Zhukov knew well that 'even without Konev I would suffer that fate if we lost the capital'.[89]

Stalin fought for his political life and for his country, which were the same in his view. His reaction to the news that his own son, Iakov, had been taken prisoner in July 1941 was characteristic. Stalin equated being taken prisoner with treason, and many families of Soviet POWs were exiled. Subsequently, Stalin had his own daughter-in-law arrested on suspicion that she might have been a party to Iakov's 'betrayal'. When an exchange of Iakov for the German Field Marshal Friedrich von Paulus (who surrendered at Stalingrad) was proposed, Stalin rejected it. He asked, 'How many sons of Ivanovs, Petrovs, Sidorovs' were in captivity? 'No, I don't have the right to an exchange. *Otherwise, I'd cease to be Stalin.*' He pitied the son he had once disowned,[90] but according to Stalin's daughter Svetlana, Stalin's reaction was different; he said, 'I have no son called Jacob [Iakov].'[91]

Stalin may not have realised it, but work had worn him down physically. Colonel General P.A. Belov, who had not seen Stalin since 1933, noted on his meeting with him in November 1941: 'He was greatly changed since that time. Before me stood a short man with a tired, haggard face. In eight years he seemed to have aged twenty. His eyes [had] lost their old steadiness; his voice lacked assurance.' Stalin was rude, brutal and cruel, but he also studied intently to learn things military. His earlier breakdown at Stalin's insult notwithstanding, Zhukov was not always intimidated by Stalin and sometimes argued with him. In late July 1941 Stalin questioned Zhukov's decision to abandon Kyiv, flaring up: 'What kind of nonsense is this?' Zhukov responded, 'If you think that the Chief of the General Staff is capable of only talking nonsense, there is nothing for him to do here. I ask to be relieved of the duties of the Chief of the General Staff and to be sent to the front.' Stalin needed Zhukov's talent at the front, so he met his request, appointing in his place Marshal B.M. Shaposhnikov, a former tsarist army officer and the only Soviet military leader whom Stalin addressed formally, that is, by his name and patronymic.[92] Stalin and Zhukov got along well all the same. Belov noted with surprise how Stalin and Zhukov interacted: 'He [Zhukov] spoke in a sharp, commanding tone. It looked as if Zhukov were really the superior officer here. And Stalin accepted this as proper. At times a kind of bafflement even crossed his face.'[93]

Thanks in part to the command of Zhukov, Konev and others, thanks in part to the approaching winter and thanks in large part to the brave soldiers of the Red Army, Moscow did not fall after all, and Stalin did not leave Moscow for a safer place during the battle. On 6 November 1941 he addressed representatives of Moscow in the hall of the Maiakovskii Metro station, appealing to Russian national sentiments: the Nazi imperialists 'without honour or conscience'

> have the effrontery to call for the extermination of the great Russian nation – the nation of Plekhanov and Lenin, of Belinsky and Chernyshevsky, of Pushkin and Tolstoy, of Gorki and Chekhov, of Glinka and Tchaikovsky, of Sechenov and Pavlov, of Suvorov and Kutuzov! The German invaders want a war of extermination against the peoples of the Soviet Union. Very well then! If they want a war of extermination they shall have it! (*Prolonged, stormy applause.*) Our task now . . . will be to destroy every German, to the very last man, who has come to occupy our country. No mercy for the German invaders! Death to the German invaders! (*Stormy applause.*)

The following morning, on the anniversary of the October Revolution, Stalin addressed the Soviet soldiers at Red Square with the sounds of battle audible in the distance:

> The war you are waging is a war of liberation, a just war. May you be inspired in this war by the heroic figures of our great ancestors, Alexander Nevsky, Dmitri Donskoi, Minin and Pozharsky, Alexander Suvorov, Michael Kutuzov! May you be blest by [the] great Lenin's victorious banner! Death to the German invaders! Long live our glorious country, its freedom and independence!

Stalin's litany of Russian heroes who had fought against foreign invaders had a 'tremendous effect' on the people. As Werth noted, the people 'felt the deep *insult* of the German invasion – it was something more deeply *insulting* than anything they had known before'.[94] By December 1941 the Soviet army was able to stage a successful counterattack on the Moscow front.

Leningrad did not fall, but it fared far worse than Moscow; it was besieged for 900 days by German forces which, instead of capturing it, let the city starve. Nearly a million people died in the siege. According to General I.I. Fediuninskii, when he and other Leningrad leaders had a conversation with Stalin after the siege had been lifted, he showed little sympathy:

> Death was cutting down not only Leningraders. People were also dying at the front and in the occupied territories. I agree that death is appalling when there is no way out of the situation, and the starvation was just such a situation. There was nothing more we could do for Leningrad. Moscow itself was hanging by a thread. Death and war are inseparable. Leningrad was not the only place to suffer from that swine Hitler.[95]

The hard-won victory on the Moscow front was a turning point: it was the first major victory by an opponent over the 'invincible Wehrmacht' since the war began in 1939. It was not so much a military turning point as a moral–psychological turning point for all nations fighting against Hitler's war machine.[96] It was also an important turning point for Stalin. As Werth noted, the Soviet people began to feel that although Stalin had 'bungled things terribly at the beginning of the war', 'here was a man with nerves of steel, who, when things looked blackest of all, had pulled himself together and had not lost his head'. Thus, after the battle of Moscow 'Stalin's stock went up and the poets began to sing his praises again'.[97]

Privately, however, Stalin's stock may not have gone up. After the retreat of the German forces, Stalin took a trip by armoured Packard towards the front along the Minsk highway, which had been cleared of mines. It is said that he wanted to generate rumours that he had gone to the front, though he did not actually get very close to it. Suddenly he had to relieve himself. He asked whether the area around a bush off the highway was mined, but no one was prepared to give him any assurance of safety. So the Supreme Commander ended up by pushing his trousers down and defecating on the asphalt in front of everyone – generals, officers and bodyguards.[98]

The war proved extraordinarily deadly. By December 1941 the Red Army 'lost 2,663,000 killed in action, 3,350,000 taken prisoner. For every German soldier killed, twenty Soviet soldiers died.'[99] This was just the beginning, however: territorial losses were enormous, too. Most land to the west of the line Leningrad–Moscow–Rostov on the Don was lost. German assaults continued. 'Until the battle of Stalingrad' of 1942–3, the historian Dmitrii Volkogonov wrote of Stalin, 'his orders tended to be somewhat impulsive and erratic, superficial and incompetent.'[100] The Kharkiv battle in the spring of 1942, for example, turned out to be a disaster owing to Stalin's insistence on an offensive. Nearly a quarter million lives were lost. There followed another serious defeat in the Crimea. After these failures, Stalin issued the infamous Order

227 'Not a Step Back!' which obliged the soldiers to fight to the death. Stalin appointed Zhukov his Deputy Supreme Commander. Zhukov initially turned down the appointment on the grounds that given his, Zhukov's, personality, it would be difficult for him and Stalin to work together. Stalin proposed that their personalities be subordinated to the interests of the motherland and Zhukov accepted the appointment. Zhukov testified that after that, Stalin no longer made operational decisions without consulting him, and he enjoyed Stalin's trust for the remainder of the war. Zhukov further noted that Stalin's understanding of military issues became quite good. However, Stalin's vanity was such that he manoeuvred to monopolise military credit, just as in 1813 Alexander I had stolen the glory of the victory over Napoleon from Kutuzov. 'It was very difficult to understand Stalin,' Zhukov wrote, 'he spoke very little and formulated his thoughts in few words.'[101]

The Soviet defeat in the Kharkiv offensive opened the way to Stalingrad for the Nazi invaders. As Zhukov noted, Stalin did not interfere with the defence strategy devised by the military. This 'in itself was a revolutionary development'.[102] Stalingrad withstood five months of fierce onslaught, until the Germans and their allied forces eventually surrendered in February 1943. More than a million lives were lost in the battle.[103] Half a century later, in the open fields near the city, the *balki* ('the gullies and slopes of the steppe') were still 'littered with sun-bleached bones'.[104] This epic struggle was a true military turning point in the war. It became and still is a nightmare for the Germans: 'Stalingrad: the word touches on a trauma that lies buried beneath the hardened lava crusts of the German soul.'[105]

The victory at Stalingrad was followed by another remarkable victory at the battle of Kursk in the summer of 1943, 'the largest tank engagement of the war', with 850 Soviet tanks against more than 600 German. One of the most celebrated battleground commanders of the Red Army was K.K. Rokossovskii, a half-Pole and a former tsarist army officer who had been arrested in the 1937 terror, withstood torture in prison, denied all the charges, implicated no one, and was released in 1940 to active service. (He was also a hero in the battles of Moscow and Stalingrad. After Stalingrad, Stalin held Rokossovskii in such high regard that he began to address Rokossovkii formally, as he did Shaposhnikov. After the war he became the Minister of Defence in Poland.)[106] The Kursk battle was won at a cost of 'only' 70,000 lives, and the subsequent offensive to break the German line cost another 183,000. 'But these are still extraordinary figures,' as Richard Overy has noted: 'In two months of fighting the Red Army lost almost as many men as the United States or the British Empire did in the entire war.' The heavy loss of human life was the norm for the Soviet army from the beginning to the end, including the capture of Berlin in 1945. On average 7,950 lives were lost each day in the Great Patriotic War. As ghastly as this figure is, it was not substantially larger than the loss of lives under the Tsar in the Great War from 1914 to 1917, averaging 7,000 casualties a day.[107] Encouraged by the victories, in August 1943 Stalin made what is said to have been his only visit to the front, although he stayed far from it. Upon returning to Moscow, he made a point of writing to Churchill and Roosevelt apologising for not responding sooner because he had been busy visiting the front.

The road to Berlin and the final victory was long, steep and brutal with millions of lives lost along the way.[108] Yet Stalin was already thinking of the post-war settlement of the world. As Alexander I did in the Patriotic War, Stalin wanted the Soviet troops to march all the way to where the war had begun – in this case Berlin, instead of Paris. (In 1947, however, he confessed to the French communist Maurice Thorez that he had dreamt of going all the way to Paris.)[109] According to Sudoplatov, in 1943 Stalin abandoned his original orders to assassinate Hitler, because he feared that if Hitler were killed, his 'Nazi henchmen would be purged by the German military and a separate treaty would be signed with the Allies without Soviet participation'. Soviet intelligence also reported to Stalin that the Vatican, using the German ambassador to Turkey Franz von Papen, was scheming to bring Germany to a separate peace with Britain and the USA: if peace were achieved, von Papen would form an alternative government with the support of Britain and the United States. Stalin was so angry that he ordered von Papen to be killed, but von Papen survived any attempts on his life.[110]

Stalin feared, almost certainly without any grounds, that Churchill was contemplating a separate peace treaty with Germany, even though the Soviet ambassador I.M. Maiskii reported to Stalin that it was unlikely: Britain would not gain anything from the defeat of the Soviet Union (although Maiskii did add that there were forces in Britain in favour of peace with Germany and the defeat of the Soviet Union). Certainly, despite Churchill's promise to open a second front, no second front was opened in the west until 1944. Stalin could not interpret Churchill's inaction in any other light than as a conspiracy against the Soviet Union.[111] During his visit to the Kremlin in 1942, Churchill humbly admitted his past anti-Soviet sentiments: 'You know, I was not friendly to you after the last war. Have you forgiven me?' Stalin avoided a clear answer: 'All that is in the past. It is not for me to forgive. It is for God to forgive.'[112] Perhaps Churchill was naïve. Maybe he did not understand Stalin well. According to Stalin's interpreter, Valentin

Berezhkov, during his visit to Moscow in 1944 Churchill told Stalin that the question of Poland, a Catholic state, could complicate the Allies' relations with the Vatican. Churchill was taken aback by Stalin's response: 'And how many divisions does the Pope have?'.[113] Churchill later wrote that it was to the French Foreign Minister Pierre Laval that Stalin posed the question: in 1935 when, in negotiating a pact of mutual assistance, Laval naïvely asked Stalin, 'Can't you do something to encourage religion and the Catholics in Russia?', Stalin said, 'Oho! The Pope! How many divisions has *he* got?'[114]

Stalin enjoyed disagreeing with Churchill. After the war, at Potsdam, according to the British diplomat William Hayter who attended the 1945 meeting, Churchill denounced Bulgaria, insisting that she should be punished for her conduct during the war. Stalin disagreed, using 'his favourite technique of short sentences interrupted by pauses for interpretation':

> 'I do not', he said, 'wish to give my colleagues a lesson on policy' (Pause). 'But if I may say so I do not think policy should be based on considerations of revenge'. (Pause, during which we wondered what he would say it should be based on; justice, the interests of the masses, the preservation of peace?) 'In my opinion', he went on, 'policy should be based on the calculation of forces'.[115]

With the calculation of forces in mind, Stalin did not trust his old foe from Britain.

As in 1940–1, however, Stalin seems to have fallen into a self-made trap. He had his agents (the 'Cambridge spies') placed in the heart of the British intelligence services. Despite his own warnings, Stalin probably ignored the facts and relied on those intelligence reports that confirmed his own prejudice and suspicion and neglected those that did not.[116] Considering that he maintained a spy ring inside the British Government, Stalin appeared both devious and sincere in August 1942, when he hosted Churchill and the American envoy W. Averell Harriman in the Kremlin: Stalin extolled military spies who were 'good people' dedicated to the service of their country. It was 'false shame' not to speak of them. They should be the 'eyes and ears' for their state. Stalin even gave a lecture on the weakness of British intelligence during the First World War.[117] As Jonathan Haslam has noted, Stalin could not understand 'the basic thrust of British policy' while Britain failed to understand 'the true extent of these dark suspicions' of Stalin. This bode ill for the post-war years.[118]

Stalin, however, enjoyed his (and the Soviet Union's) debut on the world scene as one of the 'Big Three'. It was Churchill, Charles de Gaulle, Franklin D. Roosevelt and a host of other world leaders who trekked to the Soviet Union during the war. Stalin never visited Britain, France or the USA. After the war broke out, Stalin went abroad only twice, to Tehran and Potsdam. The Tehran conference in November 1943 symbolised Stalin's elevated status in the world. Stalin, Churchill and Roosevelt engaged in amicable yet tense negotiations. Even though by nature he remained suspicious of his allies, Stalin appreciated the Grand Alliance in one critical respect: through Lend-Lease it had helped the Red Army to fight effectively. At Tehran Stalin managed to get Britain and the USA to promise to open a second front in the spring of 1944. This time the promise was kept: the massive Operation Overlord, elaborately prepared, was launched successfully in June 1944. At Tehran, Churchill presented a sword of honour to Stalin from His Majesty King George VI. Its blade bore the inscription: 'To the steel-hearted citizens of Stalingrad, a gift from King George VI as a token of the homage of the British People'. Stalin 'held it reverently in his hands for a long moment and then, with tears in his eyes, raised it to his lips and kissed it'.[119] On his trip to Tehran, Stalin paid a visit to the Shah. Stalin must have felt some camaraderie with him, given the historical ties between his homeland Georgia and Persia. The Shah later recalled that Stalin was 'particularly polite and well-mannered', but he turned down Stalin's offer of arms because it came with strings. Stalin, according to Molotov who accompanied him, 'tried to make an ally of the Shah right there, but that didn't work. . . . The English and the Americans . . . kept tabs on him.'[120]

D-Day created a race to Berlin between the Soviet and the British–American forces. It was also a race for the control of Europe. There is little evidence, however, that at that time Stalin was scheming for world domination; he appeared to be more interested in securing the gains of the war, maintaining some kind of modus vivendi with Britain and the USA, and making the Soviet Union more presentable on the world scene and more influential and hence more secure in a dangerous world. In May 1943 Stalin formally abolished the Comintern (In fact, two years previously Stalin told Dimitrov that the Comintern had lost its significance and that the national tasks of the various countries 'stand in the forefront': the communist parties should 'turn into national com[munist] parties with various names – the Workers' Party, the Marxist Party, etc. The name does not matter. What matters is that they put down roots in their own peoples and concentrate on their own proper tasks.')[121] In September 1943 Stalin struck a concordat with the Russian Orthodox Church (which, according to Sudoplatov, was 'fully infiltrated by the NKVD')[122] and reinstated the election of its patriarch. Then in late 1943 Stalin adopted a new national anthem in place of the

Internationale. All these served as good propaganda tools, making the Soviet Union more presentable to both the western borderlands (where Soviet power had been eliminated) and Europe, including the parts of occupied Europe about to be occupied by the Red Army beyond the Soviet borders.

When de Gaulle visited him in December 1944, Stalin was in a jovial mood. He had the morbid habit of terrorising people by asking, 'Haven't you been arrested yet?' or 'Haven't you been shot yet?' Stalin resorted to outright threats, too, saying that if such and such work was not done properly, an execution would result.[123] Stalin was now confident enough about his power to joke about terror. Stalin introduced A.A. Novikov to de Gaulle, saying he was 'the supply director [of the Air Force]. It is his job to bring men and material to the front. He'd better do his best. Otherwise he'll be hanged for it – that's the custom in our country,' and referring to Kaganovich, Stalin said that if the trains did not come on time, 'he'll be shot'. Stalin laughed, adding that 'People call me a monster, but as you see I even make a joke of it. So I'm not so horrible after all.'[124] Perhaps Stalin wanted to present himself in a good light to de Gaulle, but almost certainly he failed. De Gaulle returned home, believing that the Soviet system was despotic, and despaired: 'We'll be stuck with these people for one hundred years!' His interpreter Jean Laloy thought that Stalin was indeed a 'monster'.[125]

By the time of the Tehran conference Stalin was certain of victory in the war. Having overcome the most serious crisis in his life and the life of the country he had built, Stalin appeared to be very confident. After the Tehran conference, according to Molotov, Stalin complained to him that he was 'sickened by the way they were deifying him, and that there were no saints. There was no such man as Stalin was depicted, but if the people created such a Stalin, if they believed in him, it meant this was necessary in the interests of the proletariat and should therefore be supported.'[126] Stalin may not have believed in saints, but he knew that he represented the Soviet state. He understood that he was a Soviet tsar. This was probably why he told Churchill that 'no country needed a monarchy as much as Great Britain, because the Crown was the unifying force throughout the Empire, and no one who was a friend of Britain would do anything to weaken the respect shown to the Monarchy'.[127]

His view of himself and the Soviet state also formed the basis for his views of other state leaders. After the war was over, Stalin said that Churchill was a 'strong and cunning politician' and Roosevelt 'a big statesman' with progressive views. Hitler was an adventurist, but was in no way insane. 'Hitler was a gifted politician. Only a gifted man could unite the German people like that. Whether one likes it or not is another matter. The Soviet Army crossed the German border, entered German soil and reached Berlin, but the German working class did not stage a single action against the existing fascist regime. Could a mad man have united the nation like that?'[128]

Hitler, in turn, admired his arch-enemy in a similar vein. During the war, Hitler intimated that 'Stalin is half beast, half giant': 'He is a beast, but he's a beast on the grand scale'.[129] According to the German Foreign Minister Joachim von Ribbentrop, who had a 'very revealing talk with Hitler' after Germany's defeat at the battle of Stalingrad:

> He [Hitler] spoke, as he often did, of his great admiration for Stalin. In him, he said, one could perceive what one man could mean to a nation. Any other nation would have broken down under the blows of 1941 and 1942. Russia owed her victory to this man, whose iron will and heroism had rallied the people to renewed resistance. Stalin was his great opponent, ideologically and militarily. If he were ever to capture Stalin he would respect him and assign to him the most beautiful palace in Germany. He added, however, that he would never release such an opponent. Stalin had created the Red Army, a grandiose feat. He was undeniably a historic personality of very great stature.[130]

Stalin saw a reflection of himself in Hitler and vice versa.

Notes

[1] Quoted in Gustav Hilger and Alfred G. Meyer, *The Incompatible Allies: A Memoir-History of German-Soviet Relations, 1918–1941* (New York, 1953), 305.

[2] *The Diary of Georgi Dimitrov, 1933–1949* (New Haven, Conn., 2003), 65.

[3] For more detailed information on the Trotskii family, see *Izvestiia TsK KPSS*, 1990, no. 2, 112–13, and Valery Bronstein, 'Stalin and Trotsky's Relatives in Russia', in Terry Brotherstone and Paul Dukes (eds), *The Trotsky Reappraisal* (Edinburgh, 1992).

[4] Machiavelli, *The Discourses*, book three, ch. III. Lars Lih's comments have led me to consider this point. Jörg Baberowski, *Der rote Terror: Die Geschichte des Stalinismus* (Munich, 2003), 15, 179, 181, 205 attributes the style of Stalin's terror to the culture of 'Trans-Caucasian' ('non-European') robber gangs.

[5] Pavel Sudoplatov and Anatoli Sudoplatov, *Special Tasks* (Boston, Mass., 1994), 67.

[6] *The Stalin–Kaganovich Correspondence*, 350.

[7] For *The Short Course* as Stalin's autobiography, see Tucker, *Stalin in Power*, 533.

[8] RGASPI, f. 17, op. 163, d. 1217, ll. 51–2. This speech was published in *Voprosy istorii*, 2003, no. 4, 21. See also Aleksandr Vatlin, 'Iosif Stalin auf den Weg zur absoluten Macht: Neue Dokumente aus Moskauer Archiven', *Forum für osteuropäische Ideen- und Zeitgeschichte*, 4:2 (2000), 105.

9RGASPI, f. 588, op. 2, d. 155, l. 107.

10Pollock, 49.

11 *The Diary of Georgi Dimitrov*, 70.

12Ibid., 89.

13The original literally means 'Freedom and the hungry existence of people are incompatible.' Nevezhin, 152, 161.

14Stephen Kotkin, *Magnetic Mountain: Stalinism as a Civilization* (Berkeley, Calif., 1997).

15Volkogonov, 279.

16Sheila Fitzpatrick, 'Stalin and the Making of a New Elite, 1928–1939', *Slavic Review*, 38:3 (September 1979).

17RGASPI, f. 17, op. 163, d. '1217, l. 50. *Voprosy istorii*, 2003, no. 4, 20.

18Quoted in Sebag Montefiore, 4. See also *Novoe vremia*, 2003, no. 11, 29 (Iurii Bogomolov).

19Evgenii Gromov, *Stalin: iskusstvo i vlast'* (Moscow, 2003), 209. See also Catriona Kelly, *Comrade Pavlik: The Rise and Fall of a Soviet Boy Hero* (London, 2005), 15, 151.

20Vladimir Loginov, *Teni Stalina* (Moscow, 2000), 25.

21David Brandenberger and A.M. Dubrovsky, ' "The People Need a Tsar": The Emergence of National Bolshevism as Stalinist Ideology, 1931–1941,' *Europe–Asia Studies*, 50:5 (July 1998).

22RGASPI, f. 629, op. 1, d. 54, l. 29. See also *Slovo tovarishchu Stalinu*, 474.

23Zhdanov, *Vzgliad v proshloe: vospominaniia ochevidtsa* (Rostov on the Don, 2004), 172.

24See essays in Balázs Apor, Jan C. Behrends, Polly Jones and E.A. Rees (eds.), *The Leader Cult in Communist Dictatorships* (New York, 2004), Frank J. Miller, *Folklore for Stalin: Russian Folklore and Pseudofolklore of the Stalin Era* (Armonk, New York, 1990). See also Jeffrey Brooks, *Thank You, Comrade Stalin!: Soviet Public Culture from Revolution to Cold War* (Princeton, NJ, 2001) and David L. Hoffmann, *Stalinist Values: The Cultural Norms of Soviet Modernity, 1917–1941* (Ithaca, New York, 2003).

25Stalin, *Sochineniia*, 1 (14):254.

26RGASPI, f. 558, op. 11, d. 28 (13 October 1941 memorandum).

27V.K. Romanovskii, 'Nikolai Vasil'evich Ustrialov', *Otechestvennaia istoriia*, 2002, no. 4.

28 *Istoricheskii arkhiv*, 1994, no. 5, 13.

29Note of Churchill's interpreter Major A.H. Birse, Public Records Office, Prem. 3/7612, 35–7, reproduced in O.A. Rzheshevskii, 'Operatsiia "Braslet" ', *Istoricheskaia nauka na rubezhe vekov* (Moscow, 2001), 60.

30For a recent discussion of the 1938–9 crisis based on new Russian and Romanian archival documents, see Hugh Ragsdale, *The Soviets, the Munich Crisis, and the Coming of World War II* (Cambridge, 2004).

31R.W. Davies and et al. (eds), *The Economic Transformation of the Soviet Union, 1913–1945* (Cambridge, 1994), 299.

32 *Molotov Remembers*, 22.

33Joachim C. Fest, *Hitler* (London, 1974), 742.

34 *Molotov Remembers*, 192.

[35] William J. Chase, *Enemies within the Gates?: The Comintern and the Stalinist Repression, 1934–1939* (New Haven, Conn., 2001), 286–89.

[36] *The Ribbentrop Memoirs* (London, 1954), 113, 114.

[37] John Scott, *Behind the Urals* (Cambridge, Mass., 1942), 264.

[38] Alexander Werth, *Russia at War, 1941–1945* (New York, 1984), 47.

[39] *Molotov Remembers*, 12.

[40] Adam B. Ulam, *Expansion and Coexistence: Soviet Foreign Policy, 1917–1973* (New York, 1974), 277.

[41] *Tak govoril Kaganovich*, 90.

[42] Hilger and Meyer, *The Incompatible Allies*, 304.

[43] Lev Bezymenskii, 'Sekretnyi pakt s Gitlerom pisal lichno Stalin', *Novoe vremia*, 1998, no 1, 31.

[44] *The Diary of Georgi Dimitrov*, 115.

[45] *Khrushchev Remembers*, 128.

[46] *The Diary of Georgi Dimitrov*, 116.

[47] *Lituanus*, 14:2 (Summer 1968), 92, 34:2 (Summer 1989), 10, 14, and Jonathan Haslam, 'Soviet Foreign Policy, 1939–1941: Isolation and Expansion', *Soviet Union/Union Soviétique*, 18:1–3 (1991), 111. Ignacy Mościcki (1867–1947), Edward Rydz-Śmigły (1886–1941) and Józef Bek (1894–1944) were all prominent statesmen in inter-war Poland. Stalin is said to have told the Lithuanians: 'Our troops will help you put down a communist insurrection should one occur in Lithuania'! This remark is so unlikely that it is probably apocryphal.

[48] Pons, 178.

[49] *The Diary of Georgi Dimitrov*, 116, 121.

[50] Ibid., 120.

[51] *Stalin and the Soviet–Finnish War, 1939–1940* (London, 2002), 263–4.

[52] *Khrushchev Remembers*, 154, 156.

[53] Ibid., 180, and *The Diary of Georgi Dimitrov*, 128.

[54] *The Diary of Georgi Dimitrov*, 128.

[55] *Stalin and the Soviet–Finnish War*, 192.

[56] Ibid., 267–74.

[57] *Khrushchev Remembers*, 133, 166.

[58] *The Diary of Georgi Dimitrov*, 133–4.

[59] 'Peregovory V.M. Molotova v Berline v noiabre 1940 goda', *Voenno-istoricheskii zhurnal*, 1992, nos. 6–7.

[60] Robert C. Tucker, *Stalin in Power: The Revolution from Above* (New York, 1990), 615.

[61] N.V. Novikov, *Vospominannia diplomata. Zapiski o 1938–1947 gg.* (Moscow, 1989), 79.

[62] Sudoplatov and Sudoplatov, 121.

[63] For this controversy provoked by Viktor Suvorov, see Gabriel Gorodetsky, *Grand Delusion: Stalin and the German Invasion of Russia* (New Haven, Conn., 1999).

[64] *Istoricheskii arkhiv*, 1995, no. 2, 30.

[65] *Voenno-istoricheskii zhurnal*, 1995, no. 3, 41 and Gorodetsky, 209–10.

[66] *Izvestiia TsK KPSS*, 1990, no. 4, 221 (emphasis Stalin's). Some scholars claim that Stalin was deceived by Hitler's private assurances that Germany would not

attack. See, for example, David E. Murphy, *What Stalin Knew: The Enigma of Barbarossa* (New Haven, Conn., 2005), ch. 18.

[67] John Erickson, *The Road to Stalingrad* (London, 1985), 168–9.

[68] Mikoian, 388–9.

[69] Ibid., 390.

[70] Radzinsky, 458 and *Khrushchev Remembers: The Glasnost Tapes* (Boston, Mass., 1990), 101. See also *Molotov Remembers*, 39, which uses 'We blew it.' For other variations, see Sebag Montefiore, 330–1.

[71] Seweryn Bialer (ed.), *Stalin and His Generals* (New York, 1969), 209.

[72] *Molotov Remembers*, 22.

[73] Alexander Orlov, *Handbook of Intelligence and Guerrilla Warfare* (Ann Arbor, Mich., 1963), 10.

[74] Mikoian, 391.

[75] Stalin, *Sochineniia*, 2 (15):1–10.

[76] Werth, 165–6.

[77] *Khrushchev Remembers*, 169.

[78] Ibid., 168.

[79] John Barber, 'Popular Reactions in Moscow to the German Invasion of June 22, 1941', *Soviet Union/Union Soviétique*, 18:1–3 (1991).

[80] For the home front in general, see John Barber and Mark Harrison, *The Soviet Home Front, 1941–1945* (London, 1991).

[81] Mikoian, 359–60.

[82] Kuromiya, *Freedom and Terror in the Donbas*, 259–62.

[83] For the Holocaust in the Soviet Union, see, for example, Lucjan Dobroszycki and Jeffrey S. Gurock (eds), *The Holocaust in the Soviet Union* (Armonk, New York, 1993). For the barbarisation of the eastern front, see Omer Bartov, *The Eastern Front, 1941–45: German Troops and the Barbarisation of Warfare* (Basingstoke, 1985).

[84] Eugenia Ginzburg, *Within the Whirlwind* (New York, 1981), 27.

[85] Kuromiya, *Freedom and Terror in the Donbas*, 261.

[86] K.M. Simonov, *Glazami cheloveka moego pokoleniia* (Moscow, 1988), 398.

[87] *Voenno-istoricheskii zhurnal*, 1995, no. 3, 44; Harold Shukman (ed.), *Stalin's Generals* (New York, 1993), 350–1; and Volkogonov, 413.

[88] Carl Boyd, *Hitler's Japanese Confidant: General Ōshima Hiroshi and Magic Intelligence, 1941–1945* (Lawrence, Kan., 1993), ch. 7.

[89] Shukman (ed.), 351.

[90] Mgeladze, 198 (emphasis added). Iakov was killed in German captivity, but his relatives believe that he died at the front. See Galina Dzhugashvili-Stalina, *Vnuchka vozhdia* (Moscow, 2003).

[91] Alliluyeva, *Only One Year*, 370.

[92] Shukman (ed.), 229.

[93] *Otechestvennaia istoriia*, 2003, no. 3, 159 and Bialer (ed.), 296.

[94] Werth, 246, 249–50.

[95] Volkogonov, 435–6.

[96] *Voenno-istoricheskii zhurnal*, 1995, no. 3, 45.

[97] Werth, 591.

[98] Mikoian, 563.

[99] Richard Overy, *Russia's War* (London, 1997), 117.

[100] Volkogonov, 419.

[101] See his recollections in *Politicheskoe obrazovanie*, 1988, no. 9, 70–1.

[102] Overy, 169.

[103] Antony Beevor, *Stalingrad* (London, 1998).

[104] *New Yorker*, 1 February 1993, 58 (Timothy W. Ryback).

[105] Ibid., 60, citing an article from the German national weekly *Stern*.

[106] *Molotov Remembers*, 295. When Stalin summoned Rokossovkii at the beginning of the war, Stalin asked him, 'I haven't seen you lately. Where did you disappear?' Rokossovskii replied, 'I was arrested, Comrade Stalin, I sat in gaol.' Stalin said, 'So you found the time to sit,' and went on to discuss the military situation at the front (*Sovershenno sekretnno*, 2003, no. 3, 14.) Rokossovskii was not afraid of contradicting Stalin in military decision-making, and Stalin accepted his authority. (Bialer [ed.], 461.) Stalin once asked him whether they 'beat him up there'. 'They did, Comrade Stalin,' to which Stalin replied: 'We still have a lot of yes-men in our country.' *Molotov Remembers*, 295–6.

[107] Overy, 208, 212, 214–15.

[108] John Erickson, *The Road to Berlin* (London, 1983).

[109] *Istoricheskii arkhiv*, 1996, no. 1, 13.

[110] Sudoplatov and Sudoplatov, 116–7. Von Papen was acquitted at the Nuremberg trial. There may have been an attempt on Stalin's life by German agents in 1944, but of course, if it existed, it did not succeed. *Sluzhba bezopasnosti*, 1993, no. 2, 13–23, and *Lubianka 2* (Moscow, 1999), 253–6.

[111] O.A. Rzheshevskii, *Stalin i Cherchill'* (Moscow, 2004), 376–7.

[112] W. Averell Harriman and Elie Abel, *Special Envoy to Churchill and Stalin* (New York, 1975), 161.

[113] V.M. Berezhkov, *At Stalin's Side* (N.Y., 1994), 310.

[114] Winston S. Churchill, *The Gathering of Storm* (Boston, Mass., 1948), 135. Churchill's account is right: see Hubert Cole, *Laval: A Biography* (New York, 1963), 61. Stalin is said to have asked the same question of the US Presidents Roosevelt at Yalta and Truman at Potsdam. For Truman's testimony, see his 1948 address in the *New York Times*, 14 September 1948, 24.

[115] William Hayter, *The Kremlin and the Embassy* (New York, 1966), 28.

[116] For Stalin and his foreign intelligence, see Christopher Andrew and Julie Elkner, 'Stalin and Foreign Intelligence,' in Harold Shukman (ed.) *Redefining Stalinism* (London, 2003).

[117] Nevezhin, 306. At the time, however, Stalin probably still suspected that the Cambridge spies were British double agents.

[118] Jonathan Haslam, 'Stalin's Fears of a Separate Peace, 1942', *Intelligence and National Security*, 8:4 (October 1993).

[119] Sebag Montefiore, 414.

[120] Mohammed Reza Pahlavi, *Mission for My Country* (London, 1961), 80, and *Molotov Remembers*, 50.

[121] *The Diary of Georgi Dimitrov*, 155–6.

[122] Sudoplatov and Sudoplatov, 191.

[123] See I.I. Nosenko in *Sovershenno sekretno*, 2003, no. 3, 14, and N.K. Baibakov, *Ot Stalina do Iel'tsina* (Moscow, 1998), 64.

[124] Charles de Gaulle, *Salvation: 1944–1946* (New York, 1960), 84, and Nevezhin, 420, 423.

125 Jean Laloy, 'A Moscou: Entre Staline et de Gaulle', *Revue des Études Slaves*, 54:1–2 (1982), 151, 152.

126 *Molotov Remembers*, 302.

127 Winston S. Churchill, *Triumph and Tragedy* (Cambridge, Mass., 1953), 634.

128 Mgeladze, 137.

129 *Hitler's Table Talk, 1941–44: His Private Conversations* (London, 1973), 624, 657.

130 *The Ribbentrop Memoirs*, 169–70.

Chapter 7

Twilight of the God

Stalin won the war, beating Hitler who, faced with capture, killed himself.[1] Both Stalin the leader and Stalin the Soviet system had survived the ordeal of war. Humbled by his grave mistakes at the beginning of the war but immensely proud of his leadership at the end, Stalin regarded the victory as an affirmation of his rule. Stalin was 66 years old when the war ended, and the post-war years must have been a sort of epilogue for him; he was exhausted and began to feel his own mortality. He hinted that he would like to retire but, like all dictators, he in fact could not or did not really want to retire, because he neither wanted to relinquish his power nor trusted other people. He enjoyed the international status he and his system had achieved through the war, but just when his power seemed unshakable, it was being undermined by a spontaneous de-Stalinisation. Looking forward, he saw so many problems, both domestic and international, that he was compelled to carry on. Deified to an overwhelming extent, he was still irritable, capricious, and extraordinarily suspicious. His last years proved to be a dark time in the Soviet Union, and his death in 1953 marked the end of an extraordinary era and the Soviet 'God'.

Victory

Stalin had aged greatly during the war, becoming increasingly conscious of his personal mortality. Facing victory in the war, Stalin said to de Gaulle in December 1944, 'After all it is only death who [sic] wins,' even pitying Hitler, 'a poor wretch who won't escape from this one'. De Gaulle invited Stalin to Paris, 'Will you come to see us in Paris?' but Stalin said, 'How can I? I'm an old man. I'm going to die soon.'[2] Numerous rumours about the state of his health circulated in Moscow from 1945 onwards. Stalin's daughter Svetlana noted, probably incorrectly, that 'When the war was over, he [Stalin] fell apart and became ill.

They thought he would die. But it was kept a state secret – they didn't even tell me at the time. I had no idea what was wrong'.[3] After the war, Stalin cursed his old age, complaining that the war had made his hair greyer and that 'no one has power over time'.[4] In 1946 Stalin told the Yugoslavs who visited him that he would not live long and that physiological laws could not be repealed. Having said so, however, Stalin reassured them that he still had his strength.[5] In December 1946 he said, 'Stalin is old. Stalin will die soon.'[6] He lived for more than six years after that. By 1948, however, the Yugoslav communist Milovan Djilas noticed a sharp decline in Stalin's intellect: 'It was incomprehensible how much he had changed in two or three years. When I had last seen him in 1945, he was still lively, quick-witted, and had a pointed sense of humour. But that was during the war, and it had been, it would seem, Stalin's last effort and limit. . . . In one thing, though, he was still the Stalin of old: stubborn, sharp, suspicious whenever anyone disagreed with him.'[7]

Molotov remarked that after the war Stalin wanted to retire. According to Kaganovich, Stalin said that people should retire from direct leadership after they reached 70 years of age. Stalin would say, 'Let Viacheslav [Molotov] go to work now. He is younger.' Yet, true to form, Stalin did not entirely trust Molotov. Stalin reportedly said to Molotov just after the war, 'What will become of you without me if there is a war? You take no interest in military affairs. No one takes such an interest or knows military affairs. What will become of you? The imperialists will strangle you.'[8] Svetlana recalled that having grown old, her father 'wanted peace and quiet', or rather 'he didn't know himself just what it was he wanted'.[9] His entire life had been politics without which he could not live. Victory in the war did not mean the end of politics: it created a new, complex political situation. Stalin felt compelled to work.

The war ended, just as it had begun, with enormous human casualties. Many Red Army soldiers marched on Berlin in American boots and American lorries (acquired through Lend-Lease), but the race to capture Berlin was not just with the American and British forces but also among the Soviet commanders (Zhukov and Konev) and it took an unnecessarily large toll. The Berlin offensive from 10 April to 8 May 1945 cost more than 350,000 Soviet soldiers, about 12,500 deaths a day. About 125,000 Berliners are believed to have died in the siege. Along the way to Berlin and during the Soviet occupation of part of Germany and other countries, the behaviour of the Red Army did not always endear it to the local population. Looting and rape by Red Army soldiers were reported everywhere.[10] Such was the case, too, when the Red

Army advanced on Manchuria (Manzhou) in August 1945. As Svetlana testified, Stalin 'officially allowed the armed forces to loot the conquered countries of Europe': ' "We'll show them how to gut people!" he would say malevolently of the Germans.'[11] To Yugoslav communists concerned about the 'political difficulties' created by the conduct of Red Army soldiers there, Stalin replied dismissively:

> Yes, you have, of course, read Dostoevsky? Do you see what a complicated thing is man's soul, man's psyche? Well then, imagine a man who has fought from Stalingrad to Belgrade – over thousands of kilometers of his own devastated land, across the dead bodies of his comrades and dearest ones! How can such a man react normally? And what is so awful in his having fun with a woman, after such horrors? . . . The Red Army is not ideal. The important thing is that it fights Germans – and it is fighting them well, while the rest doesn't matter. . . . We lecture our soldiers too much; let them have some initiative![12]

To another Yugoslav visitor, Andrija Hebrang, Stalin angrily attacked Djilas's remark that the 'moral–political make-up' of the Soviet officers was lower than that of the English officers. He admitted, however, that there were some shameful incidents and promised to shoot those responsible.[13]

Exactly how many were killed in the war is difficult to establish. It appears that 8.6 million Soviet soldiers and 17 million civilians died from all causes. These figures are approximate and the margin for error may amount to one or two million. The number of dead may include those killed by the Soviet regime. Of 'the 34.5 million men and women mobilized an incredible 84 per cent were killed, wounded or captured'.[14] James Millar has estimated that 'the economic cost of the war was equal to, and possibly even somewhat greater than, the total wealth created during the industrialization drive of the 1930s'. Through all these losses, Stalin remained in power, whereas Roosevelt died before the war ended and Churchill failed to be re-elected after the victory. Millar has appropriately noted that no other nation or state in modern times 'has withstood such terrible costs in war and survived intact as a political and economic system'.[15]

For all this, Stalin hoped with reason that victory had justified his pre-war policies of industrialisation and collectivisation. During the war, even some of the die-hard opponents of Stalin's rapid industrialisation came to appreciate its significance: 'What would we have done without our *pyatiletki* [Five-Year Plans] against a Germany that is fighting us with all the industry of western Europe?' One Ukrainian academician was secretly recorded as saying, 'I think of Stalin and kneel before his intellect.'[16] Soon after the victory, on 24 May 1945, Stalin frankly made clear to his military commanders that the Soviet Government had made 'many mistakes', but that even in the most desperate times of 1941–2 the Russian people ('the most remarkable of all the nations of the Soviet Union') did not tell the Government to go, but believed in it and kept fighting to defeat Germany. Stalin thanked the Russian people for their trust, and in February 1946 went further, declaring that 'our victory means above all that our social system has won and that the Soviet social system has successfully withstood the test of the fire of war and demonstrated its full viability'.[17] Indeed, the peasant question and the food-supply problems that had doomed the tsarist government and the Provisional Government during the First World War and nearly destroyed the Soviet state during the Civil War did not undermine the Soviet Government this time. During the war, the whole nation lived in utter poverty, but no significant disturbances threatened the nation. Whereas the Soviet Government procured some 15 million tons of grain in 1918–21 with force, it managed to procure as many as 70 million tons in 1941–45 without outright force.[18] (The collective farm system facilitated grain collection, which is why the German occupiers maintained the 'second serfdom' largely intact.) Molotov therefore contended that 'our success in collectivization was more significant than victory in World War II. If we had not carried it through, we would not have won the war'.[19] It is interesting to note that Stalin believed that Churchill, the man who led Britain to victory, would certainly be re-elected. Churchill lost the post-victory election, however, and Molotov later confessed that 'to this day [in 1972] I cannot understand how he lost the election in 1945! I need to know English life better.'[20]

Even in the area of military matters, according to some observers, Stalin's brutal terror worked to his advantage in the end. Seweryn Bialer, for example, emphasised this point: 'The success of Hitler's political designs depended to a large extent on his ability to subordinate the military establishment to his will. Stalin started the war with an army which was his creation from the lowest command levels to the highest during the years of the Great Purge and after; never was his effective control over Red Army commanders in doubt'. Holding his generals in contempt, Hitler relied on 'his own initiative and judgment concerning military operations', whereas Stalin 'never considered the conception and planning of military operations his paramount strength, his major interest, or the measure of his absolute authority. He was more willing to listen to his generals, more willing to correct his errors (while, of course, refusing to acknowledge them).'[21] In other words, according to this reasoning, Stalin successfully solved the problem of 'Red' versus 'expert' in the military sphere by creating military experts from politically reliable people. Indeed, Stalin's 24 May 1945 speech admitting his own mistakes was received emotionally and approvingly by the military commanders present, including Sudoplatov who later recalled: 'it seemed to me that he [Stalin] looked at us young generals and admirals as the generation he had raised, his children and his heirs'.[22]

Where Stalin succeeded, Hitler failed. Towards the end of the war when he knew he had lost to Stalin, Hitler came to regret not having brought up his own elite. It would have taken twenty years for him to 'bring his new elite to maturity. Instead the war came too soon': 'We lacked men molded in the shape of our ideal. . . . Our generals and diplomats, with a few, rare exceptions, are men of another age, and their methods of waging war and conducting our foreign policy also belong to an age that is passed.'[23]

Stalin was confident enough to make jokes about his terror, as he did with de Gaulle, but his jokes about terror are grim and 'usually no one laughed'. An example was 'about a Chekist and a professor who lived in the same apartment [block]. One day the professor, irritated by his neighbor's ignorance, exclaimed, "Oh, you! You don't even know who wrote *Yevgeny Onegin*!" [Aleksandr Pushkin did.] The Chekist felt insulted (because he really did not know). Soon afterward he arrested the professor, boasting to his friends: "I got him to confess it! *He was the author!*" '[24] Another concerned Stalin's pipe. Stalin complains that he has lost his favourite pipe, saying that he will give a handsome reward to whoever finds it. A few days later Beriia calls Stalin, telling him that his pipe has been found. Stalin replies that he has found his pipe himself under the sofa. Beriia exclaims, 'It can't be! Three people have already confessed to stealing it!'[25]

Characteristically, Stalin used the threat of terror for communication. During the war, Nikolai Baibakov, then a 31 year-old Deputy People's Commissar for the Petroleum Industry, was told by Stalin that if he surrendered even a ton of oil to the advancing Germans in the northern Caucasus, he would be shot, but then again if he destroyed the oil wells prematurely, leaving the Red Army without oil, then he would be shot all the same. Stalin's threat was not a joke, and Baibakov was very likely horrified. As terrible as it was, the threat was almost certainly not meant to be taken literally – it was Stalin's way of communicating the gravity of the task to Baibakov.[26] Stalin never stopped using terror, but in cases like this he appeared to use it metaphorically because now he could afford to do so. In 1937–8 he had summarily killed hundreds of thousands of people without so much as a threat.

Stalin was confident, but he was also well aware of new problems brought on by the war. War may unite people against a common enemy, but victory often divides them. Just as overcoming the famine crisis of 1932–3 intensified the already conflicting attitudes towards Stalin, the Soviet victory in the war appeared to articulate two distinct attitudes towards him: approval of and even admiration for Stalin who as the leader had led the country to victory against fearful odds; and disapproval and even rejection of Stalin who as the leader had committed grave mistakes and sacrificed untold numbers of human lives. To continue to rule the Soviet Union, Stalin had to contain the latter, but this was no easy task.

After the Red Army liberated the occupied territory of the former Soviet Union, Soviet order had to be restored there. Suspected collaborators were identified and isolated or liquidated. Yet in many parts, particularly in western Ukraine, civil war between nationalists and Soviet military forces continued into the 1950s. As harsh as the German occupation had been, in one respect it was more lenient than the atheist Soviet system: the churches were allowed to operate freely. In fact, the Nazi policy, presented as a policy of 'God against the Devil', probably worked against the occupiers, because many churches became hotbeds of resistance. Religious revival posed a worrisome problem to the returning Soviet power. In the western borderlands in particular, where the Greek Catholic (the Uniate) and other churches were strong, the Soviet Government faced even more obstacles to controlling the population. The 1943 concordat with the Russian Orthodox Church (which the Soviet secret police had thoroughly infiltrated) was a measure in part directed at re-establishing and consolidating Soviet power in those borderlands.[27] In 1946 Stalin disbanded the Greek Catholic (Uniate) Church.

As the Soviet troops repelled the German forces, marching beyond the borders of the Soviet Union, Stalin must have wondered what would happen when these soldiers, until then almost completely shielded from the outside world but now exposed to the materially richer and politically heterogeneous outside world, returned to the Soviet Union. Stalin was an avid reader of history. Even during the intense crises of the war, he read history books in his spare time. He knew what had happened to those who marched on Paris in the war against Napoleon: they acquired critical attitudes towards autocracy and eventually rebelled against it (Decembrists). Tens of millions of people lived under German occupation and millions more lived as POWs or as forced labourers in the Reich. To contain the 'contamination' of these people by alien cultures and ideas was a Herculean task. Fear of 'Decembrism' began to emerge as early as 1942.[28]

As a matter of fact, the problems ran even deeper. 'This [1941-2] was a period of *spontaneous de-Stalinization*. We were in full crisis. Stalin's totalitarian system had fallen apart in the face of the invasion and occupation. People were suddenly forced to make their own decisions, to take responsibility for themselves. Events pressed us into becoming truly independent human beings'.[29] Even those who lived through the dreadful siege of Leningrad testify that they felt freer than ever before, freer of the grips of Moscow's terror. The poetess Ol'ga Berggol'ts even suggested paradoxically that the siege was a liberation: 'In mud, in darkness, in hunger, in grief / Where death, like a shadow, dragged at our heels / We were so happy, / We breathed such stormy freedom, / That our grandchildren might envy us'. Similarly, Boris Pasternak suggested in his famous novel *Doctor Zhivago* (1965) that 'when the war broke out, its real horrors, its real dangers, its menace of a real death were a blessing compared with the inhuman reign of the lie, and they brought relief because they broke the spell of the dead letter'.[30] Moreover, Mikoian, who worked closely with Stalin before and during the war, also noted that war had exerted a positive impact on the country: the war forced Stalin's deputies to work in close cooperation and with the trust of Stalin. Mikoian believed that 'a process of democratisation' would begin. The war became a 'school' for those who came in contact with Western Europe: they became 'different human beings', their experiences – an impediment to tyranny.[31] Even Svetlana noted that it was during the war that her 'first stirrings of doubt' about her father emerged (when in 'the eyes of everyone around me my father's name was linked with the will to win the war, with the hope of victory and an end to the war').[32]

As it happened, a new Decembrist movement or organisation did not emerge, yet Stalin was not content. Marshal Zhukov, for example, had become as much an icon of victory as Stalin. Popular expectations for change were high: 'Now, it's time to live.' Sentiments like this were widespread: '[A]fter the demobilization of the Red Army, our country will be led by Marshall Zhukov, and Stalin will retire. Zhukov will disband the collective farms, and the people will live as individuals.' Zhukov's prestige among the military and his popularity among the Soviet population was such that Stalin appeared to be fearful and envious. Stalin recalled Zhukov from Berlin to Moscow in March 1946, had a group of military leaders arrested, and had one of them write a denunciation of Zhukov to the effect that Zhukov was power-hungry, that he had made anti-Stalin remarks and that Zhukov was a Bona-partist. (Zhukov, however, took offence at this last remark: 'Napoleon? Napoleon lost [his] war, but I have won mine!') In June 1946 Stalin convened the Supreme Military Council attended by all members of the Politburo, marshals and generals. Although Stalin had Molotov and others attack Zhukov, the marshals defended him. Konev, in particular, whom Zhukov had rescued in 1941 from Stalin's wrath, spoke up and categorically denied the charges against Zhukov. 'When Stalin retorted with charges of Zhukov's alleged usurpation of war glory, Konev re-sponded: "Well, it's a trifle".' Konev later recalled this episode, explain-ing his courage as a desire to prevent a repeat of 1937 and as a result of their becoming more courageous during the war. The commanders now confronted Stalin. It was a remarkable change from 1937 and Stalin had to accept the change. Reminding Zhukov of the modesty of the great Russian military leaders such as Suvorov and Kutuzov, 'Stalin scolded Zhukov for his alleged lack of modesty and simply demoted him.'[33]

The spectre of Decembrism died hard all the same: new, critical thinking emerged among the military and in society in general. The Soviet people were hungry. War veterans sang clandestinely:

Shed my blood
For people's causes,
And returned victorious
But hungry again.

Another song challenged Stalin:

Generalissimo [Stalin],
You are dear to us,
When, instead of medals,
Will you give us crusts of bread?

Stalin would not have wanted to hear the following one:

I was in Germany –
Saw everything there!
I wish we the victors
Could live like them![34]

The 1946–7 famine that struck Ukraine had a particularly gloomy im-pact on the population: people wondered why their mighty country, which had beaten Germany, could not even feed its own population. Stalin did not want to acknowledge this crisis, saying to Khrushchev who was in charge of Ukraine at the time, 'You're being soft-bellied! They're [i.e., the Ukrainians are] deceiving you. They're counting on being able to appeal to your sentimentality when they report things like that. They're trying to force you to give them all your reserves.' All the same, unlike in 1932–3, Stalin accepted foreign aid and extended substantial (albeit not enough) help to Ukraine: 'The Ukraine is being ruined, which could be a disaster for our whole country.'[35] Stalin had changed, and so had others. People became more vocal and critical. The case of several military commanders, G.I. Kulik, F.T. Rybal'chenko and V.N. Gordov, is instructive. According to secretly tapped conversations, they questioned why Stalin, travelling by train to the south, could not see that everyone was unhappy. (Probably Stalin saw it, but refused to admit it.) They even noted that 'all collective farmers hate Stalin and are waiting for his end' and that if the collective farms were disbanded, everything would be fine – 'Let people live, they have the right to live'. Whether they actually made these remarks or whether their critical remarks were embellished by the prosecutors is not known. They were executed in any case.[36]

Those Soviet citizens repatriated from abroad (former POWs and *Ostarbeiter* or forced labourers) were scrutinised upon re-entry for ideological contamination and the crime of working for foreign intelligence. Their correspondence was intercepted and monitored by the police for the same reason. The police found critical attitudes everywhere: 'When I entered Soviet territory, I felt as if I had fallen into a dirty hole,' 'I regret very much having left [Germany],' 'In Germany there are no collective farms. The Germans live better. Were it not for collective farms here, there would be more grain', 'In foreign countries elections have long been held. There is real democracy, because several parties freely propose their candidates. Our elections won't be democratic, because there is only one party' and the like.[37] One cannot take these remarks at face value, because the police often fabricated them. It is also the case, however, that the police reported such remarks as a matter of fact, not necessarily for the purpose of making arrests. What is noteworthy is that before the war even those with the slightest connection to foreign countries were imprisoned or even executed, whereas after the war the vast majority of those who returned from abroad survived (including even those who took up arms against the Soviet state, such as the 'Vlasovites').[38]

It is true that war against the nationalists in the western borderlands, in western Ukraine in particular, was executed brutally and relentlessly.[39] More than 100,000 Ukrainians are believed to have been killed; numerous people were arrested and executed or exiled. Several minority ethnic groups (such as the Chechens and Crimean Tatars) were deported wholesale for the alleged collaboration of some of their members with the German forces.[40] Tellingly, the population of the labour camps increased after the war with, among others, the influx of nationalists from the western borderlands. In 1950, the peak year, the Gulag population exceeded 2.5 million. Draconian labour laws and other harsh legislation criminalised a vast section of the population. 'From 1946 to 1952, approximately 14 million people were convicted in the ordinary Soviet courts; at least 5.9 million of them were subjected to custodial sentences.'[41] However, one reason why the Gulag population increased is that people were put in camps instead of being executed outright.

The camps and the places of exile themselves bred critical thinking because those with suspect ideas, such as foreigners (Germans, Poles, Japanese, Italians and others) and Ukrainian and other nationalists mixed, with ordinary Soviet citizens in the camps. Towards the end of Stalin's life, the camps became increasingly unruly with hunger strikes and uprisings.[42]

Stalin enforced a personal rule on the country, and faced no apparent challenger to his power. Like the tsars or kings, Stalin used his power as he saw fit. Even at the top of the hierarchy, there was little formal procedure any more. Stalin bullied, abused and even terrorised his most trusted aide Molotov, and Molotov always repented of his 'mistakes', saying, 'the party's [i.e. Stalin's] trust is something that I value more than life itself'.[43] Khrushchev described Stalin's post-war political style: 'At that point in Stalin's life, there were no meetings of any kind in the real sense of the word, with a secretary, a protocol, proposals, exchange of ideas, formal decisions. There was none of it. Stalin behaved like Almighty God with a host of angels and archangels. He might listen to us, but the main thing was that he spoke and we listened.'[44] Stalin tolerated no sign of disloyalty or dishonesty towards him or usurpation of his power. Thus, when he began to question the loyalty of the Soviet Jews, he demanded evidence of loyalty from his loyal follower Molotov: Molotov was forced to divorce his beloved Jewish wife Polina Zhemchuzhina who was arrested. (He mustered enough courage, however, to abstain from the vote of the Politburo to expel his wife from the party, but three weeks later he changed his mind, admitted his mistake and supported the Politburo decision!)[45] When some Leningrad leaders, emboldened by their sense of entitlement stemming from their heroic battle during the war, exhibited a small degree of independence, Stalin cracked down on them. In 1949–51 a large number of Leningraders were arrested, and six of the top leaders (including N.A. Voznesenskii, a Politburo member regarded as the patron of Leningraders) were executed.[46]

As if to purify the souls of the Soviet citizens contaminated by alien culture during and after the war and to enforce Soviet ideology, Stalin began to attack Soviet intellectuals and cultural figures. (This campaign, whose figurehead was Zhdanov, came to be called *Zhdanovshchina*, the era of Zhdanov.)[47] In 1947 Stalin praised Ivan the Terrible for being a 'national tsar' who did not allow foreign influence into Russia, comparing him favourably with the Tsar Peter I ('Peter the Great') who opened the gate to Europe and let too many foreigners in, Germanising Russia. Catherine the Great had made the same mistake. The courts of Alexander I and Nicholas I, Stalin said, were not Russian but German.[48]

The poet Anna Akhmatova and the humourist Mikhail Zoshchenko, both based in Leningrad, were singled out for attack. Akhmatova, an old (or 'bourgeois') intellectual who never accepted the dogma of socialist realism, believed that her 1945 encounter with the then British diplomat Isaiah Berlin, himself from Leningrad (Petrograd), started the Cold War: Stalin, so paranoid about this meeting, said, 'So our nun has been receiving British spies' and then 'cursed so obscenely that twenty years later Anna Akhmatova was embarrassed to repeat his alleged words to Berlin'. Akhmatova survived by writing a series of poems praising Stalin.[49] Stalin privately enjoyed Zoshchenko's humorous stories, but politically could not tolerate his 'lack of ideals and principles'. Zoshchenko's view, according to Stalin, was: 'There is no respite from your [communist] ideas, so we want to rest, joke and laugh.'[50] Stalin still took ideology seriously. It was his obsession with ideology that gave credence to pseudo-science such as the infamous anti-genetics theory held by Trofim Lysenko.

Like Akhmatova, according to some scholars, the composer Dmitrii Shostakovich was forced to compromise his artistic integrity: outwardly he toed the Soviet line for fear of persecution, but in fact inwardly he criticised the Soviet system through cryptic musical messages. However, recent research suggests an even more complex picture. Stalin patronised Shostakovich as a gifted composer. Fearful though Shostakovich may have been, he was also handsomely rewarded materially by the Soviet Government, for which he remained personally grateful to Stalin.[51] Like kings and tsars, Stalin both terrorised and patronised poets, writers and artists, who, in turn, feared their patron but were also charmed by him.[52]

Having achieved a divine-like status, Stalin 'appeared to value order and continuity' and, unless his power was constrained, 'to recognize the advantage of a smooth and effective system of administration'.

Although his rule was whimsical and unpredictable, 'a regular, specialized committee-based system of decision making' aimed at 'maximizing the long-term productive potential of the Soviet economic system' was emerging under Stalin. Some scholars have called this political development 'neo-patrimonial'. The paradox was perhaps inevitable given that a modern complex body politic could not be ruled in personal and patrimonial fashion, and Stalin knew it. Once after the war he confided: 'The managers understand that I cannot know everything; all they want from me is a stamp with my signature. Yes, I cannot know everything, that is why I pay particular attention to disagreements, objections, I look into why they start, to find out what is going on.'[53]

This was naturally an unstable system fraught with tension. Stalin kept the option of terror and used it, but never resorted to a repeat of 1937. In 1949 Stalin invited Rokossovskii to his dacha. Stalin personally went to the garden, made a bouquet of white roses (gardening was Stalin's only hobby) and presented it to Rokossovskii as a sign of his gratitude for Rokossovskii's service to the fatherland. Stalin asked him to go to Poland as Defence Minister, 'otherwise we may lose Poland'. Rokossovskii was mindful of a repeat of terror in case things went wrong in Poland, but Stalin assured him that the year 1937 would not be repeated.[54] After the Second World War, according to Iurii Zhdanov, A.A. Zhdanov's son who became Stalin's son-in-law in 1949, Stalin told the narrow circle of Politburo members (who included Iurii's father): 'The war showed that there were not as many internal enemies as had been reported to us and as we had reckoned. Many have suffered in vain. The people might have driven us out for it, with a kick in the pants. We ought to repent.'[55] There is no evidence to show that Stalin did actually repent. What is certain is that Stalin did not renounce terror, but used it selectively after the war so as not to de-stabilise the system of his creation.

Cold War

As Stalin pondered the post-war world, two concerns preoccupied him: the maintenance of the Soviet Union's new superpower status (one of the 'Big Three') and the international security of the country. The latter required the friendship of East-Central Europe (including the new Germany). Contrary to the perception prevalent in the West, Stalin did not have a master plan to communise East-Central Europe immediately after the war, though the war-time alliance based on mutual distrust could not last long. Seeds of discord among the allies were legion. In the final analysis, the alliance ended in the Cold War and Eastern Europe was Sovietised.

For all the parties concerned Poland remained the thorniest issue, on account of which the war had begun in the first place. Stalin wanted a new, malleable Poland under Soviet tutelage. This overriding concern influenced the ways in which Stalin dealt with Poland. Putting on a friendly face, Stalin often praised the Poles as brave fighters, the third most 'dogged' soldiers after the Russians and Germans. Yet, with reference to Gaston Palewski, an aide to de Gaulle and apparently of Polish origin, Stalin once declared with a slip of the tongue that a 'Pole will always be a Pole'.[56] (Subsequently, in 1947, Stalin told the French communist Maurice Thorez that Palewski was a British agent.)[57] In a conversation with Stalin in October 1944 Churchill remarked that when two Poles get together, regrettably they only fight, to which Stalin responded: 'if a Pole is by himself, he'll start a fight with himself'.[58]

Stalin has been widely accused of letting the Germans slaughter the Poles in the summer of 1944 during the Warsaw Uprising, in which nearly a quarter of a million Polish civilians perished. This accusation is not entirely fair. The Soviet Army had its own military engagements and the Poles had decided to fight so as to pre-empt if not forestall the Soviet advance. Stalin's lack of sympathy with the Poles was evident, however, when he refused for more than a month during the battle to allow Anglo-American aircraft to use Soviet air bases in order to drop arms and supplies to the insurgents. This incident became the bitterest bone of contention among the allies during the war, bringing about an important turning point in their relations by causing the West to suspect Stalin's commitment to international cooperation. Stalin had already broken with the Polish government in exile in London in 1943 owing to disputes regarding the Katyn massacres, and just before the Warsaw Uprising Stalin installed a puppet 'government' (the 'Lublin Committee') in Lublin, Poland.

At an August 1944 meeting with Stanisław Mikołajczyk, the Prime Minister of the Polish Government in London, Stalin made clear that he would keep in Soviet hands the former territory of Poland that he had first gained through the 1939 Soviet–German agreement and then abrogated after the declaration of war between the two countries in June 1941. This shocked Mikołajczyk. Earlier, at meetings with Polish representatives in December 1941, Stalin had been eager for Polish support against Germany and had implicitly if evasively acknowledged that L'viv was a Polish city, promising that he would not quarrel over border issues. (When Władysław Anders complained about pro-German Ukrainians in L'viv, Stalin responded, 'They are your Ukrainians, not ours. We'll work together to obliterate them'!)[59] Mikołajczyk protested that the Poles would not accept the loss of L'viv and Vilnius and that a magnanimous gesture by Stalin would win the gratitude of the Polish nation, which would then become an ally. Stalin replied that he could insult neither the Ukrainian nor the Belarusan peoples and that the Poles could have Breslau (Wrocław) instead. Stanisław Grabskii, who accompanied Mikołajczyk, interjected that L'viv was intimately connected with Polish history and traditions, at which Stalin noted that it was also intimately connected with Ukrainian history and traditions. Grabskii responded that the Ukrainians have Kyiv, but Stalin retorted, 'The Poles have Cracow and Warsaw.'[60] Mikołajczyk and Grabski did not say that the Ukrainians have Chernihiv and Kharkiv: they knew that the former eastern Poland was already in Stalin's hands.

Stalin justified his territorial claim, which coincided roughly with the so-called 'Curzon line', on the grounds that it was devised neither by Russians nor by Poles (in fact by the former British foreign Secretary Lord Curzon in 1919–20). Both Britain and the USA as well as France, the traditional patron of Poland, accepted the Soviet claim without too much fight, but they were unwilling to concede the nature of the future Polish government. De Gaulle, who met with Stalin in Moscow in December 1944, reported that the Polish question was 'the principal object of his [Stalin's] passion and the centre of his policy'. Stalin 'declared that Russia had taken "a major turn" with regard to this nation which for centuries had been its hereditary enemy and which it henceforth wished to regard as a friend'. 'Poland', Stalin added, 'has always served as a corridor for the Germans to attack Russia. This corridor must be closed off, and closed off by Poland herself.' For this purpose it was critical to place the western border of Poland on the Oder and the Neisse. Then Stalin proclaimed that 'there is no strong state which is not democratic'. De Gaulle remembered Stalin's remarks as being 'full of hatred and scorn for the "London Poles", praising the "Lublin Committee" formed under the Soviet aegis and declaring that the latter was the only expected and desired government in Poland'. De Gaulle drew the line at accepting Stalin's persistent demand that France recognise the Lublin 'government', and insisted instead that the future government of Poland should be decided by the Poles themselves through universal, free elections. De Gaulle returned home with the impression that 'the Soviets were resolved to deal just as they chose with the states and territories occupied or about to be occupied by their forces'.[61]

Stalin's linking of the strength of the state to democracy probably appeared to de Gaulle to be hypocritical. De Gaulle, like almost everyone else, found it hard to understand Stalin's thinking. He surely wanted the facade of democracy – after all, he thought that the Soviet system was more democratic than the capitalist ones. He even had the post-war Soviet-style regimes call themselves 'people's democracies' rather than socialist or communist. In October 1944, according to Mikołajczyk, Stalin expressly denied that he intended to communise Poland after the war: 'No, absolutely not. Communism does not fit the Poles. They are too individualistic, too nationalistic!'[62] All the same, de Gaulle feared Stalin's control of Poland. In April 1945 Stalin told Djilas: 'This war is not as in the past; whoever occupies a territory also imposes on it his own social system. Everyone imposes on it his own system as far as his army can reach. It cannot be otherwise.' Yet Stalin also implied that socialism did not necessarily mean a Soviet system (just as Stalin had disbanded the Comintern, claiming that the communist parties should become national parties): 'Today socialism is possible even under the English monarchy. Revolution is no longer necessary everywhere. . . . Yes, socialism is possible even under an English king.' For now, Stalin appeared to want a 'pan-Slavic' configuration: 'If the Slavs keep united and maintain solidarity, no one in the future will be able to lift a finger. Not even a finger!' Then Stalin foresaw a more assertive future: 'The war shall soon be over. We shall recover in fifteen or twenty years, and then we'll have another go at it.'[63] In March 1945 Stalin denied to the Czechoslovaks that the Soviet Union wanted to impose a Soviet system on the Slav peoples, stressing that the Soviet system could not be exported at will and that he wanted 'genuinely democratic governments' in the Slav lands.[64]

These remarks by Stalin suggest that he wanted a 'democratic' (and even 'socialist') East-Central Europe that had to be friendly to the Soviet Union. (In practice this meant that the governments, like the 1930s people's front, could be a coalition of democratic forces but that the socialists must have the controlling influence in them.) Meanwhile, British–American rivalry would allow the Soviet Union to maintain cooperation with both. A new Europe would guarantee peace for 15–20 years. By then, Stalin hoped, conflicts among imperialist powers (particularly Britain and the USA) might reach a breaking point, which would help spread genuinely socialist revolutions and deal a fatal blow to the capitalist system. Indeed, none of the major Soviet diplomats (Maiskii, Gromyko, Litvinov) foresaw or recommended a Sovietised East-Central Europe after the war.[65]

In negotiating with Britain and the USA, Stalin implied that he was entitled to considerable concessions from the allies, given the enormous sacrifice the Soviet Union had made to contribute to the defeat of Germany. Thus the Soviet Union pushed its interests as far as it could but did not intend to risk direct confrontation, regarding the maintenance of the alliance as critical to international peace.[66] The Yalta Conference may have achieved little of substance (with regard to Germany in particular), leaving the future of Europe undecided, except for the Far East where Stalin agreed to participate in the war against Japan after the surrender of Germany. Peace and comity remained of paramount concern to the 'Big Three'. According to Gromyko, Stalin said at a dinner of the Big Three:

> History has recorded many meetings of statesmen following a war. When the guns fall silent, the war seems to have made these leaders wise, and they tell each other they want to live in peace. But then, after a little while, despite all their mutual assistance, another war breaks out. Why is this? It is because some of them change their attitudes after they have achieved peace. We must try to see that doesn't happen to us in the future.

Gromyko recalled that Roosevelt replied, 'I agree with you entirely. The nations can only be grateful for your words. All they want is peace.'[67] Stalin also supported the creation of the United Nations.

Everyone found it difficult to comprehend Stalin. He appeared to keep his thoughts to himself, considering it a disadvantage in negotiation to show his hand. Stalin, according to Khrushchev, 'knew how to wear a mask of impenetrability'.[68] In 1945 Stalin advised the Yugoslavs on dealing with 'bourgeois' politicians: 'Regarding bourgeois politicians, it is necessary to be careful. They are very touchy and vindictive. You have to control your feelings. Otherwise, you'll lose. . . . Lenin did not think that we could be allied with one flank of the bourgeoisie and to fight against the other one. We managed to do it [during the Second World War]. We are guided not by feelings, but by reason, analysis, calculation.' A year later Stalin advised Bulgarian communists on how to negotiate with other political parties: 'You got it wrong. You should not have started with a written statement of conditions. You should have started with oral negotiations and orally forced your opponents to give up their positions step by step. Only after that is it possible to let them state their demands. But now you have tied the hands of your opponents. It'll be difficult for them to retreat. It seems that you don't have enough experience of negotiations with [other] parties.'[69] Stalin was an extremely shrewd negotiator.

Stalin's behaviour could be even more difficult to understand. At Yalta, for example, Stalin managed to get Britain and the USA to agree to form a Polish government based on an enlarged Lublin Committee (by then the 'Provisional Government') with the promise of free elections. (Stalin declared that 'It is in Russia's interest that Poland should be strong and powerful, in a position to shut the door of this corridor [through which the enemy, the Germans, passed into Russia] by her own force. . . . It is necessary that Poland should be free, independent in power. Therefore, it is not only a question of honour but of life and death for the Soviet state.')[70] However, after the conference Stalin had many Polish national fighters arrested and did not seem to be interested in guaranteeing genuinely free elections in practice: he was afraid that 'free elections could turn against us [the Soviet Union]'.[71] The Allies suspected a hidden agenda: Stalin was cleverly hiding his actual intention to export revolution to Poland and other countries under Soviet control. At the July 1945 Potsdam Conference, Churchill, before being replaced by the new Prime Minister Clement Atlee, expressed his deep concern to Stalin. According to Churchill, 'Stalin said that in all the countries liberated by the Red Army the Russian policy was to see a strong, independent, sovereign State. He was against Sovietisation of any of those countries. They would have free elections, and all except Fascist parties would participate.' Churchill told Stalin 'how anxious people were about Russia's intentions'. Churchill 'drew a line from the North Cape to Albania, and named the capitals east of that line which were in Russian hands. It looked as if Russia were rolling on westwards. Stalin said he had no such intention; on the contrary, he was withdrawing troops from the West.'[72] All the same, Western fears were not assuaged.

It does not seem to be the case that either side had intended to partition Europe in 1945. The Allies explored ways in which peace could be maintained without sacrificing their own particular interests (which tended to be inimical). This was at least the spirit of Yalta. Europe would be placed under the respective 'spheres of influence' of the allies (particularly Britain and the Soviet Union), but they had vital interests in each others' spheres. In Soviet thinking, Europe was to be not so much divided as weakened.[73] How much they knew about one another's intentions and fears is not entirely clear. The Soviet Union must have known quite a bit since it had spies at the heart of the British government and at least in the Manhattan (atomic bomb) Project in the USA. During the war the USA engaged in a super-secret intelligence operation ('Venona') to monitor and decrypt Soviet diplomatic and intelligence communication in the United States,[74] and in turn, the Soviet Union bugged the Allies' diplomatic missions in Moscow and elsewhere. The extensive intelligence operations of the Soviet Union helped Stalin greatly in his negotiations with the Allies. Of course, Stalin did not blindly trust intelligence information, but 'Stalin's extreme suspiciousness, verging at times on paranoia, limited his ability to derive maximum benefits from the intelligence he received.'[75] He suspected, for example, that the Manhattan Project might be American disinformation. Just before the Potsdam Conference the USA succeeded in exploding its first atomic bomb, and President Harry Truman, who took a more hawkish position towards the Soviet Union than Roosevelt, wanted to negotiate from a position of strength – the atomic bomb. Stalin was taken by surprise at the news of the atomic bomb, but understood its significance: 'Hiroshima has shaken the whole world. The balance has been broken. Build the Bomb – it will remove the great danger from us.'[76]

Stalin had his own complaints about his allies. He characterised as unjust the British and American opposition to reparations for the Soviet Union: 'Truman doesn't even know the meaning of justice.' He also said, 'The English and the Americans want to throttle us. But never mind, we got through the Civil War – we'll get through this too.' Regarding the atomic bomb, Stalin said, 'Roosevelt clearly felt no need to put us in the picture. He could have done it at Yalta. He could simply have told me the atom bomb was going through its experimental stage. We were supposed to be allies.' Then he added, 'No doubt Washington and London are hoping we won't be able to develop the bomb ourselves for some time. And meanwhile, using America's monopoly, in fact America's and Britain's, they want to force us to accept their plans on questions affecting Europe and the world. Well, that's not going to happen!' and he 'cursed in ripe language'.[77] In order not to be intimidated by the US nuclear monopoly which he claimed was 'meant to frighten those with weak nerves', Stalin immediately ordered the development of a Soviet atomic bomb, putting Beriia in charge and mobilising all available resources. The bomb itself did 'not lead to a re-evaluation of the foreign policy line' but it seriously undermined the war-time alliance.[78] The spring 1945 'Berne incident' (the Western Allies' clandestine contacts with Nazi representatives regarding a German surrender) also heightened Soviet suspicions of the USA and Britain.[79]

Yet even in May 1946, Stalin still did not have outright Sovietisation in mind. In a conversation with Osóbka-Morawski and other Polish communists in the Polish provisional Government, Stalin said:

> There is no dictatorship of the proletariat in Poland and there is no need for one . . . The structure that has arisen in Poland – this is a democracy, this is a new type of democracy. It has no precedent. Neither the Belgian nor the English nor the French democracies can serve you as examples or models. Your democracy is special. You do not have a class of big-time capitalists. You carried out the nationalization of industry in 100 days, while the English have been trying to do that over the course of

100 years. . . . The democracy that you have established in Poland, in Yugoslavia, and in Czechoslovakia, in part, is a democracy that brings you closer to socialism without the necessity of establishing a dictatorship of the proletariat or a Soviet structure. . . . In fact, the dictatorship of the proletariat doesn't exist even in the Soviet Union. What we have is Soviet democracy.[80]

Stalin appeared to suggest that a coalition government in which the communists played a leading role was sufficient for now and that such a government would ultimately lead to socialism.

Intensive archival work during the last decade or so after the formerly closed Soviet archives began to open up has not produced convincing evidence for a Soviet master plan to bolshevise the countries under Soviet occupation. The possibility cannot be excluded that the entire scheme of the 'people's democracy' was pure deception by Stalin to serve as a cover for a cleverly hidden script of Sovietisation, but this appears unlikely. If it were true, as Norman Naimark has noted, 'Stalin becomes almost superhuman in his ability to get what he wants' and other people 'appear to be gullible, innocent, and unaware'.[81] True, Stalin enjoyed deception. In his May 1946 conversation with Stalin, the Yugoslav communist leader J. Broz Tito boasted to Stalin, 'We always had measures to suppress them [opposition parties]. The parties exist only formally, though in fact they don't exist. In reality, only the Communist Party exists.' Stalin 'chuckled pleasantly at this'.[82] Still, an examination of Stalin's post-war politics towards Europe suggests that 'European reactions to Soviet moves' such as 'strike movements, electoral struggles, street clashes' played as important a role in the outcome as Stalin's intentions.[83]

The Cold War and the eventual emergence of the 'Soviet bloc' almost certainly resulted from the complex interaction among the Allies after the war. Mutual distrust was a necessary but not a sufficient condition for the Cold War, which was not predetermined. Even those who think otherwise have noted, as Vojtech Mastny has, that the 'Cold War was both unintended and unexpected; it was predetermined all the same'.[84] Although Stalin's doubts about the future of the alliance emerged at Potsdam, his policy did not change immediately: in Iran, for example, Stalin voluntarily withdrew Soviet troops in 1946 instead of confronting Britain and the USA, and neither did he support the communists in the 1944–9 civil war in Greece, which, in negotiating with Churchill in 1944, he had ceded to the British sphere of influence.

Stalin did not believe that war with Britain and the USA was likely. Even in May 1946 he told Polish communists that the Soviet Union would not start war, nor would Britain or the USA risk war. 'Our enemies', using the shadow of war, are trying to 'frighten peoples of countries whose politics they don't like'. Peace would last for at least 20 years.[85] Yet in his first major post-war speech in February 1946 Stalin used the spectre of war to tighten his grip on the internal affairs of the country. Famously, though incorrectly, his speech has been regarded in the West as the declaration of the Cold War.[86] Stalin's speech was followed by the even more famous 'Iron Curtain' speech by Churchill in March 1946. By the spring and summer of 1946 Stalin had come to believe firmly that Britain and the USA were directly involved in the anti-Soviet insurgencies in the western borderland (in western Ukraine in particular).[87] He also appeared to be guided by an 'unwritten operational presumption' of 'full freedom of action' within the Soviet sphere of influence.[88] Even before the surrender of Germany, Britain and the USA suspected that the Soviet Union was secretly diverting Lend-Lease supplies to the Polish Provisional Government and other East European forces friendly to the Soviets. The alliance was perhaps already doomed by that time.

Scholars generally concur, however, that it was the Marshall Plan that finally tore the alliance apart. It was announced in June 1947 in the wake of the 'Truman doctrine' speech in March 1947. Based on information gained through espionage, Stalin believed that the Marshall Plan was a US manoeuvre to reconstruct the alliance according to US designs and, in particular, to aid German revival so as to pit a revived, strong Germany against the Soviet Union in the future. Stalin refused to participate in the plan and forced other East European countries to follow suit.[89] Ironically, the Soviet withdrawal helped the USA to implement the Marshall Plan: Soviet participation might have inclined the US Congress not to approve the vast financial commitment involved.

In response, in September 1947 Stalin set up the Cominform, Communist Information Bureau, a new, watered-down Comintern, composed of nine European Communist Parties. Even before the Truman doctrine and the Marshall Plan, Stalin made sure that he would not lose control of Eastern Europe (and Poland in particular). The 'free' *sejm* (parliament) elections in Poland in January 1947, fraught with manipulation, intimidation and sometimes outright terror, proved to be a far cry from 'free'. Stalin ensured the victory of communists and socialists in Poland where there were many willing Stalinists.[90] Poland was followed by Czechoslovakia which in 1948 came to be ruled by communists (the so-called 1948 coup). From then on Stalin no longer supported individual or national paths to communism and denounced the Yugoslav communist regime which chose to pursue its own path independent of the Soviet Union.[91] Frustrated by Western efforts to revive the (western) German economy without reaching an agreement with the Soviet Union, Stalin blockaded Berlin in 1948-9, dramatically straining relations with the West. In 1949 Germany ended up divided with the formation of West Germany (FRG) and East Germany (GDR). In that year the North Atlantic Alliance (NATO) was formed against the perceived Soviet threat. Shortly thereafter, the Soviet Union succeeded in developing its first atomic bomb, an almost exact replica of the American bomb, mainly through espionage. The wartime alliance was as good as dead.

By 1952 Stalin had lost all hope of a unified Germany friendly to the Soviet union. He told the East German communists to build their own, socialist state while maintaining their advocacy of a unified Germany for propaganda purposes. East Germany should organise 'production cooperatives' without calling them kolkhozes and without screaming about socialism. Stalin, however, cautioned the East Germans not to resort to dekulakisation, which in their case was 'no good'. When East Germans complained that many intelligentsia elements were defecting to the West, Stalin told them that they had to create their own 'intelligentsia'.[92] Perhaps Stalin had learnt a lesson from the Soviet experience: Germany needed its own politically reliable elite, but it should not resort to collectivisation through dekulakisation (which Stalin told Churchill was more difficult than the war against Hitler). In any case, a partitioned Europe was not what Stalin initially desired, but perhaps it met the minimum requirement of the security zone Stalin needed. Stalin, according to Molotov, saw the matter this way: 'World War I wrested one country from capitalist slavery; World War II created a socialist system; and the third will finish off imperialism forever.'[93]

The Far East was not as high a priority as Europe for Stalin, though he fought doggedly for a share in the occupation of Japan. Although, in the end, he was prevented by the USA from playing any meaningful role in Japan, by participating in the war against Japan in accordance with the Yalta accord, he got southern Sakhalin and the Kurile Islands, more than the losses suffered by Imperial Russia in 1905.[94] In September 1945, Stalin reminded the country of the 1904-5 humiliation by Japan:

> The defeat of the Russian forces in 1904 during the Russo-Japanese war left painful memories in the people's consciousness. It left a black stain on our country. Our people waited, believing that the day would come when Japan would be beaten and the stain eliminated. We, the people of an older generation, waited forty years for this day. And now this day has come.[95]

Moreover, Stalin gained a security zone in China itself through a 1945 treaty with Chiang Kai-shek's Nationalist China, though he soon found himself obliged to support the Chinese communists led by Mao Ze-dong, fighting against Chiang in defiance of Stalin's advice. In 1948 Stalin admitted: 'The Chinese [communists] proved to be right, and we were wrong.'[96] Mao's victory and the establishment of the People's Republic of China in 1949 must have been a surprise to Stalin, who had never quite regarded Mao as a true Marxist. However, Stalin understood China's strategic significance and sought to consolidate a new alliance with China to undercut American influence. The 1949–50 meetings between Stalin and Mao, which forged their alliance, have produced much mythology about the two dictators' 'test of wills'.[97] Recently declassified Soviet records of the meetings suggest, however, that the negotiations were nothing less than business-like.[98]

Another militant Asian Communist, Kim Il Sung, proved to be more troublesome. Just as Mao united China by war, Kim wanted a war for unification through the 'liberation' of South Korea. Stalin could not deny Kim what Mao had achieved, but he feared that Kim's adventure might provoke a wider war with the involvement of the USA. In the end, Stalin approved of Kim's dangerous undertaking, at the same time shielding the Soviet Union from being drawn directly into the ground war and encouraging China to assist Kim. Kim invaded South Korea in June 1950. The war soon involved multinational forces headed by the USA under the aegis of the United Nations. Initially somewhat reluctant, China eventually participated in the conflict partly out of loyalty to the Soviet Union and partly for strategic reasons regarding China's own security.[99] In urging China to fight in the war in October 1950, Stalin sounded optimistic: 'Should we fear this [a big war]? In my opinion, we should not, because together we will be stronger than the USA and England, while the other European capitalist states, without Germany which is unable to provide any assistance to the United States now, do not present a serious military force.'[100] The Soviet Union provided air cover and both military matériel and military advisers to Kim and Mao. After a number of gains and losses, the war soon reached a stalemate without any gain for Kim. Stalin nevertheless savoured this state of affairs, which he said was 'getting on America's nerves', and the 'North Koreans have lost nothing, except for casualties that they suffered during the war'! Stalin even said in a 1952 conversation with Zhou Enlai of China that the war 'has shown America's weakness':

[The] Germans conquered France in 20 days. It's been already two years, and the USA has still not subdued little Korea. What kind of strength is that? . . . They are pinning their hopes on the atom bomb and air power. But one cannot win a war with that. One needs infantry, and they don't have much infantry; the infantry they do have is weak. They are fighting with little Korea, and already people are weeping in the USA. What will happen if they start a large-scale war? Then, perhaps, everyone will weep.

Stalin was a shrewd observer and practitioner. For him the only loss of the war was Korean lives (in fact, as many Chinese, approximately 900,000, were killed). Perhaps this loss seemed negligible, for it revealed an important fact: America's 'weakness'. So Stalin advocated 'endurance and patience': 'One must be firm when dealing with America.'[101] Peace on the Korean peninsula was not achieved until after his death in March 1953.

Death

Towards the end of his life, the official cult of Stalin had become grotesquely absurd. Homage was paid all over the country and beyond: 'the greatest humanist of our time', 'the greatest genius of humanity', 'the Father of Nations' and so on. Stalin may have privately enjoyed all the adulation, although he sometimes complained about its absurdity. He also knew how to present himself as a self-effacing leader. In 1938, for example, he had 'categorically opposed' Ezhov's proposal to rename Moscow 'Stalinodar', meaning 'Stalin's Gift'. In 1945 he vetoed a new attempt to rename the capital of the country 'Stalin'.[102] On the other hand, when he was editing a new, short biography of himself in 1947, he added that Stalin was an 'outstanding pupil of Lenin' and that 'Stalin never allowed his work to be marred by the slightest hint of vanity, conceit or self-adulation'.[103]

At the extravagant official celebration of his seventieth (in fact seventy-first) birthday in December 1949, Stalin skipped the various speeches given by dignitaries and went backstage where he smoked gloomily. He saw the Hungarian communist Mátthiás Rákosi there and asked him how old he was. Rákosi said, 'Fifty-six.' Stalin replied, '[You are still] a Komsomol'.[104] From August 1951 to February 1952 Stalin did not even go to the Kremlin but made important decisions at a dinner table in his dacha, to which his entourage were invited at his whim. He was getting older and his health declined, and Djilas noted that Stalin 'exhibited gluttony' and that there 'was something both tragic and ugly in his senility'.[105] Stalin generally avoided doctors and trusted only one, V.N. Vinogradov, who noted at the beginning of 1952 'a marked deterioration in the leader's state of health. Despite flying into a rage and having Vinogradov dismissed, Stalin eventually came to heed his doctor's advice'.[106] Stalin was so afraid of assassination by poisoning that he would dump the medicine he got from the

Kremlin pharmacy into the toilet and have one of his bodyguards go out to buy the same drugs at a country pharmacy 'for his [the body-guard's] grandmother'.[107] Stalin gave up smoking and, according to Svetlana, 'was very pleased with himself', though when she saw her father at the end of 1952 she was 'worried at how bad he looked'. By then Vinogradov had been arrested and Stalin 'wouldn't let any other doctor near him'.[108] His memory, too, declined. At one point, he could not remember the name of N.A. Bulganin (a member of the Politburo) sitting opposite him. Death was obviously on his mind. Even during the war, according to Molotov, Stalin said, 'After my death a heap of trash will be dumped on my grave. But the wind of history will blow it away pitilessly!'[109]

Stalin was a lonely man with no close friend or even family member. Nadezhda had long been dead, and Iakov died during the war. As Stalin aged, he shared some fond memories of his wife with Svetlana, but they met rarely. Another son, Vasilii, an air force pilot, was a spoilt brat and an alcoholic. He became so ill at one time that he 'could no longer fly his own planes'. In this case Stalin 'scolded him mercilessly. He humiliated him and browbeat him like a little boy in front of everyone.' Still, Vasilii cared only about the authority of his father.[110] In 1947 and 1948 Stalin had Svetlana'a aunts (Evgeniia Allilueva, wife of Pavel Alliluev, Nadezhda's brother, who died under mysterious circumstances in 1938, and Anna Redens, sister of Nadezhda and wife of Stalinslav Redens, executed in 1938) arrested on the grounds that they knew too much and talked too much, which Stalin reasoned helped his enemies. He was, however, fond of Marshal A.M. Vasilevskii, who was liked by everyone around him. Like Stalin and Mikoian, he once trained to become a priest, but instead became a soldier. He said that he had cut his ties with his father, a priest, in 1926. During the war, however, Stalin told Vasilevskii that 'one shouldn't forget one's parents'. After the war Vasilevskii found out that Stalin had been sending Vasilevskii's father money orders regularly without telling him. Vasilevskii was moved.[111] When Stalin became nostalgic about his childhood, he sent money to his childhood friends or invited them to spend time with him, but he remained terribly lonely. As Svetlana said, he 'seemed to be living in a vacuum' and 'hadn't a soul he could talk to'.[112]

His loneliness and his mania reinforced each other. Again, as Svetlana noted, Stalin 'saw enemies everywhere. It had reached the point of being pathological, a persecution mania, and it was all a result of being lonely and desolate.'[113] Gromyko remarked on Stalin's last years: 'He was constantly on the watch for the threat of a conspiracy. . . . To the end of his life, Stalin never lost his ingrained, pathological suspiciousness. . . . Stalin's paranoia grew more acute with time, and more and more people fell victim to it.'[114] In 1951, according to Khrushchev, Stalin 'said to no one in particular, "I'm finished. I trust no one, not even myself".'[115] Thus, Svetlana recalled later, the last years of Stalin's rule were 'terribly trying': 'The whole country was gasping for air. Things were unbearable for everyone.'[116] Many people indeed fell victim to Stalin's suspicion. In 1952 two of his closest associates, Molotov and Mikoian, fell out of favour.

Stalin's paranoia was also fuelled by the 1948 foundation of the state of Israel. Stalin supported Israel initially, recognising it immediately and hoping that the new state, assuming a pro-Soviet stance, would help drive out British influence from the Middle East. He soon found, however, that the mere fact of the foundation of Israel led to an explosion of enthusiasm for the new state among the Soviet Jewry. When, for example, Golda Meir, the Israeli ambassador to Moscow, visited a synagogue in Moscow on Rosh Hashana in 1948, she was greeted by a spontaneous demonstration of Moscow Jews. The street in front of the synagogue

> was filled with people, packed together like sardines, hundreds and hundreds of them, of all ages, including Red Army officers, soldiers, teenagers and babies carried in their parents' arms. Instead of the 2,000-odd Jews who usually came to the synagogue on the holidays, a crowd of close to 50,000 people was waiting for us. For a minute I couldn't grasp what had happened – or even who they were. And then it dawned on me. They had come – those good, brave Jews – in order to be with us, to demonstrate their sense of kinship and to celebrate the establishment of the State of Israel. . . . I was on the verge of fainting, I think. But the crowd still surged around me, stretching out its hands and saying *Nasha Golda* (our Golda) and *Shalom, shalom*, and crying.[117]

Stalin had been suspicious of Soviet Jews for some time. When in 1943 Svetlana fell in love with Aleksei Kapler, a Jew, Stalin slapped her and said, 'A writer! He can't write decent Russian. She couldn't even find herself a Russian!'[118] During the war, he had encouraged Jewish international contact in order to solicit the material and other support of world Jewry (particularly in the USA) for the war, even allowing the formation of the Jewish Anti-fascist Committee (EAK) in the Soviet Union for this purpose. Yet its extensive international contacts began to appear to Stalin to be politically inexpedient and even dangerous after the war. The EAK was disbanded in 1948 and in 1949 its chairman, S.M. Mikhoels, was murdered, on Stalin's order, under the guise of a traffic accident. Many of the EAK leaders were secretly tried and executed in 1952,[119] and Soviet Jews came to be attacked as 'rootless cosmopolitans'. Strangely, however, they were simultaneously accused of being nationalists or Zionists! According to Svetlana, Stalin declared, 'The entire older generation is contaminated with Zionism, and now they're teaching the young people, too.'[120]

Stalin had always been suspicious of medical doctors, and the fact that there were many Jews among them now made Stalin extraordinarily suspicious of both groups of people. In December 1952, Stalin was recorded as saying, 'Any Jew is a nationalist, he is an agent of American intelligence. The Jewish nationalists think that they were saved by the USA (where it's possible to be rich and bourgeois). They consider themselves beholden to the Americans. Among the doctors there are many Jewish nationalists.'[121] He had many doctors arrested and even ordered them to be beaten to confess, which led to the so-called 'Doctors' Plot', an affair in which a 'terrorist' group of prominent Soviet doctors, including Stalin's personal doctors, were accused of plotting to poison Soviet leaders.[122] To the Politburo, according to Khrushchev's 1956 'secret speech', Stalin uttered in despair, 'You are blind like young kittens; what will happen without me? The country will perish because you do not know how to recognize enemies.'[123] Because of the new situation as he saw it, Stalin insisted on reforming the Soviet intelligence services. He declared that the Soviet Union's 'chief enemy' was now America and that one had to 'utilise what God has granted us', changing tactics and methods all the time. 'One mustn't be naïve in politics, but particularly in espionage one mustn't be naïve.' 'Espionage,' Stalin emphasised, 'is a sacred and sublime business for us.'[124] He was certainly obsessed with American espionage, marking American diplomats (George Kennan, Charles Bohlen and others) as spies.[125] He also suspected that Mao was surrounded by American and British spies.[126]

Trusting no one, Stalin meddled in almost everything, from linguistics and political economy to the censoring of films by Aleksandr Dovzhenko and Sergei Eizenshtein and to the editing of the 1952 Polish Constitution. Even towards the end of his life, Stalin continued to read a self-imposed quota of several hundred pages a day. Concerned about the future of the Soviet Union, he read closely Charles Montesquieu's *Considerations on the Causes of the Greatness of the Romans and their Decline* (1734) and lectured his subordinates using Ancient Rome as his example.[127] Stalin could not name his successor because no one appeared to be qualified, although, probably in 1950, Stalin had supported Bulganin for an important government position:

Who will we appoint chairman of the Council of Ministers after me? Beria? No, he is not Russian, but Georgian. Khrushchev? No, he is a worker, we need someone more educated. Malenkov? No, he can only follow someone else's lead. Kaganovich? No, he won't do, for he is not Russian but a Jew. Molotov? No, he has already aged, he won't cope. Voroshilov? No, he is really not up to it. Saburov? Pervukhin? These people are only fit for secondary roles. There is only one person left and that is Bulganin.[128]

Indeed, Bulganin was appointed the first deputy chairman of the council, but this was only a manoeuvre by Stalin and Bulganin lost the position by the spring of 1951. Bulganin was not to be his successor. At one point, Stalin could not even remember his name in his presence, as was mentioned earlier.

Stalin died without naming his successor. On the night of 27 or 28 February 1953 Stalin, despite his hypertension, took a steam bath near his dacha. He had a stroke during the early hours of 1 March after dining with his entourage. When he did not emerge from his room the following day his bodyguards began to worry, though they were afraid of entering his room without permission. Stalin thus lay paralysed by himself for nearly a day, much more than the few hours that are critical following a stroke. In the early hours of 2 March Politburo members gathered in his dacha, but they were wary of sanctioning medical treatment for fear of Stalin's rage when (or if) he recovered – hence the persistent rumours later that Stalin was killed or at least was left to die by his entourage. According to Molotov, Beriia himself told Molotov after Stalin's death, 'I did him in!' and 'I saved all of you,'[129] although no firm evidence of Beriia's involvement has emerged.[130] In all probability, none of the Politburo members desired Stalin's recovery. Stalin died on 5 March after considerable suffering. Svetlana, who was present, recorded the death of her father:

> At what seemed like the very last moment he suddenly opened his eyes and cast a glance over everyone in the room. It was a terrible glance, insane or perhaps angry and full of the fear of death and the unfamiliar faces of the doctors bent over him. The glances swept over everyone in a second. Then something incomprehensible and awesome happened that to this day I can't forget and don't understand. He suddenly lifted his left hand as though he were pointing to something above and bringing down a curse on us all. The gesture was incomprehensible and full of menace, and no one could say to whom or at what it might be directed. The next moment, after a final effort, the spirit wrenched itself free of the flesh.[131]

According to Molotov, as narrated to Gromyko, Stalin pointed his hand at a 'photograph with a simple subject: a little girl feeding a lamb with milk through a horn. With the same slow movement of his finger, Stalin then pointed to himself. It was his last act'. 'Those present took it as a typical example of Stalin's wit – the dying man was comparing himself with a lamb.'[132] The 'lamb' was dead, and everyone sighed.

Notes

[1] Stalin was not immediately convinced of Hitler's suicide and feared that he had fled and might resume his fight against the Soviet Union from aboard. See Henrik Eberle and Matthias Uhl (eds), *Das Buch Hitler* (Bergisch Gladbach, 2005), 23, 469–70, 482–3.

[2] De Gaulle, 88–9.

[3] Richardson, 170, 210, and Alliluyeva, *Twenty Letters*, 198.

[4] A.V. Pimanov, S.V. Deviatov, V.V. Pavlov and V.P. Zhiliaev, *Stalin. Tragediia sem'i* (Moscow, 2004), 19, and Mgeladze, 125, 188.

[5] Nevezhin, 485, 487.

[6] *Slovo tovarishchu Stalinu*, 454.

[7] Milovan Djilas, *Conversations with Stalin* (New York–London, 1962), 152.

[8] *Molotov Remembers*, 60, 189–90, and Chuev, *Tak govoril Kaganovich*, 60.

[9] Alliluyeva, *Twenty Letters*, 200.

[10] Norman M. Naimark, *The Russians in Germany: A History of the Soviet Zone of Occupation, 1945–1949* (Cambridge, Mass., 1995), ch. 2.

[11] Alliluyeva, *Only One Year*, 392.

[12] Djilas, 110–11. Stalin liked Dostoevskii.

[13] *Vostochnaia Evropa v dokumentakh Rossiiskikh arkhivov, 1944–1953 gg.*, v. 1 (Moscow, 1997), 120.

[14] Overy, 287–8 and John Erickson, 'Soviet War Losses: Calculations and Controversies' in John Erickson and David Dilks (eds), *Barbarossa: The Axis and the Allies* (Edinburgh, 1994).

[15] Susan J. Linz (ed.), *The Impact of World War II on the Soviet Union* (Totowa, NJ, 1985), 283, and James R. Millar, *The ABC of Soviet Socialism* (Champaign, Ill., 1981), 43.

[16] Maurice Hindus, *Mother Russia* (New York, 1943), 165 and Kuromiya, *Freedom and Terror in the Donbas*, 309. See also Djilas, 75.

[17] Stalin, *Sochineniia*, 2 (15), 203–4 and 3 (16), 5. In March 1946 Stalin declared that the war demonstrated the stability of the Soviet system, and proposed to change the title of 'People's Commissar, appropriate for the formative period', to that of 'Minister'. *Istoricheskii arkhiv*, 1997, nos. 5–6, 218.

[18] Linz (ed.), 83, 89 (Alec Nove).

[19] *Molotov Remembers*, 248.

[20] Ibid., 59.

[21] Bialer (ed.), 42.

[22] Sudoplatov and Sudoplatov, *Special Tasks*, 171.

[23] Cited in Allan Bullock, *Hitler and Stalin: Parallel Lives* (New York, 1992), 881.

[24] Alliluyeva, *Only One Year*, 386.

[25] Mgeladze, 168.

[26] Baibakov, 64.

[27] Sudoplatov and Sudoplatov, *Special Tasks*, 161 and Steven Merritt Miner, *Stalin's Holy War: Religion, Nationalism, and Alliance Politics, 1941–1945* (Chapel Hill, NC, 2003).

[28] E.S. Seniavskaia, *1941–1945. Frontovoe pokolenie* (Moscow, 1995), 202–3.

[29] M.Ia. Gefter, quoted in Nina Tumarkin, *The Living and the Dead: The Rise and Fall of the Cult of World War II in Russia* (New York, 1994), 65.

[30] Lisa Kirschenbaum, 'Gender, Memory, and National Myths: Ol'ga Berggol'ts and the Siege of Leningrad', *Nationalities Papers*, 28:3 (2000), 557.

[31] Mikoian, 513.

[32] Alliluyeva, *Twenty Letters*, 180.

[33] Kuromiya, *Freedom and Terror in the Donbas*, 311, I.S. Konev, *Zapiski komanduiushchego frontom* (Moscow, 2000), 498–501 and Felikus Chuev, *Soldaty imperii* (Moscow, 1998), 317.

[34] These three were recorded in 1945 by L.D. Volkov and published in *Zavetnye chastushki*, v. 2 (Moscow, 1999), 84, 169, 185.

[35] *Khrushchev Remembers*, 235, 240–1. Stalin personally witnessed the famine on his way to the south. Alliluyeva, *Twenty Letters*, 199.

[36] *Izvestiia*, 16 July 1992 ('Podslushali i rasstreliali').

[37] Kuromiya, *Freedom and Terror in the Donbas*, 312.

[38] Ibid., 209–10. The 'Vlasovites' refer to those soldiers, mainly Soviet POWs, whom the former Red Army General A.A. Andreev, after being captured by the German forces, organised to fight against Stalin under German command. See Catherine Andreyev, *Vlasov and the Russian Liberation Movement, 1941–1945* (Cambridge, 1987).

[39] Amir Weiner, *Making Sense of War: The Second World War and the Fate of the Bolshevik Revolution* (Princeton, NJ, 2001).

[40] Norman M. Naimark, *Fires of Hatred: Ethnic Cleansing in Twentieth-Century Europe* (Cambridge, Mass., 2001), ch. 3.

[41] Yoram Gorlizki and Oleg Khlevniuk, *Cold Peace: Stalin and the Soviet Ruling Circle, 1945–1953* (Oxford, 2004), 125.

[42] Semyon Vilensky (ed.), *Resistance in the Gulag, 1923–56* (Moscow, 1992) and *Istoriia stalinskogo Gulaga*, v. 6 (Moscow, 2004).

[43] Norman M. Naimark, 'Cold War Studies and New Archival Materials on Stalin', *Russian Review*, 61:1 (January 2002), 7–11, and Vladimir M. Pechatnov, 'The Allies Are Pressing on You to Break Your Will . . . ' (Cold War International History Project Working Paper no. 26, Washington, DC, 1999), 13.

[44] *Khrushchev Remembers: The Glasnost Tapes*, 72–3.

[45] *Politbiuro TsK VKP(b) i Sovet Ministrov SSSR 1945–1953* (Moscow, 2002), 313.

[46] Gorlizki and Khlevniuk, 87.

[47] Kees Boterbloem, *The Life and Times of Andrei Zhdanov, 1896–1948* (Montreal, 2004).

[48] Mar'iamov, 85, 91.

[49] György Dalos, *The Guest from the Future: Anna Akhmatova and Isaiah Berlin* (London, 1998).

[50] *Istochnik*, 2000, no. 3, 103.

[51] See Leonid Maximenkov, 'Stalin and Shostakovich: Letters to a "Friend"' in Laurel E. Fay (ed.), *Shostakovich and His World* (Princeton, NJ, 2004). For the

heated controversy on Shostakovich, see, for example, Malcolm Hamrick Brown (ed.), *A Shostakovich Casebook* (Bloomington, Ind., 2004).

[52]See, for example, the film director Aleksandr Dovzhenko's remark: 'I am afraid of him [Stalin], but he also charms me'. George O. Liber, *Alexander Dovzhenko: A Life in Soviet Film* (London, 2002), 168.

[53]Gorlizki and Khlevniuk, 9, 64, 83, 169.

[54]Chuev, *Soldat imperii*, 350.

[55]Iu.A. Zhdanov, *Vzgliad v proshloe: vospominaniia ochevidtsa* (Rostov on the Don, 2004), 227.

[56]*Vostochnaia Evropa*, 40, Gromyko, 100 and Jean Lacouture and Roland Mehl, *De Gaulle ou l'Éternel Défi* (Paris, 1988), 210.

[57]*Istoricheskii arkhiv*, 1996, no. 1, 16.

[58]Rzheshevskii, *Stalin i Cherchill'*, 419.

[59]Władysław Anders, *Bez ostatniego rozdziału* (Newtown, Wales, 1950), 123.

[60]*Istochnik*, 1999, no. 1, 155–6.

[61]De Gaulle, 74–9, 85, 88.

[62]Stanislaw Mikolajczyk, *The Rape of Poland* (New York–London, 1948), 100.

[63]Djilas, 113–5. In December 1943 Edvard Beneš interpreted Stalin's remarks on 'Slavic cooperation' as implying a 'Slavic empire' to stem the German '*Drang nach Osten*'. *Voprosy istorii*, 2001, no. 3, 19–20.

[64]*Istochnik*, 1997, no. 5, 128.

[65]Vladimir O. Pechatnov, *The Big Three after World War II* (Cold War International History Project Working Paper No. 13, Washington, DC, 1995).

[66]There were cases of minor confrontation. According to Stalin, during the battle for Berlin, the US forces asked the Soviet military command for permission to bomb the Germans close to the Soviet–German front. When it became known that the Americans meant to bomb German factories, they were denied permission. Even so, the Americans did attempt to bomb the factories, and Soviet fighter planes shot down several American bombers. *Istochnik*, 2003, no. 3, 120.

[67]Gromyko, 87.

[68]*Khrushchev Remembers: The Last Testament* (Boston, Mass., 1974), 182.

[69]*Vostochnaia Evropa*, 132–3, 360.

[70]James F. Byrnes, *Speaking Frankly* (New York–London, 1947), 31–2.

[71]Quoted in Lacouture and Mehl, 213.

[72]Churchill, *Triumph and Tragedy*, 636.

[73]Silvio Pons, 'In the Aftermath of the Age of Wars: the Impact of World War II on Soviet Security Policy', *Annali* (Fondazione Giangiacomo Feltrinelli), 1998.

[74]John Earl Haynes and Harvey Klehr, *Venona: Decoding Soviet Espionage in America* (New Haven, Conn., 1999).

[75]Christopher Andrew and Oleg Gordievsky, *KGB* (New York, 1990), 339.

[76]Vladislav Zubok and Konstantin Pleshakov, *Inside the Kremlin's Cold War: From Stalin to Khrushchev* (Cambridge, Mass., 1996), 40, and David Holloway, *Stalin and the Bomb* (New Haven, Conn., 1994), 132.

[77]Gromyko, 109–10, 112.

[78]See Holloway, 169, 171.

[79]Harriman and Abel, 432–9.

[80]*Vostochnaia Evropa*, 457–8 and Norman M. Naimark, 'Post-Soviet Russian Historiography on the Emergence of the Soviet Bloc', *Kritika*, 5:3 (Summer 2004),

572 from which most of this translation is taken. The 1936 'Stalin Constitution' had replaced the 'dictatorship of the proletariat' with 'Soviet democracy'.

[81] Naimark, 'Post-Soviet Russian Historiography', 579, and id., *The Russians in Germany*.

[82] *Cold War International History Project Bulletin*, no. 10 (March 1998), 121.

[83] Norman M. Naimark, 'Stalin and Europe in the Postwar Period, 1945–53: Issues and Problems', *Journal of Modern European History*, 2:1 (March 2004), 55.

[84] Vojtech Mastny, *The Cold War and Soviet Insecurity: The Stalin Years* (New York, 1996), 23.

[85] *Vostochnaia Evropa*, 456–7. In 1949 Stalin repeated similar thoughts to Mao Zedong, adding, however, 'But who could be sure no madman appeared on the scene?' *Far Eastern Review* (Moscow), 1989, no. 2, 129 (Shi Zhe) and *Cold War International History Project Bulletin*, nos. 6–7 (1995–6), 5.

[86] Zubok and Pleshakov, 35.

[87] Jeffrey Burds, *The Early Cold War in Soviet West Ukraine, 1944–1948* (Pittsburgh, Pa.: Carl Beck Papers, No. 1505, 2001).

[88] Pechatnov, 22. Litvinov is said to have been deeply sceptical of what he considered to be Stalin's 'outmoded concept of security in terms of territory – the more you've got the safer you are'. He was reputed to have said to an American correspondent in 1946, 'You Americans won't be able to deal with this Soviet government. . . . Do you think this government, these hard-liners will meet you halfway in any sense? Nothing will come of your dealings with them . . . Only external pressure can help, that is, a military campaign'. *Molotov Remembers*, 68. For different assessments of Litvinov's views, see Pechatnov, 19, Zubok and Pleshakov, 38–9 and Vojtech Mastny, 'The Cassandra in the Foreign Commissariat', *Foreign Affairs*, 54:2 (January 1976).

[89] For Stalin's intimidation of Czechoslovak politicians in this regard, see *Vostochnaia Evropa*, 672–5.

[90] For them, see Teresa Toranska, *Oni: Stalin's Polish Puppets* (London, 1987).

[91] Stalin ordered the assassination of the Yugoslav leader Tito. In response, according to Zhores and Roi Medvedev, the angry Tito sent Stalin a note that read: 'Stalin. Stop sending assassins to murder me. We have already caught five, one with a bomb, another with a rifle. . . . If this doesn't stop, I will send one man to Moscow and there will be no need to send another.' *Cold War International History International Project Bulletin*, no. 10 (March 1998), 137 and Roy Medvedev and Zhores Medvedev, *The Unknown Stalin* (New York, 2004), 70.

[92] *Istochnik*, 2003, no. 3, 117, 124–5.

[93] *Molotov Remembers*, 63.

[94] For this, see Tsuyoshi Haegawa, *Racing the Enemy: Stalin, Truman, and the Surrender of Japan* (Cambridge, Mass., 2005).

[95] Stalin, *Sochineniia* 2 (15):214.

[96] Dimitrov, 443.

[97] Sergei N. Goncharov, John W. Lewis and Xue Litai, *Uncertain Partners: Stalin, Mao, and the Korean War* (Stanford, Calif., 1993).

[98] *Cold War International History Project Bulletin*, nos. 6–7 (1995–96), 5–9.

[99] This controversial issue has been much clarified by the recent declassification of some key Soviet and Chinese documents. See ibid., nos. 8–9 (Winter 1996/97),

237–42 (Shen Zhihua). For a cogent summary, see ibid., nos. 14–15 (Winter 2003–Spring 2004), 369–72 (James G. Hershberg). For more detail, see Chen Jian, *Mao's China and the Cold War* (Chapel Hill, NC, 2001), Haruki Wada, *Chōsen Sensō Zenshi* (A Complete History of the Korean War) (Tokyo, 2003) and Shen Zhihua, *Mao Zedong, Sidalin yu Chaoxian zhan zheng* (Mao Zedong, Stalin and the Korean War) (Guangzhou, 2003).

[100] *Cold War International History Project Bulletin*, nos. 14–15 (Winter 2003–Spring 2004), 376.

[101] Ibid., nos. 6–7 (Winter 1995/1996), 12–13.

[102] Chuev, *Soldat imperii*, 547.

[103] *Istoricheskii arkhiv*, 1990, no. 9, 117, 118.

[104] Chuev, *Soldaty imperii*, 553.

[105] Djilas, 152.

[106] Gorlizki and Khlevniuk, 145.

[107] Pimanov, Deviatov, Pavlov and Zhiliaev, 49.

[108] Alliluyeva, *Twenty Letters*, 216.

[109] Feliks Chuev, *Molotov: poluderzhavnyi vlasterin* (Moscow, 1999), 396. A similar remark to A.E. Golovanov in 1943 is in *Polkovodtsy* (Moscow, 1995), 31.

[110] Alliluyeva, *Twenty Letters*, 222–3. Vasilii died of alcoholism in 1962, at the age of 41. Svetlana became a Christian believer and defected abroad in 1967.

[111] *Molotov Remembers*, 303.

[112] Alliluyeva, *Twenty Letters*, 203.

[113] Ibid., 206.

[114] Gromyko, 356–7.

[115] *Khrushchev Remembers*, 307.

[116] Alliluyeva, *Twenty Letters*, 207.

[117] Golda Meir, *My Life* (New York, 1975), 250–1.

[118] Alliluyeva, *Twenty Letters*, 192.

[119] Joshua Rubenstein and Vladimir P. Naumov (eds), *Stalin's Secret Pogrom: The Postwar Inquisition of the Jewish Anti-Fascist Committee* (New Haven, Conn., 2001). For Mikhoels, see also Jeffrey Veidlinger, *The Moscow State Yiddish Theater: Jewish Culture on the Soviet Stage* (Bloomington, Ind., 2000).

[120] Alliluyeva, *Twenty Letters*, 206.

[121] *Istochnik*, 1997, no. 5, 140–1 (V.A. Malyshev).

[122] See Ia.L. Rapoport, *The Doctors' Plot of 1953* (Cambridge, Mass., 1991).

[123] Bertram D. Wolfe, *Khrushchev and Stalin's Ghost* (New York, 1957), 204.

[124] *Istochnik*, 2001, no. 5, 132.

[125] Van Ree, *The Political Thought of Joseph Stalin*, 300.

[126] *Stepan Anastasovich Mikoyan: An Autobiography* (Shrewsbury, 1999), 139.

[127] Zhdanov, 436.

[128] Gorlizki and Khlevniuk, 94, 149. For a variant, see *Khrushchev Remembers: The Glasnost Tape*, 38–9. Medvedev and Medvedev, ch. 2 claim that Stalin wanted to appoint M.A. Suslov, the editor of *Pravda* in 1950, as his successor.

[129] *Molotov Remembers*, 161, 237.

[130] For Beriia, whom Stalin introduced to Roosevelt as 'our Himmler' at Yalta, see Amy Knight, *Beria: Stalin's First Lieutenant* (Princeton, NJ, 1993).

[131] Alliluyeva, *Twenty Letters*, 22.

[132] Gromyko, 103.

Conclusion

The ghost of Stalin did not die quietly. On the day of his funeral, several hundred people waiting to pay their respects to him are said to have been crushed to death in a stampede. The whole nation appeared to cry over his death. Marshal Rokossovskii, according to Svetlana, stood at Stalin's coffin with 'his uniform drenched in tears', while the Italian communist Palmiro Togliatti 'sat there completely calm'.[1] In essence, the regime Stalin had created lasted for nearly forty more years. Perhaps the only major changes that took place after Stalin's death were the end of mass terror and Khrushchev's advocacy of 'peaceful coexistence'. Yet the 'peaceful coexistence' doctrine did not stop the Cold War. In the end, the Soviet regime collapsed in 1991. Whether, as Stalin had feared, the country perished because its new leaders did not know 'how to recognise enemies' is debatable. As Stalin once predicted, a 'heap of trash' was dumped on his grave after his death. (In 1961, at the height of de-Stalinisation, his remains were taken out of the Lenin mausoleum in Red Square and placed in the Kremlin wall.) However, few people today would say that 'the wind of history' has blown the 'heap of trash' pitilessly away. To the extent that Stalin and the Soviet regime were synonymous, Stalin's death marked the beginning of the end of the Soviet regime.

No one would contend that Stalin left an enduring intellectual legacy, although it is possible that his theories on nations and nationalism and 'socialism in one country' may be of interest to some people or nations. In comparison with, for example, Marx's grand theory on human history, whatever contribution Stalin may have made to political thought is negligible. Stalin was neither ideologue nor theorist, and Svetlana testified that Stalin had 'a distrust of erudition'.[2]

He was first and foremost a politician, a point of critical importance that many of Stalin's political rivals with intellectual pretensions misunderstood. 'His intellect', Gromyko stated, 'was not that of a scholar, but rather that of a practical man, an organiser and, above all, a very capable and subtle manipulator.'[3] A.H. Birse, Churchill's Russian interpreter, noted similarly, 'there was more than a spark in his intelligence and skill as a negotiator . . . there was something in his personality which revealed pre-eminence, a grasp of the essentials, the alert mind, which could not fail to impress and fascinate. He relied to a minimum on his assistants at the round-table; he carried all the details in his head. Nor did he miss any weakness in the argument of his opponents, on which he would pounce like a bird of prey.'[4] Accounts of Stalin's alleged desire to be recognised as a 'genius' or a 'Himalaya' or, for that matter, to receive the Order of the Red Banner during the Civil War may have been true, but Stalin did not sacrifice politics – and his quest for power – to intellectual pretence or military glory.

Stalin was a *rara avis*, a rare and even unique politician who lived and was able to live by politics alone. Stalin could be cruel because he did not allow human emotion to interfere with politics. Although, as he admitted, his personal life was 'crippled' twice by the deaths of his wives, only politics guided him. Svetlana, who was the human being closest to Stalin, understood all this: 'He gave himself fully to political interests and emotions, leaving too little room for everything else a man lives by. . . . Human feelings in him were replaced by political considerations. He knew and sensed the political game, its shades, its nuances. He was completely absorbed by it. And since, for many years, his sole concern had been to seize, hold, and strengthen his power in the Party – and in the country – everything else in him had given way to this one aim.'[5] Gromyko made a similarly interesting observation on Stalin the politician: 'Stalin was a virtuoso at hiding his thoughts, especially about other powerful figures in the party. He had an astonishing talent for finding allies at precisely the right moment. He had his own understanding of what loyalty to principles, duty and honour meant. Everything was permissible in dealing with his opponents, even with those who the day before might have been his allies. The worst of medieval Europe's scheming monarchs would not have been up to the job for Stalin's purposes.'[6]

This in itself did not necessarily make Stalin an unmitigated monster (although once, after converting to Christianity in defiance of the ghost of her atheist father, Svetlana maintained that he was a 'moral and spiritual monster').[7] Stalin in fact understood human relations well and skilfully used them for political ends. In his note to Ordzhonikidze in 1922, A.M. Nazaretian, then working under Stalin, wrote of him: 'He's very cunning. He's hard as a nut. . . . For all his, as it were, coldly savage disposition, he's a soft human being, he has a heart and knows how to assess the values of individuals.'[8] In 1940 Stalin opposed the depiction by Soviet artists of his enemies as monsters 'devoid of human characteristics': 'Why not portray Bukharin, whatever monster he may have been, so that he has some human traits as well. Trotskii [was] an enemy, but he was unquestionably an able man.

You must portray him as an enemy, but one with not merely negative characteristics.'[9]

Shrewdly, Stalin often assumed the role of the 'wise padrone', bullying and terrorising Molotov into playing the 'bad cop' and taking tough positions towards the Western allies.[10] Birse, like many others, even found Stalin to be humane: '[T]o me, a small cog in the machinery of negotiations, he [Stalin] was always amiable, friendly, and considerate, even more so than Molotov or Vyshinsky, with whom I had most to do'. Birse added, however: 'I could never quite rid myself of the thought that I was in the presence of the Absolute Dictator, and I was thankful that he was not my master.'[11] Many foreigners who dealt with Stalin have made similar observations. Anthony Eden, British Foreign Secretary during the war, said of Stalin: 'He never wasted a word. He never stormed, he was seldom even irritated. Hooded, calm, never raising his voice, he avoided the repeated negatives of Molotov which were so exasperating to listen to. By more subtle methods he got what he wanted without having seemed so obdurate.'[12] The American diplomat Charles Bohlen, who ranked Stalin 'high on the list of the world's monsters', viewing him as 'a man to whom pity and other human sentiments were completely alien', also noted that Stalin 'was patient, a good listener, always quiet in his manner and in his expression'; 'There were no signs of the harsh and brutal nature behind this mask – nothing of the ruthlessness with which he ordered the slaughter of millions of Russians. He was always polite and given to understatement.'[13] Particularly instructive are the reflections of W. Averell Harriman, the American Ambassador to the Soviet Union in 1943–6 who met with Stalin numerous times and whom Stalin held partly responsible for the deterioration of Soviet-American relations after the death of Roosevelt:

> It is hard for me to reconcile the courtesy and consideration that he showed me personally with the ghastly cruelty of his wholesale liquidations. Others, who did not know him personally, see only the tyrant in Stalin. I saw the other side as well – his high intelligence, that fantastic grasp of detail, his shrewdness and the surprising human sensitivity that he was capable of showing, at least in the war years. I found him better informed than Roosevelt, more realistic than Churchill, in some ways the most effective of the war leaders. At the same time he was, of course, a murderous tyrant. I must confess that for me Stalin remains the most inscrutable and contradictory character I have known – and leave the final judgment to history.'[14]

Stalin appears less contradictory if one realises that Stalin the tyrant understood human relations well, certainly better than Molotov or Vyshinskii, and used his understanding for political ends.

Indeed, many Western diplomats have testified as to how polite, affable and even reasonable Stalin could be, regretting those Western politicians (such as Roosevelt) who allegedly fell victim to his deceptive charm. Interestingly, both Churchill and Truman privately confessed that they liked him. On 13 October 1944 Churchill wrote to his wife Clementine from Moscow: 'I have had v[er]y nice talks with the Old Bear [Stalin]. I like him the more I see him. *Now* they respect us here & I am sure they wish to work w[ith] us – I have to keep the President [Roosevelt] in constant touch & this is the delicate side.'[15] Likewise, Truman wrote to his wife towards the close of the Potsdam meeting: 'I like Stalin. He is straightforward. Knows what he wants and will compromise when he can't get it. His foreign minister [Molotov] isn't so forthright.'[16]

Politics governed Stalin's relations with other people. Rude, suspicious and vindictive, Stalin alienated people easily, though he was also capable of appearing humble and was good at charming people. Again, as Svetlana noted, 'My father had a very negative view of human beings in general. He would see them as what they are good for, what he could make them do. . . . He was rough and tough: when he saw potential, he would go out of his way to attract it. He could be very charming when he wanted to attract and impress people; he would give them all that they needed so long as they worked for him. . . . He had a staggering capacity to inspire love, tremendous charisma.'[17] De Gaulle, too, made a similar observation: 'As a communist disguised as a Marshal, a dictator preferring the tactics of guile, a conqueror with an affable smile, he was a past master of deception. But so fierce was his passion that it often gleamed through this armour, not without a kind of sinister charm'; and he was 'possessed by the will to power. Accustomed by a life of machination to disguise his features as well as his inmost soul, to dispense with illusions, pity, sincerity, to see in each man an obstacle or a threat, he was all strategy, suspicion and stubbornness.'[18] Stalin, as Lenin had observed, was devoid of any sentimentality. He subsumed all human sentiment to politics.

The pervasive terror becomes explicable in this context. Stalin wilfully sent his own relatives, as well as untold numbers of friends, colleagues and strangers, to death. Perhaps all politicians, including those in democracies, have to accept death in an abstract form – how else do they live with the fact that in war, for example, they send so many innocent people to their deaths? They believe and contend that there are things (the life and death of democracy, for example) of higher value than individual lives. The adage, 'One death is a tragedy, but a million is a statistic,' is often attributed to Stalin.[19] The basic idea, in fact, can be traced to Erich Maria Remarque's *Der schwarze Obelisk* (*The Black Obelisk*) published in 1956, after Stalin's death, in which a German soldier wonders why he and his comrades have practically forgotten the two million dead in the Great War: '*Aber das ist wohl so, weil einzelner immer der Tod ist – und zwei Millionen immer nur eine Statistik*' ('But perhaps it is because one dead man is death and two million are merely a statistic'). The popular attribution to Stalin may be mistaken, but it surely represents Stalin's perception (except that Stalin may not have considered even one political death a tragedy). To be fair, Stalin admitted to Mgeladze that 'mistakes' were made in 1937 and that many honest people suffered. Like death, life itself was something abstract to Stalin. Once, when he was reading Trotskii's *Terrorism and Communism* (1920), Stalin marked the following passage with the note 'Right!': 'If human life in general is sacred and inviolable, we must deny ourselves not only the use of terror, not only war, but also revolution itself.'[20] Although Stalin may not have been a monster, his politics made him appear monstrous, as he did indeed to de Gaulle.[21]

Stalin knew that politics was dirty. When told that 'Stalin once said to Svetlana that politics is a filthy business,' Molotov responded, 'This must be kitchen gossip. Stalin could not have said that. He spent his whole life in politics, that so-called filthy business.'[22] Stalin almost certainly said it, however. As mentioned earlier (p. 116), he told Romain Rolland in 1935 that it is 'better to be out of politics and keep one's hands clean'. In 1940 Stalin sought to persuade Iu.A. Zhdanov, a chemist interested in politics and his future son-in-law, to focus on his scientific studies, saying, 'Politics is a dirty business. We need chemists.'[23] Stalin appeared to believe that those who thought that even in the dirty world of politics there should be some human decency would lose. He knew that politics could turn men into beasts. At Potsdam, Stalin, a former choirboy, was moved by Truman's playing of the piano at dinner. The music was the Minuet in G by the Polish composer Ignacy Paderewski. Praising the President, according to Gromyko, Stalin said laughingly, 'Ah yes, music's an excellent thing – it drives out the beast in man.'[24] In 1952, Stalin told his secret police chief S.D. Ignat'ev, who he suspected was reluctant to use terror, 'You want to keep your hands clean, do you? You can't. Have you forgotten Lenin ordered Fanny Kaplan to be shot? . . . If you're going to be squeamish, I'll smash your face in.'[25]

Unlike Hitler, Stalin was not consumed by his emotions or tastes, adhering only to Marxism (which he believed represented the objective laws of history) and dismissing non-Marxist ideas and theories such as liberalism, racism and nationalism. Stalin, according to Truman, said, 'it would be incorrect to be guided by injuries or feelings of retribution': such feelings are 'poor advisers in politics'.[26] He did, however, use whatever prejudices and preconceptions were politically expedient at any given time. Thus he was not averse to singling out national groups for repression or deporting certain national groups *in toto*. He also used anti-Semitism to control the country towards the end of his life,[27] though by and large he did not allow, for example, anti-Polonism, anti-Teutonism or anti-Semitism to dictate or sway his politics in general (in 1948 he very promptly recognised the newly founded state of Israel). In 1932, as discussed earlier, Stalin attacked the 'common narrow-minded mania of "anti-Polonism"' and concluded a non-aggression pact with Poland. In 1945 Stalin said to the Czechoslovaks, 'I hate the Germans, but hatred must not hinder us from objectively assessing them. The Germans are a great people, very good technical people and organisers. Good, innately brave soldiers. It's impossible to eliminate them. They'll stay.'[28] Stalin's contrast with Hitler, who treated the Slavs as *Untermenschen*, could not have been starker.

Similarly, although Stalin believed that Russia formed the core of the Soviet Union and he may have laid the foundations for the development of Russian nationalism after his death,[29] he did not allow chauvinistic Russian nationalism to develop. Contrary to some scholars' contentions, Stalin was not a Russian nationalist. When the Polish communists themselves dared not mention Russia's former colonial rule of Poland in their 1952 constitution draft, Stalin edited the Polish draft to include in its preamble the phrase 'the national enslavement imposed by the Prussian, Austrian and Russian conquerors and colonizers'.[30] Likewise, in 1948 Stalin frankly declared to the Hungarians that 'the Russia of the tsars was guilty' of 'helping the Habsburgs suppress the Hungarian revolution' in 1848.[31] Stalin's motto was, 'What is useful to the proletariat and the State is honest.'[32] He identified himself not with Russia but with the Soviet socialist regime, with collectivised agriculture and heavy industry. The Soviet regime was patently not Russia.

His personal identification with the Soviet regime allowed him seemingly to renounce 'private' concerns in favour of the political. He often referred to himself in the third person singular, implying that he was not 'Stalin', which he equated with Soviet power. Arvo Tuominen, who had observed Stalin closely in the 1930s, noted:

> Stalin's autocracy was genuine, and hence he could assume a different attitude than Hitler and Mussolini. These men emphasized themselves, flaunted their power, whereas Stalin did not speak of himself but of the party and the government and the Soviet people. Had I not been aware of

the limitlessness of his power, I would have been greatly misled in seeing him at meetings. He never sought to dictate but always said, 'Why speak of me? Speak of the matter at hand.'[33]

It is true that, like every politician, he wanted power. Once in power, however, his personal concerns became matters of state. If he symbolised the state which realised the objective laws of history as explained by Marxism, a struggle against Stalin was a struggle against historical inevitability and for the restoration of capitalism.

Power always invites fear and awe to some extent, and Stalin certainly used his power, the 'all-conquering power of Bolshevism', to intimidate the people. According to a 'forbidden anecdote' dating to 1931, the OGPU chief Iagoda asked Stalin, 'Which would you prefer, Comrade Stalin: that Party members should be loyal to you from conviction or from fear?' Stalin: 'From fear.' Iagoda: 'Why?' Stalin: 'Because convictions can change; fear remains.'[34] This Machiavellian anecdote is probably apocryphal, but it reflects the style of Stalin's rule.[35] Khrushchev later observed, 'I used to think that this urge to glorify himself was a weakness unique to Stalin, but apparently men like Stalin and Mao are very similar in this respect: to stay in power, they consider it indispensable for their authority to be held on high, not only to make the people obedient to them, but to make the people afraid of them as well.' Khrushchev had to admit, however: 'I will give Stalin credit for one thing: he didn't simply come with a sword and conquer our minds and bodies. No, he demonstrated his superior skill in subordinating and manipulating people – an important quality necessary in a great leader. In everything about Stalin's personality there was something admirable and correct as well as something savage.'[36]

Fear was necessary, but it was not sufficient. When asked by Emil Ludwig why it was 'necessary to inspire fear in the interests of strengthening the regime', Stalin replied that Ludwig was mistaken: 'Do you really believe that we could have retained power and have had the backing of the vast masses for 14 years by methods of intimidation and terror? No, that is impossible.'[37] Almost certainly it was belief, shared to some degree by the leader and the led alike, that sustained the Stalinist regime: belief in the future, belief in salvation, belief in the rightness of socialism and belief in the laws of history. It was belief that justified his terror. In this sense, the Soviet system was not unlike a religious order with Stalin as its God. Stalin deified himself, but at the same time disdained (or pretended to disdain) this deification, which he justified as necessary for political purposes.

Unlike Hitler, Stalin had created a new, Soviet elite who shared his belief and who were free of the legacy of the old regime, politically loyal and professionally competent. Thus, during the Second World War, for example, despite numerous frictions, Stalin and the Soviet military high command worked together much better than Hitler and the Wehrmacht generals whose loyalty Hitler could not entirely trust. Stalin suspected the loyalty of the older generation of cadres. He could not work with them during the Civil War and could not have done so during the Second World War.

Stalin was confident. He believed that history would justify him. Although his regime was secretive, he knew that 'One cannot hide anything. In the end, everything will be known, everything will become public.'[38] Of course, one does not know everything about Stalin, but one knows far more now than, say, 15 years ago. Stalin maintained that the laws of history spoke through him.

This is not to say that he believed everything he said.[39] His speeches and official statements were not revelations but political tools. As discussed in Chapter 7, he did not believe in the accusations of foreign espionage against 'all those Trotskists and Bukharinists'. When talking with his doctor M.G. Shneiderovich in the mid-1930s, Stalin even said, 'You are a clever doctor, and have to understand that there is not a word of truth in them [Soviet newspapers such as *Pravda*, meaning 'Truth', and *Izvestiia*, meaning 'News']'. Shneiderovich, taken aback, did not know what to say, so Stalin laughed and made a joke of it. One does not know whether Stalin was being cynical or provocative (he even asked the doctor whether he sometimes wished to poison him!).[40] At the Potsdam Conference, the British Foreign Minister Ernest Bevin, a Labour Party member and Minister of Labour under Churchill, happened to stand beside Stalin in the men's washroom. Bevin made a joke through his interpreter: 'This is the only place in the capitalist world where workers can rightfully take the means of production into their own hands.' Stalin smiled and replied, 'The same is true in the socialist world.'[41] Stalin's remark may have been merely a joke, but it is also possible that he was being cynical – or, again, the remark may be apocryphal.

Stalin was familiar with Machiavelli, and followed at least some of his precepts. Yet Machiavelli's precepts, like everyone else's except for those of Marx (and those of Lenin as well), were a mere tool for Stalin. According to Molotov's account, as related by his interlocutor, Stalin believed that Machiavellian political philosophy was alien to the 'spirit' of Soviet society: 'Stalin spoke the truth, but Machiavelli always found ways to present a lie as a truth. Or sometimes vice versa.'[42] Stalin understood that politicians, including Kamenev who was accused of using Machiavelli to criticise party rule, were all Machiavellian. Stalin, however, considered himself to be much more than a mere Machiavellian. It was Marxism that guided Stalin, though naturally he interpreted Marxism in his own way, calling his interpretation 'creative Marxism'. He was proud of his achievement of the Soviet Union and identified himself with it. Obviously the country was not yet a communist Utopia, but he held that it had laid the foundations for a new, post-capitalist world – no mean achievement.

As a Marxist, he spoke for the people of the Soviet Union, but there is no evidence that he manifested a special interest in their material life. Perhaps he sincerely believed that the Soviet people lived better than the workers in the capitalist world, struck as they were by the Depression and then by the war. In 1950 Stalin told Soviet economists that 'Americans boast about their high standard of living, but according to their own statistics two out of three workers don't make a living wage. All of these capitalist tricks need to be exposed.'[43] Moreover, he emphasised that the exploitation of man by man had been eliminated in the Soviet Union and that the working people in the Soviet Union, unlike those in the capitalist countries, have the right to employment, rest and leisure, education, superannuation and free medical service. Stalin himself cared little for material luxury, although, unlike the ordinary Soviet citizen, he did not suffer from hunger or lack of necessities and often indulged in sumptuous gluttony. Unlike Mao, Stalin was ascetic and monkish in his peculiar way.[44] In this regard, he was similar to Tsar Nicholas I (ruled 1825–1855) who was puritanical, stern and severe and always slept on a cot with a straw pallet.[45] Stalin, who always slept on a divan, indeed seemed to have liked Nicholas's Spartan habits.[46] Like Nicholas, he probably knew that the Russian people were hungry and not free, and even noted in 1937 that 'Freedom and hunger are incompatible.' Like Nicholas, Stalin may have feared the potential for rebellion by the hungry and unfree masses of people. The Soviet labour camps, for example, became increasingly restless and unruly towards the end of his life. Speaking in 1950 to East German communists about West Germany, Stalin said, 'the people are afraid and silent, but sometimes the silence of such a patient people is more dangerous than open demonstrations'.[47] He probably knew that his remark applied to the Soviet people as well.

Despite everything, Stalin survived. Moreover, as Ernest Gellner aptly notes, 'Marxism survived Stalinist terror.' As Gellner argues, Stalin's terror 'even established a kind of testimony to the new revelation, by signalling that something tremendous was happening'. 'Marxism failed to survive Brezhnevite squalor', however, which was 'most conspicuous in the very sphere of life, the economic, which was meant to be the location of a "second coming" '.[48] Stalin personified what Gellner called 'something tremendous' – a great transformation accompanied by a great struggle. Stalin was proud of his creation, and believed that he was the personification of the Soviet system. However, the great transformation could not overtake, let alone surpass, advanced capitalism in the economic sphere; eventually the comparative economic misery of socialism left it doomed. In the end, Stalin proved to be right: 'Freedom and hunger are incompatible' – 'The genuine freedom of people can exist only when they are strong economically.'[49]

Notes

[1] Alliluyeva, *Only One Year*, 378.

[2] Ibid., 382.

[3] Gromyko, 362.

[4] A.H. Birse, *Memoirs of an Interpreter* (New York, 1967), 212.

[5] Alliluyeva, *Only One Year*, 366, 372.

[6] Gromyko, 373.

[7] Alliluyeva, *Only One Year*, 364.

[8] *Bol'shevistskoe rukovodstvo. Perepiska. 1917–1927* (Moscow, 1996), 263. See also Service, *Stalin*, 226.

[9] *Surovaia drama naroda* (Moscow, 1989), 501.

[10] Naimark, 'Cold War Studies', 10.

[11] Birse, 212.

[12] *The Memoir of Anthony Eden: The Reckoning* (Boston, Mass., 1965), 595. Elsewhere, however, Eden wrote: 'A meeting with him [Stalin] would be in all respects a creepy, even a sinister experience if it weren't for his readiness to laugh, when his whole face creases and his little eyes open. He looks more and more like bruin.' Ibid., 479.

[13] Charles E. Bohlen, *Witness to History, 1929–1969* (New York, 1973), 339, 340.

[14] Harriman and Abel, 535–6.

[15] *Winston and Clementine: The Personal Letters of the Churchills* (Boston, Mass., 1999), 506.

[16] His letter dated 29 July 1945 in *Dear Bess: The Letters from Harry to Bess Truman, 1910–1959* (New York and London, 1983), 522.

[17] Quoted in Richardson, 201–2.

[18] De Gaulle, 68, 69.

[19] See, for instance, Martin Amis, *Koba the Dread: Laughter and the Twenty Million* (London, 2002), 276–7.

[20] *Pravda*, 21 December 1994, 3 (Boris Slavin). The passage is L. Trotsky, *The Defence of Terrorism (Terrorism and Communism)* (London, 1921), 59.

[21] Apparently, however, Stalin liked de Gaulle who was 'firm' (*tverdyi*, perhaps like steel), because 'If you are weak, of course, you'll be crushed.' Nevezhin, 418.

[22] *Molotov Remembers*, 304.

[23] Zhdanov, *Vzgliad v proshloe*, 69.

[24] Gromyko, 113. See also *Memoirs by Harry S. Truman*, v. 1 (New York, 1955), 361. Stalin probably had a weakness for music. In 1935 he said, 'Don't let's

trouble the musicians.' The musical profession as a whole escaped the Great Terror lightly. Caroline Brooke, 'Soviet Musicians and the Great Terror', *Europe–Asia Studies*, 54:3 (May 2002), 397.

[25] Rayfield, *Stalin and His Hangmen*, 434.

[26] *Memoirs by Harry S. Truman*, 364.

[27] Svetlana testified that in the end Stalin grew doubtful of what he had created – the 'Doctors' Plot'. Richardson, 247 and Alliluyeva, *Twenty Letters*, 217. For Stalin's contradictory attitudes towards Jews, see Leonid Luks, 'Zum Stalinschen Antisemitismus – Brüche und Widersprüche,' *Jahrbuch für Historische Kommunismusforschung*, 1 (1997).

[28] *Istochnik*, 1997, no. 5, 128.

[29] See David Brandenberger, *National Bolshevism: Stalinist Mass Culture and the Formation of Modern Russian National Identity, 1931–1956* (Cambridge, Mass., 2002). Note the following curious incident. At the 24 May 1945 meeting mentioned earlier (p. 172), according to A.A. Zhdanov, as narrated to his son, when Stalin proposed a toast to the Russian people, there was a loud response from the floor, 'To the Soviet people.' Stalin was silent for a moment and repeated 'To the Russian people.' This exchange was not reported in the press. See Zhdanov, 135.

[30] *Cold War International History Project Bulletin*, 11 (Winter 1998), 150, 151.

[31] Nevezhin, 503.

[32] Quoted in Enzo Biagi, *Svetlana: An Intimate Portrait* (New York, 1967), 57.

[33] Arvo Tuominen, *The Bells of the Kremlin* (Lebanon, NH, 1983), 170.

[34] Alexander Weissberg, *The Accused* (New York, 1951), 510.

[35] Machiavelli preferred fear to love, 'for love is held by a chain of obligation which, men being selfish, is broken whenever it serves their purpose; but fear is maintained by a dread of punishment which never fails'. Machiavelli, *The Prince*, ch. XVII.

[36] *Khrushchev Remembers*, 6, 7.

[37] Stalin, *Works*, 13:111.

[38] Quoted in Mgeladze, 116.

[39] For a contrary view, see Jörg Baberowski, *Der rote Terror: Die Geschichte des Stalinismus* (Munich, 2003), 12.

[40] *Istochnik*, 1998, no. 2, 72.

[41] Valentin Berezhkov, *Riadom so Stalinym* (Moscow, 1998), 324.

[42] Iulian Semenov, 'Nenapisannye romany', *Neva*, 1988, no. 6, 78.

[43] Pollock, 32.

[44] Unlike Stalin, who stopped writing poems in his teens, Mao continued to write poems into his old age.

[45] W. Bruce Lincoln, *Nicholas I: Emperor and Autocrat of All the Russias* (Bloomington, Ind., 1978), 159.

[46] Sebag Montefiore, 101.

[47] *Istochnik*, 2003, no. 3, 111.

[48] Ernest Gellner, 'Civil Society in Historical Context', *International Social Science Journal*, 43:3 (1991), 505.

[49] Nevezhin, 152, 161.

Bibliography

This bibliography lists only important and frequently used books and articles, though a few items not referred to in the notes are also listed for further reading. Others such as archival sources and historical documents reproduced in Russian periodicals are listed in footnotes.

Alliluyeva, Svetlana, *Twenty Letters to A Friend.* New York, 1968.

— *Only One Year.* New York, 1969.

Anders, Władysław, *Bez ostatniego Rozdiału: Wspomnienia z lat 1939– 1946.* 2nd ed. Newtown, Wales, 1950.

Andrew, Christopher and Julie Elkner. 'Stalin and Foreign Intelligence', in Shukman, Harold (ed.), *Redefining Stalinism.* London, 2003.

Argenbright, Robert, 'Red Tsaritsyn: Precursor of Stalinist Terror', *Revolutionary Russia*, 4:2 (December 1991).

Arsenidze, P., 'Iz vospominanii o Staline', *Novyi zhurnal*, 72 (1963).

Baibakov, N.K., *Ot Stalina do Iel'tsina.* Moscow, 1998.

Banac, Ivo (ed.), *The Diary of Georgi Dimitrov, 1933–1949.* New Haven, Conn., 2003.

Bazhanov, Boris, *Vospominaniia byvshego sekretaria Stalina.* Paris, 1980.

Berlin, Isaiah and Ramin Jahanbegloo. *Conversations with Isaiah Berlin.* New York, 1991.

Bialer, Seweryn (ed.), *Stalin and His Generals.* New York, 1969.

Birse, A.H., *Memoirs of an Interpreter.* New York, 1967.

Brackman, Roman, *The Secret File of Joseph Stalin: A Hidden Life.* London, 2001.

Brandenberger, David and A.M. Dubrovsky, ' "The People Need a Tsar": The Emergence of National Bolshevism as Stalinist Ideology, 1931- 1941,' *Europe–Asia Studies*, 50:5 (July 1998).

Bullock, Allan, *Hitler and Stalin: Parallel Lives.* New York, 1992.

Chuev, Feliks, *Tak govoril Kaganovich.* Moscow, 1992.

— *Soldaty imperii.* Moscow, 1998.

Churchill, Winston S., *Triumph and Tragedy*. Cambridge, Mass., 1953.

Cohen, Stephen F., *Bukharin and the Bolshevik Revolution: A Political Biography, 1888–1938*. New York, 1973.

Conquest, Robert, *Stalin: Breaker of Nations*. London, 1991.

Danilov, V., R. Manning and L. Viola (eds), *Tragediia Sovetskoi derevni: Kollektivizatsiia i raskulachivaniie*. 5 vols. Moscow, 1999–2004.

Davies, R.W. and Stephen G. Wheatcroft *The Years of Hunger: Soviet Agriculture, 1931–1933*. London, 2004.

Davies, R.W., Oleg V. Khlevniuk and E.A. Rees (eds) *The Stalin–Kaganovich Correspondence 1931–1936*. New Haven, Conn., 2003.

Davrichewy, Joseph, *Ah! Ce qu'on rigolait bien avec mon copain Staline*. Paris, 1979.

De Gaulle, Charles, *Salvation: 1944–1946*. New York, 1960.

Djilas, Milovan, *Conversations with Stalin*. New York and London, 1962.

Ellison, Herbert J., 'Stalin and His Biographers: The Lenin–Stalin Relationship,' in Elwood, Ralph Carter (ed.), *Reconsiderations on the Russian Revolution*. Cambridge, Mass., 1976.

Figes, Orlando, *A People's Tragedy: A History of the Russian Revolution*. New York, 1997.

Getty, J. Arch and Oleg V. Naumov, *The Road to Terror: Stalin and the Self-Destruction of the Bolsheviks, 1932–1939*. New Haven, Conn., 1999.

Gorlizki, Yoram and Oleg Khlevniuk, *Cold Peace: Stalin and the Soviet Ruling Circle, 1945–1953*. Oxford, 2004.

Gromov, Evgenii, *Stalin: iskusstvo i vlast'*. Moscow, 2003.

Gromyko, Andrei. *Memoirs*. New York, 1989.

Harriman, W. Averell and Elie Abel. *Special Envoy to Churchill and Stalin*. New York, 1975.

Himmer, Robert, 'On the Origin and Significance of the Name "Stalin"' *Russian Review*, 45:3 (July 1986).

— 'The Transition from War Communism to the New Economic Policy: An Analysis of Stalin's Views', *Russian Review*, 53:4 (October 1994).

— 'First Impressions Matter: Stalin's Initial Encounter with Lenin, Tammerfors 1905', *Revolutionary Russia*, 14:2 (December 2001).

Holloway, David, *Stalin and the Bomb*. New Haven, Conn., 1994.

Hughes, James, *Stalin, Siberia and the Crisis of the New Economic Policy*. Cambridge, 1991.

Iosif Stalin v ob'iatiiakh sem'i. Moscow, 1993.

Ilizarov, B.S., *Tainaia zhizn' Stalina*. Moscow, 2002.

Iremaschwili, J., *Stalin und die Tragödie Georgiens*. Berlin, 1931.

Jansen, Marc and Nikita Petrov, *Stalin's Loyal Executioner: People's Commissar Nikolai Ezhov, 1895–1940*. Stanford, Calif., 2002.

Kak lomali NEP: Stenogrammy plenumov TsK VKP(b) 1928–1929 gg. 5 vols. Moscow, 2000.

Khlevniuk, Oleg, 'The Objectives of the Great Terror, 1937–1938', in Cooper, J., M. Perrie, and E.A. Rees (eds), *Soviet History, 1917–53: Essays in Honour of R.W. Davies*. London, 1995.

Khrushchev Remembers. Boston, Mass., 1970.

Khrushchev Remembers: The Last Testament. Boston, Mass., 1974.

Khrushchev Remembers: The Glasnost Tapes. Boston, Mass., 1990.

Kun, Miklós, *Stalin: An Unknown Portrait*. Budapest, 2003.

Kuromiya, Hiroaki, *Stalin's Industrial Revolution: Workers and Politics, 1928–1932*. Cambridge, 1988.

— *Freedom and Terror in the Donbas: A Ukrainian–Russian Borderland, 1870s–1990s*. Cambridge, 1998.

— 'Accounting for the Great Terror', *Jahrbücher für Geschichte Osteuropas*, 53:1 (2005).

Laloy, Jean, 'A Moscou: Entre Staline et de Gaulle', *Revue des Études Slaves*, 54:1–2 (1982).

Laquer, Walter, *Stalin: The Glasnost Revelations*. London, 1990.

Lenin, V.I., *Collected Works*, 45 vols. Moscow, 1960–1970.

Lih, Lars T., Oleg V. Naumov and Oleg V. Khlevniuk (eds), *Stalin's Letters to Molotov, 1925–1936*. New Haven, Conn., 1995.

Linz, Susan J. (ed.), *The Impact of World War II on the Soviet Union*. Totowa, NJ, 1985.

Löwe, Heinz-Dietrich, *Stalin: Der entfesselte Revolutionär*. Zurich, 2002.

Luks, Leonid. 'Zum Stalinschen Antisemitismus – Brüche und Widersprüche,' *Jahrbuch für Historische Kommunismusforschung*, 1 (1997).

McNeal, Robert H., *Stalin: Man & Ruler*. London, 1988.

Mar'iamov, G., *Kremlevskii tsenzor: Stalin smotrit kino*. Moscow, 1992.

Medvedev, Roy, *Let History Judge*. New York, 1989.

Mgeladze, Akakii. *Stalin kakim ia ego znal*. N.p., 2001.

Mick, Christoph. 'Frühe Stalin-Biographien 1928–1932', *Jahrbücher für Geschichte Osteuropas*, 36:3 (1988).

Mikoian, Anastas Ivanovich, *Tak bylo. Razmyshleniia o minuvshem*. Moscow, 1999.

Molotov Remembers: Inside Kremlin Politics. Chicago, Ill., 1993.

Naimark, Norman M., 'Cold War Studies and New Archival Materials on Stalin', *Russian Review*, 61:1 (January 2002)

— 'Post-Soviet Russian Historiography on the Emergence of the Soviet Bloc,' *Kritika*, 5:3 (Summer 2004).

Nevezhin, V.A., *Zastol'nye rechi Stalina.* Moscow, 2003.

Ostrovskii, Aleksandr, *Kto stoial za spinoi Stalina.* Moscow, 2002.

Overy, Richard, *Russia's War.* London, 1997.

Pechatnov, Vladimir O., *The Big Three after World War II* (Cold War International History Project Working Paper No. 13). Washington, DC, 1995.

Pimanov, A.V. S.V. Deviatov, V.V. Pavlov and V.P. Zhiliaev, *Stalin. Tragediia sem'i.* Moscow, 2004.

Pokhlebkin, V.V., *Velikii psevdonim.* Moscow, 1996.

Pollock, Ethan, *Conversations with Stalin on Questions of Political Economy* (Cold War International History Project Working Paper No. 33). Washington, DC, 2001.

Pomper, Philip, *Lenin, Trotsky and Stalin.* New York, 1990.

Popov, V.P., 'Gosudarstvennyi terror v sovetskoi Rossii. 1923–1953 gg. (istochniki i ikh interpretatsiia)', *Otechestvennye arkhivy*, 1992, no. 2.

Radzinsky, Edvard, *Stalin.* New York, 1997.

Rancour-Laferriere, Daniel. *The Mind of Stalin: A Psychoanalytic Study.* Ann Arbor, Mich., 1988.

Rayfield, Donald, 'Stalin the Poet', *PN Review*, 11:3 (1984).

— *Stalin and His Hangmen.* London, 2004.

Richardson, Rosamond, *The Long Shadow: Inside Stalin's Family.* London, 1994.

Rieber, Alfred J., 'Stalin, Man of the Borderlands', *American Historical Review*, 106:5 (December 2001).

Rzheshevskii, O.A., *Stalin i Cherchill'.* Moscow, 2004.

Sakharov, V.A., *'Politicheskoe zaveshchanie' Lenina. Real'nost' istorii i mify politiki.* Moscow, 2003.

Samuelson, Lennart *Plans for Stalin's War Machine: Tukhachevskii and Military–Economic Planning, 1925–1941.* London, 2000.

Sebag Montefiore, Simon, *Stalin: The Court of the Red Tsar.* London, 2003.

Serebriakova, Galina, 'Smerch', *Pod"em*, no. 7 (1988).

— 'Oni delali chest' idee, kotoroi sluzhili', *Izvestiia*, 30 January 1989.

Service, Robert, *Stalin: A Biography*. London, 2004.

Shukman, Harold (ed.), *Stalin's Generals*. New York, 1993.

Slovo tovarishchu Stalinu. Moscow, 2002.

Slusser, Robert M., *Stalin in October: The Man Who Missed the Revolution*. Baltimore and London, 1987.

Smith, Edward Ellis, *The Young Stalin*. New York, 1967.

Sokolov, B.V., *Stalin. Vlast' i krov'*. Moscow, 2004.

Souvarine, Boris, *Stalin: A Critical Survey of Bolshevism*. New York, 1939.

Stalin, I.V. *Works*, vols. 1–13. Moscow, 1952–55.

— *Sochineniia*, vols. 1–3 (14–16). Stanford, Calif., 1967.

Stalin and the Soviet-Finnish War, 1939–1940. London, 2002.

Sudoplatov, Pavel and Anatoli Sudoplatov, *Special Tasks*. Boston, Mass., 1994.

Suny, Ronald Grigor, 'After the Fall: Stalin and His Biographers', *Radical History Review*, 54 (Fall 1992).

— 'Beyond Psychohistory: The Young Stalin in Georgia', *Slavic Review*, 50:1 (Spring 1991).

Trotsky, Leon, *Stalin*. New York, 1967.

Tucker, Robert C., *Stalin as Revolutionary, 1879–1929*. New York, 1973.

— *Stalin in Power: The Revolution from Above*. New York, 1990.

Tucker, Robert C. (ed.), *The Lenin Anthology*. New York, 1975.

Ulam, Adam B., *Stalin: The Man and His Era*. London, 1973.

Uratadze, Grigorii, *Vospominaniia gruzinskogo sotsial-demokrata*. Stanford, Calif., 1968.

Van Ree, Erik, 'Stalin's Bolshevism: The First Decade,' *International Review of Social History*, 39:2 (August 1994).

— 'Stalin and the National Question,' *Revolutionary Russia*, 7:2 (December 1994).

— ' "Lenin's Last Struggle" Revisited,' *Revolutionary Russia*, 14:2 (December 2001).

— *The Political Thought of Joseph Stalin*. London, 2002.

Volkogonov, Dmitri, *Stalin: Triumph and Tragedy*. New York, 1991.

Vostochnaia Evropa v dokumentakh Rossiiskikh arkhivov, 1944–1953 gg., v. 1. Moscow, 1997.

Zhdanov, Iu.A, *Vzgliad v proshloe: vospominaniia ochevidtsa*. Rostov on the Don, 2004.

Index

1905 Revolution, 13

Akhmatova, Anna, 179
Alexander I, 158, 159, 179
Alliluev, Pavel, 192
Allilueva, Evgeniia, 192
Allilueva, Nadezhda, 28, 37,
       38, 70
   and life with Stalin, 107
   suicide (1932), 107–110
Allilueva, Svetlana, 9, 21, 109,
       169, 170, 192, 200n,
       201, 202, 204
   on Great Terror, 126
   on war, 175
Anders, Władysław, 181
Andreev, A.A., 82
'Anti-Comintern pact', 131n,
       142
Antonov rebellion (1921), 51
Argenbright, Robert, 41
Atlee, Clement, 185
Austria, 133
Austria–Hungary, 22, 27, 36

Babel', Isaak, 43, 114
Baberowski, Jörg, 163n
Baibakov, N.K., 97, 173
Baku, 17, 149
Baltic states, 36, 148
Barbusee, Henri, 69
Batumi, 10, 149
Batumi massacres (1902), 10

Bazhanov, Boris, 58, 60, 64,
       107, 121
Belarus, western, 143
Belov, P.A., 155
Beneš, Edvard, 198n
Berezhkov, Valentin, 159
Berggol'ts, Ol'ga, 175
Beriia, L.P., 151, 195
Berlin, 170, 189, 198n
Berlin, Isaiah, 32, 35, 36
   and Akhmatova, 179
Berman-Iurin, K.B., 118
'Berne incident' (1945), 186
Bessarabia, 148
Bevin, Ernest, 208
Bialer, Seweryn, 172
Birse, A.H., 32, 201–203
Bliukher, V.K., 124
Bliumkin, Ia.G., 90
Bogdanov, A.A., 18
Bohlen, Charles, 194, 203
Bolsheviks, 12, 15, 17
Bosphorous, strait of, 148
Brest-Litovsk, treaty of, 37, 43
Brezhnev, L.I., 97
Britain, 44, 68, 122, 140, 143,
       182, 183
   and Poland, 141
Budenyyi, S.M., 124
Bukharin, N.I., 20, 43, 58, 59,
       76, 81–83, 84, 106,
       119, 123
   on Great Terror, 127

and Lenin's 'testament', 63
on NEP, 51
and police reports (1928), 81
Bukovyna, northern, 148
Bulgakov, Mikhail, 43, 90
Bulganin, N.A., 192, 194–195

'Cambridge spies', ix, 160
Chaianov, A.V., 95
Chamberlain, Neville, 141
Chechens, 177
Cheka, see secret police
Chernov, V.M., 33
Chiang Kai-shek, 189
China, 68, 80, 104, 122, 189–190
Church, Greek Catholic, 174
Church, Russian Orthodox, 161, 174
Churchill, Winston, ix, 103, 139, 159, 185, 188, 203–204
  in Tehran, 161
  on Bulgaria, 160
  on Poles, 181
Clemenceau, Georges, 119, 121
Cold War, 180–191
collectivisation, 90–93, 96
Cominform, 188
Comintern, 57, 68, 118, 139
  abolished (1943), 161
'congress of victors' (1934), 112
constituent assembly (1918), 39
Crimean Tatars, 177
Cripps, Stafford, 148
Curzon line, 182
Czechoslovakia, 114, 133, 141
  1948 coup in, 188

Dardanelles, strait of, 148

David, Fritz (I.I. Kruglianskii), 118
Davrichewy, Joseph, 2, 10, 16
Day, Richard, 53
de Gaulle, Charles, 44, 160, 162, 169, 182, 183, 204
de-Stalinisation, 175, 201
Decembrism, 176
Decembrists, 174
defence budget, 105
dekulakisation, 90–93
Dimitrov, G.M., 136, 148, 161
Djilas, Milovan, 170, 171, 191
'Doctors' Plot' (1953), 194
Donbas, 115
Dostoevskii, F.M., 171, 196n
Dovzhenko, Aleksandr, 198n
Dzerzhinskii, F.E., 32
Dzhugashvili, Ekaterina, 1–3, 4, 8, 23n, 45, 46, 122
Dzhugashvili, Iakov, 16, 18, 58, 155, 166n
Dzhugashvili, Iosif, see Stalin, I.V.
Dzhugashvili, Vissarion, 1

Eden, Anthony, 203, 210n
Efron, Sergei, 118
Egorov, A.I., 44, 124
Eismont, N.B., 107
Eizenshtein, S., 35, 140
Elizabeth, Queen, 123
Enakievo, Ukraine, 102
Engels, Friedrich, 114
Enukidze, A.S., 70, 116
Estonia, 143
Ezhov, N.I., 118, 121, 123, 125, 132n

famine (1921–2), 52
famine (1932–3), 102–105

deaths, 103
grain exports, 103
grain production, 103
famine (1946–7), 176
February Revolution (1917),
        28–29
Fediuninskii, I.I., 156
Finland, 36, 116, 124, 144, 148
Finns, ethnic
    operation against
        (1937–38), 125
First World War, 27, 43
Fot'eva, L.A., 60
France, 114, 122, 140, 141,
        143, 182
    non-aggression pact with
        USSR (1932), 104

Gellner, Ernest, 209
Genghis Khan, 8, 123
George VI, 161
Georgia, 1, 8, 36, 44, 45, 62
Germans, ethnic
    deportations of (1935), 115
    operation against
        (1937–38), 125
    survey of (1934), 115
Germany, 22, 27, 36, 37, 43,
        114, 116, 121, 122,
        124, 138, 140, 141,
        143
    divided, 189
    revolution in (1923), 57
Gor'kii, Maksim, 3, 106
Gordov, V.N., 177
Gori, Georgia, 1
GPU, see secret police
Grabski, Stanisław, 182
grain procurement, 172
Gramsci, Antonio, 53
Great Terror, 120–128, 172
    statistics, 125

Greece, 149, 187
Greeks, ethnic
    operation against
        (1937–38), 125
Groman, V.G., 95
Gromyko, A.A., 97, 192, 201,
        202
Gulag, 97, 154, 178

Harriman, W. Averell, 160, 203
Haslam, Jonathan, 160
Hayter, William, 160
Hebrang, Andrija, 171
Hitler, Adolf, 104, 113, 114,
        119, 149, 163
    annexation of Austria, 133
    compared with Stalin, 172,
        205–208
    and his elite, 173
    Munich accord, 140
    murder of Röhm (1934),
        115
    seizure of Prague, 141
    seizure of Sudetenland, 133
Holocaust, 154
Hugo, Victor, 6
Hungary, 149

Iagoda, G.G., 59, 82, 116, 207
Iakir, I.E., 124
Ierusalimskii, A.S., 149
Ignat'ev, S.D., 205
'Industrial Party', 95
industrialisation, 85–86, 88,
        89, 93, 140, 171
Iran, 161, 187
Iremaschwili, I., 2, 3, 7, 18, 45
    exiled (1922), 57
Israel, 206
Italy, 121
Ivan the Terrible, 123, 179

Japan, 113, 114, 138, 155, 189

and Manchukuo, 104
non-aggression treaty with,
    149
Jewish Anti-fascist Committee,
    193
Jews, 12, 141, 154, 193–194,
    206
July Incident (1917), 33

Kaganovich, L.M., 83, 110,
    118, 126, 142, 170
Kalinin, M.I., 42, 67
Kamenev, L.B., 6, 22, 28, 29,
    32, 33, 42, 58, 59, 60,
    68, 121
    and Bukharin, 82–83
    and Lenin's 'testament', 61,
    63
    and Machiavelli, 120, 131n
    and October Revolution, 35
    and 'Riutin affair', 106
Kaplan, Fanny, 39
Kapler, Aleksei, 193
Katyn massacre, 143
Keke, see Dzhugashvili,
    Ekaterina
Kennan, George, 194
Kerenskii, A.F., 33, 47n
Khalkin Gol, battle at (1939),
    134, 141
Kharkiv, 158
Khlevniuk, Oleg, 121
Khoper experience (1929), 87
Khrushchev, N.S., 97, 153, 176,
    178, 184, 193, 207
    and Nadezhda Allilueva,
    108
Kim Il Sung, 190
Kirov, S.M., 67, 115
Koba, see Stalin, I.V.
Koestler, Arthur, 127
Kolyma, 154

Kondrat'ev, N.D., 95
Konev, I.S., 154, 155, 176
Kopelev, Lev, 102
Korean War, 190–191
Koreans, ethnic, 114
    operation against (1937),
    125
korenizatsiia (indigenisation),
    56
Kornilov affair (1917), 34
Kosygin, A.N., 97
Kotkin, Stephen, 137
Kovalev, M.P., 146
Krasin, Leonid, 16
Kravchenko, Galina, 108
'Kremlin affair' (1935), 117
Kronstadt rebellion (1921), 51
Krupskaia, Nadezhda, 27,
    59–61, 64
Kuibyshev, city of, 154
Kuibyshev, V.V., 77
'kulak operation' (1937–8), 124
Kulik, G.I., 151, 177
Kursk, battle of, 158
Kuzakova, M.O., 19
Kyiv, 43, 153

L'viv, 44, 154, 181, 182
L'vov, Prince, 33, 69
Lake Khasan, battle at (1938),
    133–134
Laloy, Jean, 162
'Lashevich Affair' (1926), 67
Laval, Pierre, 160
League of Nations, 101, 114
Left SRs, 35, 37, 39
Lenin, V.I., 1, 13, 14, 15–16,
    21, 26, 30, 33, 39, 41,
    42, 43, 44, 54
    April Theses, 30
    and church, 57
    death, 53

and 'Decree on Peace', 36
and Duma, 15
'expropriations', 16
February Revolution, 27
land reform, 15
Malinovskii, 54
Martov, 38
Mensheviks, 55
and NEP, 51
October Revolution, 34–35
and Polish campaign
  (1920), 43
revolutionary defeatism, 13
on success of NEP, 55–56
on terror, 41
'testament', 59–63
and Trotskii, 31, 46, 60, 61
Leningrad, siege of, 156
Leningrad affair (1949–51),
  178
'Leningrad Opposition', 66
Lih, Lars, 47n, 163n
Lithuania, 143
Litvinov, M.M., 104, 141, 199n
Louis XI, 123
Louis XVI, 123
Ludwig, Emil, 207
Lyons, Eugene, 97
Lysenko, Trofim, 179

Machiavelli, Niccolò, x, xiiin,
  22, 120, 128, 131n,
  134, 208, 211n
Maiskii, I.M., 159
Malenkov, G.M., 151
Malinovskii, Roman, 19, 21
Manchukuo, 104, 124
Mandel'shtam, Osip, 105
Manhattan Project, 185
Mao Zedong, 80, 189, 190,
  199n, 211n

compared with Stalin, x,
  209
Marshall Plan, 188
Martin, Terry, 57
Martov, Iu.O., 37–38
Marx, Karl, 86
Mastny, Vojtech, 187
Matchavariani, David, 11
Meir, Golda, 193
Mensheviks, 12, 17, 29, 32, 35
  in Georgia, 45–46
Menzhinskii, V.R., 95
Merkulov, V.N., 150, 153
Mgeladze, A.I., 126, 205
Mikhoels, S.M., 193
Mikoian, A.I., 115, 152, 175,
  193
Mikołajczyk, Stanisław,
  181–183
Miliukov, P.N., 30, 31, 128
Millar, James, 171
Molotov, V.M., 19, 28, 29, 123,
  141, 151, 170, 178,
  193, 202–203, 205,
  208
  on Churchill, 172
  on collectivisation, 172
  on English life, 172
  and expulsion of 'social
    aliens' (1935), 119
  on Great Terror, 127
  and intelligence reports,
    152
  Molotov–Ribbentrop pact,
    143
  trip to Berlin (1940), 149
  on Ukraine, 102
  and Zhemchuzhina, 178
Molotov–Ribbentrop pact
  (1939), 141
Montesquieu, Charles, 194
Morozov, Pavlik, 137

Moscow show trials (1936–8), 121–123
Moscow, battle of (1941), 156
Munich accord (1938), 139
Muranov, M.N., 28

Naimark, Norman, 187
NATO, 189
Nazaretian, A.M., 202
NEP, 51–53, 74–75, 86
    crisis of, 75–80
New Economic Policy, see NEP
Nicholas I, 179, 209
Nicholas II, 13, 27, 28, 39
Nikolaev, L.V., 115–116
NKVD, see secret police
Nosovich, General, 40
Novikov, A.A., 162
Nussimbaum, Lev, 11

October Revolution (1917), 34–35
OGPU, see secret police
Onufrieva, P.G., 19
Ordzhonikidze, G. (Sergo) K., 18, 45, 82, 84
Osóbka-Morawski, E., 186
Ostarbeiter, 177
Ottoman Empire, 22
Overy, Richard, 158

Paderewski, Ignacy, 205
Palewski, Gaston, 181
Paris Commune, viii, 34
Pasternak, Boris, 175
Pavlov, D.G., 153
peasant uprisings, 105
Petrovskaia, S.L., 19
Piatakov, G.L., 61, 88, 122
Piłsudski, Józef, 43, 104
Plekhanov, G.V., 31
pogroms (1905), 17
pogroms (1918–20), 43

Poland, 36, 104, 116, 124, 141, 143, 160, 181–183
    Constitution (1952), 206
    elections in 1947, 188
    Government in exile, 181
    intelligence on USSR, 104
    Lublin Committee, 181, 182
    Provisional Government, 184
    Ukrainians in, 181
Poles, ethnic, 114
    deportations of (1935), 115
    operation against (1937–38), 125
Polish campaign (1920), 43–44
Polish Communist Party, 118
'Polish Military Organisation' (POW), 104
Potsdam conference (1945), 122, 160, 185, 205, 208
Preobrazhenskii, E.A., 55, 86
Provisional Government (1917), 28–33

Röhm, Ernst, 115
Rákosi, Mátthiás, 191
Radek, K.B., 59, 63, 88, 122
Ramishvili, Isidor, 45
Ramzin, L.K., 95
Rappalo, treaty of (1922), 57
Rasputin, Grigorii, 27
Rayfield, Donald, 5
Red Army, 123–124, 148, 151, 154
    advanced to Poland, 143
    battle for Berlin, 170, 198n
    collectivisation, 91
    Warsaw Uprising, 181
    casualties of, 157, 159
    growth of, 140

looting and rape by,
170–171
reform of, 146
Redens, Anna, 192
Redens, Stanislav, 192
religious revival, postwar, 174
Remarque, E.M., 205
Richardson, Rosamond, 108
'Riutin affair' (1932), 105
Riutin, M.N., 94
Rokossovskii, K.K., 158, 167,
180, 201
Rolland, Romain, 116
Romania, 149
Roosevelt, Franklin D., 160,
162, 184
Russian Social Democratic
Party (RSDRP), 5, 9,
12
Russo-Japanese War, 13
Rustaveli, Shota, 8
Rybal'chenko, F.T., 177
Rykov, A.I., 59, 66

Sakharov, V.A., 60, 72n
Second World War, 143,
150–162
Soviet deaths in, 171
secret police, 57, 69, 84, 94, 97,
104, 115, 117, 154
and Bliumkin, 90
and collectivisation, 91
Great Terror, 120–128
infiltration of church by,
161
intelligence reports, 81
and Kirov murder, 116
show trial (1930), 95
in Tbilisi, 45
in Tsaritsyn, 40
Sen, Amartya, 103
Sergeev, Artem, 137

Service, Robert, 7
Shah Pahlavi, 161
'Shakhty affair' (1928), 79–80
Shaposhnikov, B.M., 156
Shliapnikov, A.G., 116
Shneiderovich, M.G., 208
Sholokhov, Mikhail, 91
Short Course, 96, 135
Shostakovich, Dmitrii, 179
Siniavskii, Andrei, vii
Skoropadskii, Hetman, 37
Skrypnyk, M.O., 112, 117
Socialist Revolutionaries
(SRs), 15, 29, 32, 35,
39
trial of (1922), 57
Sokol'nikov, G.Ia., 66, 68, 82,
119, 122
Solzhenitsyn, A.I., 97
Soso, *see* Stalin, I.V.
Souvarine, Boris, xiii, 114
Spanish Civil War, 121
Spiridonova, Mariia, 153
'Stalin Constitution' (1936),
113, 138, 199n
Stalin, I.V.
1905 Revolution, 13–14
academic performance in
seminary, 5
address to the nation
(1941), 152
adopted pen name Stalin,
19
ageing of, 155
appointment as General
Secretary (1922), 50,
54
arrested, 9, 10, 18, 19, 20
as 'Asiatic', 8, 134
atomic bomb, 186
in Baku, 17, 44
in Batumi, 10

biographers, vii, ix
Britain, 142, 144, 162, 183, 186
Bukharin and Bukharinists, 75, 81, 83, 106, 135–136, 202
Bulganin, 192, 194–195
Charles Darwin, 4
Churchill, 128, 139, 160, 162
collectivisation, 87, 103, 136
and common criminals, 21
concordat with church (1943), 161
conduct in seminary, 4
co-opted on to party CC (1912), 19
cult of, 162, 191
de Gaulle, 162, 169, 210n
death of, 195
on death, 169, 170
on defeatism (1939), 144
dekulakisation, 87, 189
and doctors, 191–192, 194
East-Central Europe, 180, 183
on education, 137
wife Ekaterina, 16, 18
elected to Politburo (1919), 42
on Engels, 114
entered Tbilisi theological seminary, 4
exile, 11, 18, 19, 20, 21
expelled from seminary, 8
'expropriations', 16, 38
famine (1932–3), 103
famine (1946–7), 176–177, 197n
February 1946 speech, 188
France, 144, 147
on freedom and hunger, 136, 210
funeral, 201
Germans and Germany, 141, 147, 149, 206
on God, 137
in Gori school, 3
Great Terror, 120–128, 180, 205
health, 191–192
and history, 8, 192
Hitler, 114, 115, 122, 149, 154, 162, 172, 196n, 205–208
Iagoda, 116, 207
son Iakov, 16, 18, 58, 155
identification with the Soviet Union, x, 97, 206
illegitimate children, 8, 19, 21, 24n
on imperialist powers, 144, 170
industrialisation, 85, 88, 89, 93
on intelligence, 81, 104, 119, 150, 152, 160, 185, 194
on intelligentsia, 189
Ivan the Terrible, 123, 179
Japan, 13, 149, 189
on Jesus, 3
and Jews, 12, 141, 193–194, 206
jokes, 89–90, 142, 173
Kaganovich, 142
Kamenev, 6, 22, 32, 57
Kazbegi's The Patricide, 6
Kirov murder, 115
knowledge of foreign languages, 20
as Koba, 7–8

Korean War, 190–191
Krupskaia, 59, 60, 64
lack of feminine influence
    on, 109
Lenin, 7, 12, 13, 14, 15–16,
    21, 22, 31–33, 39–40,
    43, 44, 54, 60, 62, 64,
    68, 84
as listener, 7, 203
as 'little dictator', 7
loneliness, 192
Machiavelli, x, xiiin, 22,
    25n, 128, 208
Malinovskii, 19, 21
Mao, 190, 199n, 209
Martov, 37–38
Marxism, 20, 137, 208
May 1945 speech, 171–173
Mensheviks, 12, 30
military specialists, 39, 40
Molotov, 19, 29, 178,
    202–203
Molotov–Ribbentrop pact,
    141, 142
Moscow show trial (1936),
    135
on music, 205, 210n
wife Nadezhda, 37, 107,
    108, 109
and national anthem, 161
as negotiator, 184, 201–202
'neo-patrimonial' rule, 180
November 1941 address,
    156
October Revolution, 34–35
as orator, 26
on pacifism (1938), 139
'pan-Slavic' configuration,
    183
paranoia, 5
parents, 1–2
as People's Commissar of

Nationalities, 35
'people's democracy', 187
personal characteristics, 2,
    7, 9, 11–13, 21, 22,
    29, 54
physical characteristics, 3
poems, 4–5, 23
on Poland, 43–44, 104, 141,
    143, 181, 182–184,
    186–187, 206
on policy-making, 160, 206
Polish campaign (1920),
    43–44
as politician, ix, 201, 202
on politics, 11, 205
Pravda, 19, 29
as reader, 7
reasons for rise, ix, 70
Red Army, 124, 146–148,
    171
on revenge, 59, 71n
Russia and Russian people,
    85–86, 172, 206
Russian proverbs, 84, 128
in Siberia (1928), 76
on siege of Leningrad, 157
silent masses, 209
'socialism in one country',
    53, 55, 65, 183
on Soviet priests, 138
speech manner, 12
on Stalin himself, 137, 193
in Tbilisi (1921), 45–46, 48n
tendered resignation, 64, 69
on terror, 69, 78, 94, 116,
    205
on 'terrorists' (1922), 57
Tito, 187, 199n
Trotskii and Trotskists, 21,
    40, 41, 44, 61, 63,
    72n, 121, 134,
    135–136, 202

Truman, 122, 186, 205
on truth, 208
as 'tsar', 2, 73n, 137
on tsars, 134
Ukraine and Ukrainians,
102, 112, 181
USA, 183, 186, 194
views of seminary, 4
Wehrmacht, 152
wire tapping of Kremlin, 59
witnessed executions, 3
worked at Tbilisi
observatory, 9
Yugoslavs, 170
Zhukov, 151, 155–156, 158
Stalin, Vasilii, 192, 200n
Stalingrad, battle of, 158
Stalinskii, E.S., 20
Stamenov, Ivan, 155
Steinberg, I.N., 41
Stolypin, Petr, 16, 17, 28
Struve, Petr, 128
Stuart, Mary, 123
Sudoplatov, Pavel, 134, 173
Sultan-Galiev, Mirsaid, 58
Suslov, M.A., 200n
Svanidze, Aleksandr, 16, 120,
153
Svanidze, Ekaterina, 16, 18
Sverdlov, Ia.M., 21
synagogue, in Moscow, 193

Tehran conference (1943), 161
Ter-Petrosian, Semen (Kamo),
16
Thorez, Maurice, 159, 181
Timoshenko, S.K., 146, 150
Tito, J.B., 187, 199n
Togliatti, Palmiro, 201
Tolmachev, V.N., 107
Tomskii, M.P., 66
Trilisser, M.A., 82

Trotskii, L.D., 1, 9, 21, 33, 34,
35, 36, 37, 40, 44, 47,
53, 62, 72n, 119, 135
attempt at comeback
(1932), 106
and Bukharin-Kamenev
meetings (1928), 83
on Clemenceau, 119, 121
defended USSR, 128
demanded Stalin's removal
(1918), 41
exiled (1928), 68
expelled from USSR, 68
family, 134
on 'Industrial Party', 95
internationalism, 65
as Jew, 64
and Lenin, 31, 46, 60, 61
as politician, 70
Revolution Betrayed, 121
as 'superman', 61
on terror, 205
Truman, Harry S., 186,
203–204, 205
Tukhachevskii, M.N., 44, 94,
124
Tuominen, Arvo, 206–207
Turkey, 90, 148, 149

Uborevich, I.P., 124
Uglanov, N.A., 81
Ukraine, 36, 37, 103–105, 108,
111–112, 176–177
civil war, 177
western, 114, 143, 174, 177
Ul'ianova, Mariia, 54, 66, 72n
Ulam, Adam B., 119
'underground Politbuvo', 65
United Nations, 184
'United Opposition', 67
Uratadze, Gregorii, 7, 11
USA, 114, 182, 183

USSR, 54, 114
Ustrialov, Nikolai, 138

Vasilevskii, A.M., 192
Vatican, 160
Vilnius, 182
Vinogradov, V.N., 191
Vlasov, A.A., 197n
von Bismarck, Otto, 149
von Papen, Franz, 159, 167n
von Ribbentrop, Joachim, 142, 163
von Rinteln, Franz, 124
Voroshilov, K.E., 18, 40, 124, 145, 148
Voznesenskii, N.A., 178
Vyshinskii, A.Ia., 18, 111, 120

Wald, Georg, 124
Warsaw, 43, 44
Warsaw Uprising (1944), 181

Werth, Alexander, 153, 156, 157
Winter War, 145

Yalta conference, 184–185
Yugoslavia, 149

Zhdanov, Iu.A., 138, 180, 205
Zhdanovshchina, 179
Zheliabov, A., 116
Zhemchuzhina, P.S., 178
Zhou Enlai, 190
Zhukov, G.K., 150, 151, 155–156, 158, 175–176
Zinov'ev, G.E., 30, 33, 35, 58, 60, 61, 63, 64, 67, 68, 83, 121
  and Comintern, 68
  and 'Riutin affair', 106
Zoshchenko, Mikhail, 179